CONSTRUCTION – FIRE PROTECTION, FIRE DETECTION AND FIRE EXTINCTION

IMPLEMENTING

SOLAS CHAPTER II–2, 2002

The revised Chapter II–2 of the International Convention for the Safety of Life at Sea (SOLAS) Came into force 1 July 2002

Maritime and Coastguard Agency

London: TSO

Spring Place
105 Commercial Road
Southampton
SO15 1EG

Published by TSO (The Stationery Office) and available from:

Online
www.tso.co.uk/bookshop

Mail, Telephone, Fax & E-mail
TSO
PO Box 29, Norwich, NR3 1GN
Telephone orders/General enquiries: 0870 600 5522
Fax orders: 0870 600 5533
E-mail: book.orders@tso.co.uk
Textphone 0870 240 3701

TSO Shops
123 Kingsway, London, WC2B 6PQ
020 7242 6393 Fax 020 7242 6394
68-69 Bull Street, Birmingham B4 6AD
0121 236 9696 Fax 0121 236 9699
9-21 Princess Street, Manchester M60 8AS
0161 834 7201 Fax 0161 833 0634
16 Arthur Street, Belfast BT1 4GD
028 9023 8451 Fax 028 9023 5401
18-19 High Street, Cardiff CF10 1PT
029 2039 5548 Fax 029 2038 4347
71 Lothian Road, Edinburgh EH3 9AZ
0870 606 5566 Fax 0870 606 5588

TSO Accredited Agents
(see Yellow Pages)

and through good booksellers

ISBN 0 11 552576 9

Printed in the United Kingdom for The Stationery Office
88634 C5 12/03

Contents

CHAPTER II–2

Construction – Fire Protection, Fire Detection and Fire Extinction

Introduction

Chapter II–2 of SOLAS, Construction – Fire Protection, Fire Detection and Fire Extinction, has been revised and came into force on 1 July 2002. It should be noted that some parts of Chapter II–2 apply to existing ships and these are set out in Regulation 1.2.2 and 1.6.7 of Chapter II–2. Reference should be made to the Merchant Shipping (Fire Protection) Regulations 2003 and Merchant Shipping (Fire Protection) Regulations (Amendment) Regulations 2003 which implements the amendments to existing legislation where Chapter II–2 applies to existing ships.

This publication has been prepared to help ship-owners, masters, crews and industry to understand and comply with the new regulations.

The publication contains the full International Maritime Organization text of each Regulation and explanatory Guidance Notes relating to each of the Regulations. The full titles of IMO resolutions, IMO resolutions published as Codes, IMO Circulars, and other standards referenced within the Regulations or Guidance Notes are listed in the Appendix.

The Regulations and Guidance are coded as follows:

| | Text of Regulations in italics | and continuation of text in italics |

| GUIDANCE NOTES | | Guidance Notes follow Text of Regulations |

Part A – General

1   Application

1.1   Unless expressly provided otherwise, this chapter shall apply to ships constructed on or after 1 July 2002.

1.2   For the purpose of this chapter:

> *.1 the expression* ships constructed *means ships the keels of which are laid or which are at a similar stage of construction;*

> *.2 the expression* all ships *means ships, irrespective of type, constructed before, on or after 1 July 2002; and*

> *.3 a cargo ship, whenever built, which is converted to a passenger ship shall be treated as a passenger ship constructed on the date on which such a conversion commences.*

1.3   For the purpose of this chapter, the expression a similar stage of construction *means the stage at which:*

> *.1 construction identifiable with a specific ship begins; and*

> *.2 assembly of that ship has commenced comprising at least 50 tonnes or 1% of the estimated mass of all structural material, whichever is less.*

2   Applicable requirements to existing ships

2.1   Unless expressly provided otherwise, for ships constructed before 1 July 2002 the Administration shall ensure that the requirements which are applicable under chapter II–2 of the International Convention for the Safety of Life at Sea, 1974, as amended by resolutions MSC.1(XLV), MSC.6(48), MSC.13(57), MSC.22(59), MSC.24(60), MSC.27(61), MSC.31(63) and MSC.57(67), are complied with.

2.2   Ships constructed before 1 July 2002 shall also comply with:

> *.1 paragraphs 3, 6.5 and 6.7 as appropriate;*

> *.2 regulations 13.3.4.2 to 13.3.4.5, 13.4.3 and Part E, except regulations 16.3.2.2 and 16.3.2.3 thereof, as appropriate, not later than the date of the first survey after 1 July 2002;*

> *.3 regulations 10.4.1.3 and 10.6.4 for new installations only; and*

> *.4 regulation 10.5.6 not later than 1 October 2005 for passenger ships of 2,000 gross tonnage and above.*

3   Repairs, alterations, modifications and outfitting

3.1   All ships which undergo repairs, alterations, modifications and outfitting related thereto shall continue to comply with at least the requirements previously applicable to these ships. Such ships, if constructed before 1 July 2002, shall, as a rule, comply with the requirements for ships constructed on or after that date to at least the same extent as they did before undergoing such repairs, alterations, modifications or outfitting.

3.2   Repairs, alterations and modifications which substantially alter the dimensions of a ship or the passenger accommodation spaces, or substantially increase a ship's service life and outfitting related thereto, shall meet the requirements for ships constructed on or after 1 July 2002 in so far as the Administration deems reasonable and practicable.

Guidance 1

G1   Major repairs, alterations and modifications

G1.1   Paragraphs 3.1 and 3.2 are required to apply to ships undergoing repairs, alterations and modifications only within the parts of the ship in which the repairs alterations and modifications are made. However, the Regulations should not apply to existing bulkheads, decks and ceilings, linings, materials or fittings within such parts provided they are unaffected by the repairs, alterations and modifications.

4   Exemptions

4.1   The Administration may, if it considers that the sheltered nature and conditions of the voyage are such as to render the application of any specific requirements of this chapter unreasonable or unnecessary, exempt* from those requirements individual ships or classes of ships entitled to fly the flag of its State, provided that such ships, in the course of their voyage, do not sail at distances of more than 20 miles from the nearest land.

4.2   In the case of passenger ships which are employed in special trades for the carriage of large numbers of special trade passengers, such as the pilgrim trade, the Administration, if satisfied that it is impracticable to enforce compliance with the requirements of this chapter, may exempt such ships from those requirements, provided that they comply fully with the provisions of:

> *.1   the rules annexed to the Special Trade Passenger Ships Agreement, 1971; and*

> *.2   the rules annexed to the Protocol on Space Requirements for Special Trade Passenger Ships, 1973.*

5   Applicable requirements depending on ship type

Unless expressly provided otherwise:

> *.1   requirements not referring to a specific ship type shall apply to ships of all types; and*

> *.2   requirements referring to "tankers" shall apply to tankers subject to the requirements specified in paragraph 6 below.*

6   Application of requirements for tankers

6.1   Requirements for tankers in this chapter shall apply to tankers carrying crude oil or petroleum products having a flashpoint not exceeding 60°C (closed cup test), as determined by an approved flashpoint apparatus, and a Reid vapour pressure which is below the atmospheric pressure or other liquid products having a similar fire hazard.

---

*   Refer to Port State concurrence with SOLAS exemptions (MSC/Circ.606).

6.2   Where liquid cargoes other than those referred to in paragraph 6.1 or liquefied gases which introduce additional fire hazards are intended to be carried, additional safety measures shall be required, having due regard to the provisions of the International Bulk Chemical Code, as defined in regulation VII/8.1, the Bulk Chemical Code, the International Gas Carrier Code, as defined in regulation VII/11.1, and the Gas Carrier Code, as appropriate.

6.2.1   A liquid cargo with a flashpoint of less than 60°C for which a regular foam fire-fighting system complying with the Fire Safety Systems Code is not effective, is considered to be a cargo introducing additional fire hazards in this context. The following additional measures are required:

> *.1   the foam shall be of alcohol-resistant type;*
>
> *.2   the type of foam concentrates for use in chemical tankers shall be to the satisfaction of the Administration, taking into account the guidelines developed by the Organization*; and*
>
> *.3   the capacity and application rates of the foam extinguishing system shall comply with chapter 11 of the International Bulk Chemical Code, except that lower application rates may be accepted based on performance tests. For tankers fitted with inert gas systems, a quantity of foam concentrate sufficient for 20 min of foam generation may be accepted.†*

6.2.2   For the purpose of this regulation, a liquid cargo with a vapour pressure greater than 1.013 bar absolute at 37.8°C is considered to be a cargo introducing additional fire hazards. Ships carrying such substances shall comply with paragraph 15.14 of the International Bulk Chemical Code. When ships operate in restricted areas and at restricted times, the Administration concerned may agree to waive the requirements for refrigeration systems in accordance with paragraph 15.14.3 of the International Bulk Chemical Code.

6.3   Liquid cargoes with a flashpoint exceeding 60°C other than oil products or liquid cargoes subject to the requirements of the International Bulk Chemical Code are considered to constitute a low fire risk, not requiring the protection of a fixed foam extinguishing system.

6.4   Tankers carrying petroleum products with a flashpoint exceeding 60°C (closed cup test), as determined by an approved flashpoint apparatus, shall comply with the requirements provided in regulations 10.2.1.4.4 and 10.10.2.3 and the requirements for cargo ships other than tankers, except that, in lieu of the fixed fire-extinguishing system required in regulation 10.7, they shall be fitted with a fixed deck foam system which shall comply with the provisions of the Fire Safety Systems Code.

6.5   Combination carriers constructed before, on or after 1 July 2002 shall not carry cargoes other than oil unless all cargo spaces are empty of oil and gas-freed or unless the arrangements provided in each case have been approved by the Administration taking into account the guidelines developed by the Organization.**

---

*   Refer to the Guidelines for performance and testing criteria and surveys of expansion foam concentrates for fire-extinguishing systems for chemical tankers (MSC/Circ.799).

†   Refer to the information on flashpoint and recommended fire-fighting media for chemicals to which neither the IBC nor BCH Codes apply (MSC/Circ.553).

** Refer to the Guidelines for inert gas systems (MSC/Circ.353), as amended by MSC/Circ.387.

6.6   Chemical tankers and gas carriers shall comply with the requirements for tankers, except where alternative and supplementary arrangements are provided to the satisfaction of the Administration, having due regard to the provisions of the International Bulk Chemical Code and the International Gas Carrier Code, as appropriate.

6.7   The requirements of regulations 4.5.10.1.1 and 4.5.10.1.4 and a system for continuous monitoring of the concentration of hydrocarbon gases shall be fitted on all tankers constructed before 1 July 2002 by the date of the first scheduled dry-docking after 1 July 2002, but not later than 1 July 2005. Sampling points or detector heads shall be located in suitable positions in order that potentially dangerous leakages are readily detected. When the hydrocarbon gas concentration reaches a pre-set level which shall not be higher than 10% of the lower flammable limit, a continuous audible and visual alarm signal shall be automatically effected in the pump-room and cargo control room to alert personnel to the potential hazard. However, existing monitoring systems already fitted having a pre-set level not greater than 30% of the lower flammable limit may be accepted.

Guidance 1

G2   The International Bulk Chemical Code, the Bulk Chemical Code, the International Gas Carrier Code and the Gas Carrier Code are implemented in the United Kingdom by the following Regulations:

- The Merchant Shipping (Gas Carriers) Regulations 1994 (SI 2464)

- The Merchant Shipping (Dangerous or Noxious Liquid Substances in Bulk) Regulations 1996 (SI 3010) plus amendment 1998 (SI 1153)

- The Merchant Shipping (Dangerous Goods and Marine Pollutants) Regulations 1997 (SI 2367)

- The Merchant Shipping (Carriage of Cargoes) Regulations 1999 (SI 336)

G3   Application of Bulk Chemical and Gas Carrier Codes.

G3.1 The referenced Bulk Chemical and Gas Carrier Codes, as applicable, apply only in ships built prior to 1 July 1986. The International Bulk Chemical Code and International Gas Carrier Codes, as applicable, apply to ships built on or after that date.

G4   References to "the Administration" in this document, as regards ships to which the Merchant Shipping (Fire Protection) Regulations 2002 apply, may be construed as references to the Secretary of State.

REGULATION 2

Fire safety objectives and functional requirements

1.   Fire safety objectives

1.1   The fire safety objectives of this chapter are to:

    .1 prevent the occurrence of fire and explosion;

    .2 reduce the risk to life caused by fire;

    .3 reduce the risk of damage caused by fire to the ship, its cargo and the environment;

    .4 contain, control and suppress fire and explosion in the compartment of origin; and

    .5 provide adequate and readily accessible means of escape for passengers and crew.

2   Functional requirements

2.1   In order to achieve the fire safety objectives set out in paragraph 1, the following functional requirements are embodied in the regulations of this chapter as appropriate:

    .1 division of the ship into main vertical and horizontal zones by thermal and structural boundaries;

    .2 separation of accommodation spaces from the remainder of the ship by thermal and structural boundaries;

    .3 restricted use of combustible materials;

    .4 detection of any fire in the zone of origin;

    .5 containment and extinction of any fire in the space of origin;

    .6 protection of means of escape and access for fire fighting;

    .7 ready availability of fire-extinguishing appliances; and

    .8 minimization of possibility of ignition of flammable cargo vapour.

3   Achievement of the fire safety objectives

The fire safety objectives set out in paragraph 1 shall be achieved by ensuring compliance with the prescriptive requirements specified in parts B, C, D, E or G, or by alternative design and arrangements which comply with Part F. A ship shall be considered to meet the functional requirements set out in paragraph 2 and to achieve the fire safety objectives set out in paragraph 1 when either:

    .1 the ship's design and arrangements, as a whole, comply with the relevant prescriptive requirements in parts B, C, D, E or G;

    .2 the ship's design and arrangements, as a whole, have been reviewed and approved in accordance with part F; or

    .3 part(s) of the ship's design and arrangements have been reviewed and approved in accordance with part F and the remaining parts of the ship comply with the relevant prescriptive requirements in parts B, C, D, E or G.

REGULATION

3 Definitions

For the purpose of this chapter, unless expressly provided otherwise, the following definitions shall apply:

1   Accommodation spaces *are those spaces used for public spaces, corridors, lavatories, cabins, offices, hospitals, cinemas, game and hobby rooms, barber shops, pantries containing no cooking appliances and similar spaces.*

2   "A" class divisions *are those divisions formed by bulkheads and decks which comply with the following criteria:*

   .1 *they are constructed of steel or other equivalent material;*

   .2 *they are suitably stiffened;*

   .3 *they are insulated with approved non-combustible materials such that the average temperature of the unexposed side will not rise more than 140°C above the original temperature, nor will the temperature, at any one point, including any joint, rise more than 180°C above the original temperature, within the time listed below:*

class "A–60"	60 min
class "A–30"	30 min
class "A–15"	15 min
class "A–0"	0 min

   .4 *they are constructed as to be capable of preventing the passage of smoke and flame to the end of the one-hour standard fire test; and*

   .5 *the Administration required a test of a prototype bulkhead or deck in accordance with the Fire Test Procedures Code to ensure that it meets the above requirements for integrity and temperature rise.*

3   Atriums *are public spaces within a single main vertical zone spanning three or more open decks.*

4   "B" class divisions *are those divisions formed by bulkheads, decks, ceilings or linings which comply with the following criteria:*

   .1 *they are constructed of approved non-combustible materials and all materials used in the construction and erection of "B" class divisions are non-combustible, with the exception that combustible veneers may be permitted provided they meet other appropriate requirements of this chapter;*

   .2 *they have an insulation value such that the average temperature of the unexposed side will not rise more than 140°C above the original temperature, nor will the temperature at any one point, including any joint, rise more than 225°C above the original temperature, within the time listed below:*

class "B–15"	15 min
class "B–0"	0 min

   .3 *they are so constructed as to be capable of preventing the passage of flame to the end of the first half hour of the standard fire test; and*

.4 *the Administration required a test of a prototype division in accordance with the Fire Test Procedures Code to ensure that it meets the above requirements for integrity and temperature rise.*

5   Bulkhead deck *is the uppermost deck up to which the transverse watertight bulkheads are carried.*

6   Cargo area *is that part of the ship that contains cargo holds, cargo tanks, slop tanks and cargo pump-rooms including pump-rooms, cofferdams, ballast and void spaces adjacent to cargo tanks and also deck areas throughout the entire length and breadth of the part of the ship over the afore-mentioned spaces.*

7   Cargo ship *is a ship as defined in regulation I/2(g).*

8   Cargo spaces *are spaces used for cargo, cargo oil tanks, tanks for other liquid cargo and trunks to such spaces.*

9   Central control station *is a control station in which the following control and indicator functions are centralized:*

.1 *fixed fire detection and fire alarm systems;*

.2 *automatic sprinkler, fire detection and fire alarm systems;*

.3 *fire door indicator panels;*

.4 *fire door closure;*

.5 *watertight door indicator panels;*

.6 *watertight door closures;*

.7 *ventilation fans;*

.8 *general/fire alarms;*

.9 *communication systems including telephones; and*

.10 *microphones to public address systems.*

Guidance 3

G1   Central control stations

G1.1   The communications systems referred to in this definition of 'central control station' do not include fire systems which are not required by the Regulations.

10   "C" class divisions *are divisions constructed of approved non-combustible materials. They need meet neither requirements relative to the passage of smoke and flame nor limitations relative to the temperature rise. Combustible veneers are permitted provided they meet the requirements of this chapter.*

11   Chemical tanker *is a cargo ship constructed or adapted and used for the carriage in bulk of any liquid product of a flammable nature listed in chapter 17 of the International Bulk Chemical Code, as defined in regulation VII/8.1.*

12   Closed ro-ro spaces are ro-ro spaces which are neither open ro-ro spaces nor weather decks.

13   Closed vehicle spaces are vehicle spaces which are neither open vehicle spaces nor weather decks.

14   Combination carrier is a cargo ship designed to carry both oil and solid cargoes in bulk.

15   Combustible material is any material other than a non-combustible material.

16   Continuous "B" class ceilings or linings are those "B" class ceilings or linings which terminate at an "A" or "B" class division.

17   Continuously manned central control station is a central control station which is continuously manned by a responsible member of the crew.

18   Control stations are those spaces in which the ship's radio or main navigating equipment or the emergency source of power is located or where the fire recording or fire control equipment is centralized. Spaces where the fire recording or fire control equipment is centralized are also considered to be a fire control station.

Guidance 3

G2   Control stations

G2.1 Spaces in which the sprinkler pumps, drencher pumps and fire pumps are situated should not be regarded as control stations. Such spaces in passenger ships are categorised as 'auxiliary machinery spaces' and in cargo ships as 'other machinery spaces'.

G2.2 A control room situated in a machinery space, which does not contain the propulsion machinery and boilers, should still be regarded as a control station even when the space contains pumps, purifiers etc. necessary for the operation of the propulsion machinery and boilers. Moreover, spaces containing batteries which are reserve power sources for radio installations, emergency generator starting or transitional emergency power supply, are control stations.

19   Crude oil is any oil occurring naturally in the earth, whether or not treated to render it suitable for transportation, and includes crude oil where certain distillate fractions may have been removed from or added to.

20   Dangerous goods are those goods referred to in regulation VII/2.

21   Deadweight is the difference in tonnes between the displacement of a ship in water of a specific gravity of 1.025 at the load waterline corresponding to the assigned summer freeboard and the lightweight of the ship.

22   Fire Safety Systems Code means the International Code for Fire Safety Systems as adopted by the Maritime Safety Committee of the Organization by resolution MSC.98(73), as may be amended by the Organization, provided that such amendments are adopted, brought into force and take effect in accordance with the provisions of article VIII of the present Convention concerning the amendment procedures applicable to the annex other than chapter I thereof.

23 Fire Test Procedures Code *means the International Code for Application of Fire Test Procedures as adopted by the Maritime Safety Committee of the Organization by resolution MSC.61(67), as may be amended by the Organization, provided that such amendments are adopted, brought into force and take effect in accordance with the provisions of article VIII of the present Convention concerning the amendment procedures applicable to the annex other than chapter I thereof.*

24 Flashpoint *is the temperature in degrees Celsius (closed cup test) at which a product will give off enough flammable vapour to be ignited, as determined by an approved flashpoint apparatus.*

25 Gas carrier *is a cargo ship constructed or adapted and used for the carriage in bulk of any liquefied gas or other products of a flammable nature listed in chapter 19 of the International Gas Carrier Code, as defined in regulation VII/11.1.*

26 Helideck *is a purpose-built helicopter landing area located on a ship including all structure, fire-fighting appliances and other equipment necessary for the safe operation of helicopters.*

27 Helicopter facility *is a helideck including any refuelling and hangar facilities.*

28 Lightweight *is the displacement of a ship in tonnes without cargo, fuel, lubricating oil, ballast water, fresh water and feedwater in tanks, consumable stores, and passengers and crew and their effects.*

29 Low flame-spread *means that the surface thus described will adequately restrict the spread of flame, this being determined in accordance with the Fire Test Procedures Code.*

30 Machinery spaces *are machinery spaces of category A and other spaces containing propulsion machinery, boilers, oil fuel units, steam and internal combustion engines, generators and major electrical machinery, oil filling stations, refrigerating, stabilizing, ventilation and air conditioning machinery, and similar spaces, and trunks to such spaces.*

31 Machinery spaces of category A *are those spaces and trunks to such spaces which contain either:*

    .1 internal combustion machinery used for main propulsion;

    .2 internal combustion machinery used for purposes other than main propulsion where such machinery has in the aggregate a total power output of not less than 375 kW; or

    .3 any oil-fired boiler or oil fuel unit, or any oil-fired equipment other than boilers, such as inert gas generators, incinerators, etc.

32 Main vertical zones *are those sections into which the hull, superstructure and deckhouses are divided by "A" class divisions, the mean length and width of which on any deck does not in general exceed 40 m.*

33 Non-combustible material *is a material which neither burns nor gives off flammable vapours in sufficient quantity for self-ignition when heated to approximately 750°C, this being determined in accordance with the Fire Test Procedures Code.*

Guidance 3

G3   Non-combustible material

G3.1   Where non-combustible materials are required by the Regulations, they should be of an approved type. Approval is not however required for metals or any inorganic materials which are recognised as being non-combustible e.g. steel, aluminium, alloy, copper, glass, woven glass cloth, concrete, perlite, vermiculite, calcium silicate, ceramic products, natural stone etc., except when any such material is combined with a combustible material of any quantity in a product.

34   Oil fuel unit *is the equipment used for the preparation of oil fuel for delivery to an oil-fired boiler, or equipment used for the preparation for delivery of heated oil to an internal combustion engine, and includes any oil pressure pumps, filters and heaters dealing with oil at a pressure of more than 0.18 N/mm².*

35   Open ro-ro spaces *are those ro-ro spaces which are either open at both ends or have an opening at one end, and are provided with adequate natural ventilation effective over their entire length through permanent openings distributed in the side plating or deckhead or from above, having a total area of at least 10% of the total area of the space sides.*

36   Open vehicle spaces *are those vehicle spaces which are either open at both ends, or have an opening at one end and are provided with adequate natural ventilation effective over their entire length through permanent openings distributed in the side plating or deck-head or from above, having a total area of at least 10% of the total area of the space sides.*

37   Passenger ship *is a ship as defined in regulation I/2(f).*

38   Prescriptive requirements *means the construction characteristics, limiting dimensions, or fire safety systems specified in parts B, C, D, E or G.*

39   Public spaces *are those portions of the accommodation which are used for halls, dining rooms, lounges and similar permanently enclosed spaces.*

40   Rooms containing furniture and furnishings of restricted fire risk, *for the purpose of regulation 9, are those rooms containing furniture and furnishings of restricted fire risk (whether cabins, public spaces, offices or other types of accommodation) in which:*

    .1 *case furniture such as desks, wardrobes, dressing tables, bureaux or dressers are constructed entirely of approved non-combustible materials, except that a combustible veneer not exceeding 2 mm may be used on the working surface of such articles;*

    .2 *free-standing furniture such as chairs, sofas or tables, are constructed with frames of non-combustible materials;*

    .3 *draperies, curtains and other suspended textile materials have qualities of resistance to the propagation of flame not inferior to those of wool having a mass of mass 0.8 kg/m², this being determined in accordance with the Fire Test Procedures Code;*

    .4 *floor coverings have low flame-spread characteristics;*

    .5 *exposed surfaces of bulkheads, linings and ceilings have low flame-spread characteristics;*

.6 *upholstered furniture has qualities of resistance to the ignition and propagation of flame, this being determined in accordance with the Fire Test Procedures Code; and*

.7 *bedding components have qualities of resistance to the ignition and propagation of flame, this being determined in accordance with the Fire Test Procedures Code.*

Guidance 3

G4   Rooms containing furniture and furnishings of restricted fire risk

G4.1   The requirements specified in the definition should apply to furniture and furnishings in private sanitary facilities situated in cabins containing furniture and furnishings of restricted fire risk.

41   Ro-ro spaces *are spaces not normally subdivided in any way and normally extending to either a substantial length or the entire length of the ship in which motor vehicles with fuel in their tanks for their own propulsion and/or goods (packaged or in bulk, in or on rail or road cars, vehicles (including road or rail tankers), trailers, containers, pallets, demountable tanks or in or on similar stowage units or other receptacles) can be loaded and unloaded normally in a horizontal direction.*

42   Ro-ro passenger ship *means a passenger ship with ro-ro spaces or special category spaces.*

43   Steel or other equivalent material *means any non-combustible material which, by itself or due to insulation provided, has structural and integrity properties equivalent to steel at the end of the applicable exposure to the standard fire test (e.g., aluminium alloy with appropriate insulation).*

44   Sauna *is a hot room with temperatures normally varying between 80°C and 120°C where the heat is provided by a hot surface (e.g. by an electrically heated oven). The hot room may also include the space where the oven is located and adjacent bathrooms.*

45   Service spaces *are those spaces used for galleys, pantries containing cooking appliances, lockers, mail and specie rooms, store-rooms, workshops other than those forming part of the machinery spaces, and similar spaces and trunks to such spaces.*

46   Special category spaces *are those enclosed vehicle spaces above and below the bulkhead deck, into and from which vehicles can be driven and to which passengers have access. Special category spaces may be accommodated on more than one deck provided that the total overall clear height for vehicles does not exceed 10 m.*

47   A standard fire test *is a test in which specimens of the relevant bulkheads or decks are exposed in a test furnace to temperatures corresponding approximately to the standard time-temperature curve in accordance with the test method specified in the Fire Test Procedures Code.*

48   Tanker *is a ship as defined in regulation I/2(h).*

49   Vehicle spaces *are cargo spaces intended for carriage of motor vehicles with fuel in their tanks for their own propulsion.*

50   Weather deck *is a deck which is completely exposed to the weather from above and from at least two sides.*

Part B – Prevention of fire and explosion

Probability of Ignition

1. Purpose

The purpose of this regulation is to prevent the ignition of combustible materials or flammable liquids. For this purpose, the following functional requirements shall be met:

 .1 means shall be provided to control leaks of flammable liquids;

 .2 means shall be provided to limit the accumulation of flammable vapours;

 .3 the ignitability of combustible materials shall be restricted;

 .4 ignition sources shall be restricted;

 .5 ignition sources shall be separated from combustible materials and flammable liquids; and

 .6 the atmosphere in cargo tanks shall be maintained out of the explosive range.

2 Arrangements for oil fuel, lubrication oil and other flammable oils

*2.1 *Limitations in the use of oils as fuel

The following limitations shall apply to the use of oil as fuel:

 .1 except as otherwise permitted by this paragraph, no oil fuel with a flashpoint of less than 60°C shall be used;*

 .2 in emergency generators, oil fuel with a flashpoint of not less than 43°C may be used;

 .3 the use of oil fuel having a flashpoint of less than 60°C but not less than 43°C may be permitted (e.g., for feeding the emergency fire pump's engines and the auxiliary machines which are not located in the machinery spaces of category A) subject to the following:

  .3.1 fuel oil tanks except those arranged in double bottom compartments shall be located outside of machinery spaces of category A;

  .3.2 provisions for the measurement of oil temperature are provided on the suction pipe of the oil fuel pump;

  .3.3 stop valves and/or cocks are provided on the inlet side and outlet side of the oil fuel strainers; and

  .3.4 pipe joints of welded construction or of circular cone type or spherical type union joint are applied as much as possible; and

 .4 in cargo ships the use of fuel having a lower flashpoint than otherwise specified in paragraph 2.1, for example crude oil, may be permitted provided that such fuel is not stored in any machinery space and subject to the approval by the Administration of the complete installation.

---

* Refer to the Recommended procedures to prevent the illegal or accidental use of low flashpoint cargo oil as fuel adopted by the Organization by resolution A.565(14).

2.2 Arrangements for oil fuel

In a ship in which oil fuel is used, the arrangements for the storage, distribution and utilisation of the oil fuel shall be such as to ensure the safety of the ship and persons on board and shall at least comply with the following provisions.

2.2.1 Location of oil fuel systems

As far as practicable, parts of the oil fuel system containing heated oil under pressure exceeding 0.18 N/mm² shall not be placed in a concealed position such that defects and leakage cannot readily be observed. The machinery spaces in way of such parts of the oil fuel system shall be adequately illuminated.

2.2.2 Ventilation of machinery spaces

The ventilation of machinery spaces shall be sufficient under normal conditions to prevent accumulation of oil vapour.

2.2.3 Oil fuel tanks

2.2.3.1 Fuel oil, lubrication oil and other flammable oils shall not be carried in forepeak tanks.

2.2.3.2 As far as practicable, oil fuel tanks shall be part of the ship's structure and shall be located outside machinery spaces of category A. Where oil fuel tanks, other than double bottom tanks, are necessarily located adjacent to or within machinery spaces of category A, at least one of their vertical sides shall be contiguous to the machinery space boundaries, and shall preferably have a common boundary with the double bottom tanks, and the area of the tank boundary common with the machinery spaces shall be kept to a minimum. Where such tanks are situated within the boundaries of machinery spaces of category A they shall not contain oil fuel having a flashpoint of less than 60°C. In general, the use of free-standing oil fuel tanks shall be avoided. When such tanks are employed their use shall be prohibited in category A machinery spaces on passenger ships. Where permitted, they shall be placed in an oil-tight spill tray of ample size having a suitable drain pipe leading to a suitably sized spill oil tank.

2.2.3.3 No oil fuel tank shall be situated where spillage or leakage therefrom can constitute a fire or explosion hazard by falling on heated surfaces.

2.2.3.4 Oil fuel pipes, which, if damaged, would allow oil to escape from a storage, settling or daily service tank having a capacity of 500 l and above situated above the double bottom, shall be fitted with a cock or valve directly on the tank capable of being closed from a safe position outside the space concerned in the event of a fire occurring in the space in which such tanks are situated. In the special case of deep tanks situated in any shaft or pipe tunnel or similar space, valves on the tank shall be fitted, but control in the event of fire may be effected by means of an additional valve on the pipe or pipes outside the tunnel or similar space. If such an additional valve is fitted in the machinery space it shall be operated from a position outside this space. The controls for remote operation of the valve for the emergency generator fuel tank shall be in a separate location from the controls for remote operation of other valves for tanks located in machinery spaces.

2.2.3.5 Safe and efficient means of ascertaining the amount of oil fuel contained in any oil fuel tank shall be provided.

2.2.3.5.1 Where sounding pipes are used, they shall not terminate in any space where the risk of ignition of spillage from the sounding pipe might arise. In particular, they shall not terminate in passenger or crew spaces. As a general rule, they shall not terminate in machinery spaces. However, where the Administration considers that these latter requirements are impracticable, it may permit termination of sounding pipes in machinery spaces on condition that all of the following requirements are met:

.1 an oil-level gauge is provided meeting the requirements of paragraph 2.2.3.5.2;

.2 the sounding pipes terminate in locations remote from ignition hazards unless precautions are taken, such as the fitting of effective screens, to prevent the oil fuel in the case of spillage through the terminations of the sounding pipes from coming into contact with a source of ignition; and

.3 the terminations of sounding pipes are fitted with self-closing blanking devices and with a small-diameter self-closing control cock located below the blanking device for the purpose of ascertaining before the blanking device is opened that oil fuel is not present. Provisions shall be made so as to ensure that any spillage of oil fuel through the control cock involves no ignition hazard.

2.2.3.5.2 Other oil-level gauges may be used in place of sounding pipes subject to the following conditions:

.1 in passenger ships, such gauges shall not require penetration below the top of the tank and their failure or overfilling of the tanks shall not permit release of fuel; and

.2 in cargo ships, the failure of such gauges or overfilling of the tank shall not permit release of fuel into the space. The use of cylindrical gauge glasses is prohibited. The Administration may permit the use of oil-level gauges with flat glasses and self-closing valves between the gauges and fuel tanks.

2.2.3.5.3 The means prescribed in paragraph 2.2.3.5.2 which are acceptable to the Administration shall be maintained in the proper condition to ensure their continued accurate functioning in service.

2.2.4 Prevention of overpressure

Provisions shall be made to prevent overpressure in any oil tank or in any part of the oil fuel system, including the filling pipes served by pumps on board. Air and overflow pipes and relief valves shall discharge to a position where there is no risk of fire or explosion from the emergence of oils and vapour and shall not lead into crew spaces, passenger spaces nor into special category spaces, closed ro-ro spaces, machinery spaces or similar spaces.

2.2.5 Oil fuel piping

2.2.5.1 Oil fuel pipes and their valves and fittings shall be of steel or other approved material, except that restricted use of flexible pipes shall be permissible in positions where the Administration is satisfied that they are necessary.* Such flexible pipes and

---

* Refer to recommendations published by the International Organization for Standardization, in particular publications ISO 15540:1999, *Test methods for fire resistance of hose assemblies* and ISO 15541:1999, *Requirements for the test bench of fire resistance of hose asssemblies.*

end attachments shall be of approved fire-resisting materials of adequate strength and shall be constructed to the satisfaction of the Administration. For valves fitted to oil fuel tanks and are under static pressure, steel or spheroidal-graphite cast iron may be accepted. However, ordinary cast iron valves may be used in piping systems where the design pressure is lower than 7 bar and the design temperature is below 60°C.

2.2.5.2 External high-pressure fuel delivery lines between the high-pressure fuel pumps and fuel injectors shall be protected with a jacketed piping system capable of containing fuel from a high-pressure line failure. A jacketed pipe incorporates an outer pipe into which the high-pressure fuel pipe is placed, forming a permanent assembly. The jacketed piping system shall include a means for collection of leakages and arrangements shall be provided with an alarm in case of a fuel line failure.

2.2.5.3 Oil fuel lines shall not be located immediately above or near units of high temperature, including boilers, steam pipelines, exhaust manifolds, silencers or other equipment required to be insulated by paragraph 2.2.6. As far as practicable, oil fuel lines shall be arranged far apart from hot surfaces, electrical installations or other sources of ignition and shall be screened or otherwise suitably protected to avoid oil spray or oil leakage onto the sources of ignition. The number of joints in such piping systems shall be kept to a minimum.

2.2.5.4 Components of a diesel engine fuel system shall be designed considering the maximum peak pressure which will be experienced in service, including any high-pressure pulses which are generated and transmitted back into the fuel supply and spill lines by the action of fuel injection pumps. Connections within the fuel supply and spill lines shall be constructed having regard to their ability to prevent pressurised oil fuel leaks while in service and after maintenance.

2.2.5.5 In multi-engine installations which are supplied from the same fuel source, means of isolating the fuel supply and spill piping to individual engines, shall be provided. The means of isolation shall not affect the operation of the other engines and shall be operable from a position not rendered inaccessible by a fire on any of the engines.

2.2.5.6 Where the Administration may permit the conveying of oil and combustible liquids through accommodation and service spaces, the pipes conveying oil or combustible liquids shall be of a material approved by the Administration having regard to the fire risk.

2.2.6 Protection of high-temperature surfaces

2.2.6.1 Surfaces with temperatures above 220°C which may be impinged as a result of a fuel system failure shall be properly insulated.

2.2.6.2 Precautions shall be taken to prevent any oil that may escape under pressure from any pump, filter or heater from coming into contact with heated surfaces.

2.3 Arrangements for lubricating oil

2.3.1 The arrangements for the storage, distribution and utilisation of oil used in pressure lubrication systems shall be such as to ensure the safety of the ship and persons on board.

The arrangements made in machinery spaces of category A, and whenever practicable in other machinery spaces, shall at least comply with the provisions of paragraphs 2.2.1, 2.2.3.3, 2.2.3.4, 2.2.3.5, 2.2.4, 2.2.5.1, 2.2.5.3 and 2.2.6, except that:

> *.1 this does not preclude the use of sight-flow glasses in lubricating systems provided that they are shown by testing to have a suitable degree of fire resistance; and*

> *.2 sounding pipes may be authorized in machinery spaces; however, the requirements of paragraphs 2.2.3.5.1.1 and 2.2.3.5.1.3 need not be applied on condition that the sounding pipes are fitted with appropriate means of closure.*

2.3.2 The provisions of paragraph 2.2.3.4 shall also apply to lubricating oil tanks except those having a capacity less than 500 l; storage tanks on which valves are closed during the normal operation mode of the ship, or where it is determined that an unintended operation of a quick-closing valve on the oil lubricating tank would endanger the safe operation of the main propulsion and essential auxiliary machinery.

2.4   Arrangements for other flammable oils

The arrangements for the storage, distribution and utilization of other flammable oils employed under pressure in power transmission systems, control and activating systems and heating systems shall be such as to ensure the safety of the ship and persons on board. Suitable oil collecting arrangements for leaks shall be fitted below hydraulic valves and cylinders. In locations where means of ignition are present, such arrangements shall at least comply with the provisions of paragraphs 2.2.3.3, 2.2.3.5, 2.2.5.3 and 2.2.6 and with the provisions of paragraphs 2.2.4 and 2.2.5.1 in respect of strength and construction.

2.5   Arrangements for oil fuel in periodically unattended machinery spaces

In addition to the requirements of paragraphs 2.1 to 2.4, the oil fuel and lubricating oil systems in a periodically unattended machinery space shall comply with the following:

> *.1 where daily service oil fuel tanks are filled automatically, or by remote control, means shall be provided to prevent overflow spillages. Other equipment which treats flammable liquids automatically (e.g., oil fuel purifiers) which, whenever practicable, shall be installed in a special space reserved for purifiers and their heaters, shall have arrangements to prevent overflow spillages; and*

> *.2 where daily service oil fuel tanks or settling tanks are fitted with heating arrangements, a high temperature alarm shall be provided if the flashpoint of the oil fuel can be exceeded.*

3   Arrangements for gaseous fuel for domestic purposes

Gaseous fuel systems used for domestic purposes shall be approved by the Administration. Storage of gas bottles shall be located on the open deck or in a well ventilated space which opens only to the open deck.

4   Miscellaneous items of ignition sources and ignitability

4.1   Electric radiators

Electric radiators, if used, shall be fixed in position and so constructed as to reduce fire risks to a minimum. No such radiators shall be fitted with an element so exposed that clothing, curtains, or other similar materials can be scorched or set on fire by heat from the element.

4.2   Waste receptacles

Waste receptacles shall be constructed of non-combustible materials with no openings in the sides or bottom.

4.3   Insulation surfaces protected against oil penetration

In spaces where penetration of oil products is possible, the surface of insulation shall be impervious to oil or oil vapours.

4.4   Primary deck coverings

Primary deck coverings, if applied within accommodation and service spaces and control stations, shall be of approved material which will not readily ignite, this being determined in accordance with the Fire Test Procedures Code.

Guidance 4

G1   Electric space heaters

G1.1   In this Regulation 'similar materials' includes free standing furniture, particularly those items with upholstered parts, which should not be placed near to the heater.

G2   Oil and vapour barriers

G2.1   Flexible vapour barriers

G2.1.1   Any joint in a flexible oil and oil vapour barrier should be sealed with tape of the same material as the vapour barrier or a compatible material having a minimum width of 50mm using an adhesive which is also compatible. The advice of the manufacturer of the insulation or vapour barrier should be sought where there is doubt as to the compatibility of materials.

G2.1.2   It should be noted that in no case where a vapour barrier is fitted should the wire netting securing an 'A' Class insulation be dispensed with.

G2.1.3   Where there is a risk of an 'A' Class insulation becoming damaged by the shipping or unshipping of items of machinery or similar operations, then a metal oil and oil vapour barrier referred to in the following paragraph will afford some protection to the insulation. See also regulation 5.3.1.1.

G2.2   Metal vapour barriers

G2.2.1   In no case must a metal vapour barrier be fitted directly on the face of an 'A' Class insulation in lieu of the wire netting or otherwise, because fire casualties have revealed that the restraint afforded by the steel pins against expansion has buckled the metal vapour barrier causing serious damage to the insulation and forcing the spring washers off the pins resulting in the falling down of the barrier and insulation.

G2.2.2   Metal oil and oil vapour barriers should be attached to the ship's structure independently of an 'A' Class insulation with a gap of at least 20mm between the exposed face of the insulation and the vapour barrier. The number and size of the means of securing the vapour barrier to the structure should be kept to a minimum in order to ensure that heat transfer through the insulation is minimal. A penetration should not exceed 100mm^2 in cross sectional area, nor should it be spaced less than 500mm from another penetration. The metal should be unperforated.

4

G3   Deck coverings

G3.1 Primary deck coverings

G3.1.1   Each primary deck covering which is to be used in accommodation spaces, service spaces and control stations should also comply with regulation 6.3.

G3.1.2   See regulation 5.3.2.1 for information relating to approved deck coverings incorporating 'A' Class overdeck insulations.

5   Cargo areas of tankers

5.1   Separation of cargo oil tanks

5.1.1   Cargo pump-rooms, cargo tanks, slop tanks and cofferdams shall be positioned forward of machinery spaces. However, oil fuel bunker tanks need not be forward of machinery spaces. Cargo tanks and slop tanks shall be isolated from machinery spaces by cofferdams, cargo pump-rooms, oil bunker tanks or ballast tanks. Pump-rooms containing pumps and their accessories for ballasting those spaces situated adjacent to cargo tanks and slop tanks and pumps for oil fuel transfer, shall be considered as equivalent to a cargo pump-room within the context of this regulation provided that such pump-rooms have the same safety standard as that required for cargo pump-rooms. Pump-rooms intended solely for ballast or oil fuel transfer, however, need not comply with the requirements of regulation 10.9. The lower portion of the pump-room may be recessed into machinery spaces of category A to accommodate pumps, provided that the deck head of the recess is in general not more than one third of the moulded depth above the keel, except that in the case of ships of not more than 25,000 tonnes deadweight, where it can be demonstrated that for reasons of access and satisfactory piping arrangements this is impracticable, the Administration may permit a recess in excess of such height, but not exceeding one half of the moulded depth above the keel.

5.1.2   Main cargo control stations, control stations, accommodation and service spaces (excluding isolated cargo handling gear lockers) shall be positioned aft of cargo tanks, slop tanks, and spaces which isolate cargo or slop tanks from machinery spaces, but not necessarily aft of the oil fuel bunker tanks and ballast tanks, and shall be arranged in such a way that a single failure of a deck or bulkhead shall not permit the entry of gas or fumes from the cargo tanks into main cargo control stations, control stations, or accommodation and service spaces. A recess provided in accordance with paragraph 5.1.1 need not be taken into account when the position of these spaces is being determined.

5.1.3   However, where deemed necessary, the Administration may permit main cargo control stations, control stations, accommodation and service spaces forward of the cargo tanks, slop tanks and spaces which isolate cargo and slop tanks from machinery spaces, but not necessarily forward of oil fuel bunker tanks or ballast tanks. Machinery spaces, other than those of category A, may be permitted forward of the cargo tanks and slop tanks provided they are isolated from the cargo tanks and slop tanks by cofferdams, cargo pump-rooms, oil fuel bunker tanks or ballast tanks, and have at least one portable fire extinguisher. In cases where they contain internal combustion machinery, one approved foam-type extinguisher of at least 45 l capacity or equivalent shall be arranged in addition to portable fire extinguishers. If operation of a semi-portable fire extinguisher is impracticable, this fire *extinguisher may be replaced by two additional portable fire extinguishers. Main cargo control stations, control stations and accommodation and service spaces shall be arranged in such a way that a single failure of a deck or bulkhead shall not permit the entry of gas or fumes from the cargo tanks into such spaces. In addition, where deemed necessary for the safety or navigation of the ship, the Administration may permit machinery spaces containing internal combustion machinery not being main propulsion machinery having an output greater than 375 kW to be located forward of the cargo area provided the arrangements are in accordance with the provisions of this paragraph.*

5.1.4   In combination carriers only:

.1   The slop tanks shall be surrounded by cofferdams except where the boundaries of the slop tanks, are part of the hull, main cargo deck, cargo pump-room bulkhead or oil fuel bunker tank. These cofferdams shall not be open to a double bottom, pipe tunnel, pump-room or other enclosed space, nor shall they be used for cargo or ballast and shall not be connected to piping systems serving oil cargo or ballast. Means shall be provided for filling the cofferdams with water and for draining them. Where the boundary of a slop tank is part of the cargo pump-room bulkhead, the pump-room shall not be open to the double bottom, pipe tunnel or other enclosed space; however, openings provided with gastight bolted covers may be permitted;

.2   Means shall be provided for isolating the piping connecting the pump-room with the slop tanks referred to in paragraph 5.1.4.1. The means of isolation shall consist of a valve followed by a spectacle flange or a spool piece with appropriate blank flanges. This arrangement shall be located adjacent to the slop tanks, but where this is unreasonable or impracticable, it may be located within the pump-room directly after the piping penetrates the bulkhead. A separate permanently installed pumping and piping arrangement incorporating a manifold, provided with a shut-off valve and a blank flange, shall be provided for discharging the contents of the slop tanks directly to the open deck for disposal to shore reception facilities when the ship is in the dry cargo mode. When the transfer system is used for slop transfer in the dry cargo mode, it shall have no connection to other systems. Separation from other systems by means of removal of spool pieces may be accepted;

.3   Hatches and tank cleaning openings to slop tanks shall only be permitted on the open deck and shall be fitted with closing arrangements. Except where they consist of bolted plates with bolts at watertight spacing, these closing arrangements shall be provided with locking arrangements under the control of the responsible ship's officer; and

.4   Where cargo wing tanks are provided, cargo oil lines below deck shall be installed inside these tanks. However, the Administration may permit cargo oil lines to be placed in special ducts provided these are capable of being adequately cleaned and ventilated to the satisfaction of the Administration. Where cargo wing tanks are not provided, cargo oil lines below deck shall be placed in special ducts.

5.1.5   Where the fitting of a navigation position above the cargo area is shown to be necessary, it shall be for navigation purposes only and it shall be separated from the cargo tank deck by means of an open space with a height of at least 2 m. The fire protection requirements for such a navigation position shall be those required for control stations, as specified in regulation 9.2.4.2 and other provisions for tankers, as applicable.

5.1.6   Means shall be provided to keep deck spills away from the accommodation and service areas. This may be accomplished by provision of a permanent continuous coaming of a height of at least 300 mm, extending from side to side. Special consideration shall be given to the arrangements associated with stern loading.

5.2   Restriction on boundary openings

5.2.1   Except as permitted in paragraph 5.2.2, access doors, air inlets and openings to accommodation spaces, service spaces, control stations and machinery spaces shall not face the cargo area. They shall be located on the transverse bulkhead not facing the cargo area or on the outboard side of the superstructure or deckhouse at a distance of at least 4% of the length of the ship, but not less than 3 m from the end of the superstructure or deckhouse facing the cargo area. This distance need not exceed 5 m.

5.2.2   The Administration may permit access doors in boundary bulkheads facing the cargo area or within the 5 m limits specified in paragraph 5.2.1, to main cargo control stations and to such service spaces used as provision rooms, store-rooms and lockers, provided they do not give access directly or indirectly to any other space containing or providing for accommodation, control stations or service spaces such as galleys, pantries or workshops, or similar spaces containing sources of vapour ignition. The boundary of such a space shall be insulated to "A–60" class standard, with the exception of the boundary facing the cargo area. Bolted plates for the removal of machinery may be fitted within the limits specified in paragraph 5.2.1. Wheelhouse doors and windows may be located within the limits specified in paragraph 5.2.1 so long as they are designed to ensure that the wheelhouse can be made rapidly and efficiently gastight and vapourtight.

5.2.3   Windows and sidescuttles facing the cargo area and on the sides of the superstructures and deckhouses within the limits specified in paragraph 5.2.1 shall be of the fixed (non-opening) type. Such windows and sidescuttles, except wheelhouse windows, shall be constructed to "A–60" class standard.

5.2.4   Where there is permanent access from a pipe tunnel to the main pump-room, a watertight door shall be fitted complying with the requirements of regulation II–1/25–9.2 and, in addition, with the following:

> *.1   in addition to the bridge operation, the watertight door shall be capable of being manually closed from outside the main pump-room entrance; and*

> *.2   the watertight door shall be kept closed during normal operations of the ship except when access to the pipe tunnel is required.*

5.2.5   Permanent approved gastight lighting enclosures for illuminating cargo pump-rooms may be permitted in bulkheads and decks separating cargo pump-rooms and other spaces provided they are of adequate strength and the integrity and gastightness of the bulkhead or deck is maintained.

5.2.6   The arrangement of ventilation inlets and outlets and other deckhouse and superstructure boundary space openings shall be such as to complement the provisions of paragraph 5.3 and regulation 11.6. Such vents, especially for machinery spaces, shall be situated as far aft as practicable. Due consideration in this regard shall be given when the ship is equipped to load or discharge at the stern. Sources of ignition such as electrical equipment shall be so arranged as to avoid an explosion hazard.

5.3   Cargo tank venting

5.3.1   General requirements

The venting systems of cargo tanks shall be entirely distinct from the air pipes of the other compartments of the ship. The arrangements and position of openings in the cargo tank deck from which emission of flammable vapours can occur shall be such as to minimize the possibility of flammable vapours being admitted to enclosed spaces containing a source of ignition, or collecting in the vicinity of deck machinery and equipment which may constitute an ignition hazard. In accordance with this general principle, the criteria in paragraphs 5.3.2 to 5.3.5 and regulation 11.6 will apply.

5.3.2   Venting arrangements

> *5.3.2.1 The venting arrangements in each cargo tank may be independent or combined with other cargo tanks and may be incorporated into the inert gas piping.*
>
> *5.3.2.2 Where the arrangements are combined with other cargo tanks, either stop valves or other acceptable means shall be provided to isolate each cargo tank. Where stop valves are fitted, they shall be provided with locking arrangements which shall be under the control of the responsible ship's officer. There shall be a clear visual indication of the operational status of the valves or other acceptable means. Where tanks have been isolated, it shall be ensured that relevant isolating valves are opened before cargo loading or ballasting or discharging of those tanks is commenced. Any isolation must continue to permit the flow caused by thermal variations in a cargo tank in accordance with regulation 11.6.1.1.*
>
> *5.3.2.3 If cargo loading and ballasting or discharging of a cargo tank or cargo tank group which is isolated from a common venting system is intended, that cargo tank or cargo tank group shall be fitted with a means for over-pressure or under-pressure protection as required in regulation 11.6.3.2.*
>
> *5.3.2.4 The venting arrangements shall be connected to the top of each cargo tank and shall be self-draining to the cargo tanks under all normal conditions of trim and list of the ship. Where it may not be possible to provide self-draining lines, permanent arrangements shall be provided to drain the vent lines to a cargo tank.*

5.3.3   Safety devices in venting systems

The venting system shall be provided with devices to prevent the passage of flame into the cargo tanks. The design, testing and locating of these devices shall comply with the requirements established by the Administration based on the guidelines developed by the

Organization.* Ullage openings shall not be used for pressure equalisation. They shall be provided with self-closing and tightly sealing covers. Flame arresters and screens are not permitted in these openings.

5.3.4   Vent outlets for cargo handling and ballasting

5.3.4.1 Vent outlets for cargo loading, discharging and ballasting required by regulation 11.6.1.2 shall:

.1.1   *permit the free flow of vapour mixtures; or*

.1.2   *permit the throttling of the discharge of the vapour mixtures to achieve a velocity of not less than 30 m/s;*

.2   *be so arranged that the vapour mixture is discharged vertically upwards;*

.3   *where the method is by free flow of vapour mixtures, be such that the outlet shall be not less than 6 m above the cargo tank deck or fore and aft gangway if situated within 4 m of the gangway and located not less than 10 m measured horizontally from the nearest air intakes and openings to enclosed spaces containing a source of ignition and from deck machinery, which may include anchor windlass and chain locker openings, and equipment which may constitute an ignition hazard; and*

.4   *where the method is by high-velocity discharge, be located at a height not less than 2 m above the cargo tank deck and not less than 10 m measured horizontally from the nearest air intakes and openings to enclosed spaces containing a source of ignition and from deck machinery, which may include anchor windlass and chain locker openings, and equipment which may constitute an ignition hazard. These outlets shall be provided with high-velocity devices of an approved type.*

5.3.4.2 The arrangements for the venting of vapours displaced from the cargo tanks during loading and ballasting shall comply with paragraph 5.3 and regulation 11.6 and shall consist of either one or more mast risers, or a number of high-velocity vents. The inert gas supply main may be used for such venting.

5.3.5   *Isolation of slop tanks in combination carriers*

In combination carriers, the arrangements for isolating slop tanks containing oil or oil residues from other cargo tanks shall consist of blank flanges which will remain in position at all times when cargoes other than liquid cargoes referred to in regulation 1.6.1 are carried.

5.4   Ventilation

5.4.1   *Ventilation systems in cargo pump-rooms*

Cargo pump-rooms shall be mechanically ventilated and discharges from the exhaust fans shall be led to a safe place on the open deck. The ventilation of these rooms shall have

---

* Refer to MSC/Circ.677, Revised standards for the design, testing and locating of devices to prevent the passage of flame into cargo tanks in tankers, and to MSC/Circ.450/Rev.1, Revised factors to be taken into consideration when designing cargo tank venting and gas-freeing arrangements.

sufficient capacity to minimise the possibility of accumulation of flammable vapours. The number of air changes shall be at least 20 per hour, based upon the gross volume of the space. The air ducts shall be arranged so that all of the space is effectively ventilated. The ventilation shall be of the suction type using fans of the non-sparking type.

5.4.2   Ventilation systems in combination carriers

In combination carriers, cargo spaces and any enclosed spaces adjacent to cargo spaces shall be capable of being mechanically ventilated. The mechanical ventilation may be provided by portable fans. An approved fixed gas warning system capable of monitoring flammable vapours shall be provided in cargo pump-rooms, pipe ducts and cofferdams, as referred to in paragraph 5.1.4, adjacent to slop tanks. Suitable arrangements shall be made to facilitate measurement of flammable vapours in all other spaces within the cargo area. Such measurements shall be made possible from the open deck or easily accessible positions.

5.5   Inert gas systems

5.5.1   Application

5.5.1.1 For tankers of 20,000 tonnes deadweight and upwards, the protection of the cargo tanks shall be achieved by a fixed inert gas system in accordance with the requirements of the Fire Safety Systems Code, except that, in lieu of the above, the Administration, after having given consideration to the ship's arrangement and equipment, may accept other fixed installations if they afford protection equivalent to the above, in accordance with regulation I/5. The requirements for alternative fixed installations shall comply with the requirements in paragraph 5.5.4.

5.5.1.2 Tankers operating with a cargo tank cleaning procedure using crude oil washing shall be fitted with an inert gas system complying with the Fire Safety Systems Code and with fixed tank washing machines.

5.5.1.3 Tankers required to be fitted with inert gas systems shall comply with the following provisions:

.1 double hull spaces shall be fitted with suitable connections for the supply of inert gas;

.2 where hull spaces are connected to a permanently fitted inert gas distribution system, means shall be provided to prevent hydrocarbon gases from the cargo tanks entering the double hull spaces through the system; and

.3 where such spaces are not permanently connected to an inert gas distribution system, appropriate means shall be provided to allow connection to the inert gas main.

5.5.2   Inert gas systems of chemical tankers and gas carriers

The requirements for inert gas systems contained in the Fire Safety Systems Code need not be applied to:

.1 chemical tankers and gas carriers when carrying cargoes described in regulation 1.6.1, provided that they comply with the requirements for inert gas systems on *chemical tankers established by the Administration, based on the guidelines developed by the Organization;* or*

.2 chemical tankers and gas carriers when carrying flammable cargoes other than crude oil or petroleum products such as cargoes listed in chapters 17 and 18 of the International Bulk Chemical Code, provided that the capacity of tanks used for their carriage does not exceed 3,000 m3 and the individual nozzle capacities of tank washing machines do not exceed 17.5 m3/h and the total combined throughput from the number of machines in use in a cargo tank at any one time does not exceed 110 m³/h.

5.5.3   *General requirements for inert gas systems*

5.5.3.1 The inert gas system shall be capable of inerting, purging and gas-freeing empty tanks and maintaining the atmosphere in cargo tanks with the required oxygen content.

5.5.3.2 The inert gas system referred to in paragraph 5.5.3.1 shall be designed, constructed and tested in accordance with the Fire Safety Systems Code.

5.5.3.3 Tankers fitted with a fixed inert gas system shall be provided with a closed ullage system.

5.5.4   *Requirements for equivalent systems*

5.5.4.1 Where an installation equivalent to a fixed inert gas system is installed, it shall:

.1 be capable of preventing dangerous accumulations of explosive mixtures in intact cargo tanks during normal service throughout the ballast voyage and necessary in-tank operations; and

.2 be so designed as to minimize the risk of ignition from the generation of static electricity by the system itself.

5.6   Inerting, purging and gas-freeing

5.6.1   Arrangements for purging and/or gas-freeing shall be such as to minimize the hazards due to dispersal of flammable vapours in the atmosphere and to flammable mixtures in a cargo tank.

5.6.2   The procedure for cargo tank purging and/or gas-freeing shall be carried out in accordance with regulation 16.3.2.

5.6.3   The arrangements for inerting, purging or gas-freeing of empty tanks as required in paragraph 5.5.3.1 shall be to the satisfaction of the Administration and shall be such that the accumulation of hydrocarbon vapours in pockets formed by the internal structural members in a tank is minimized and that:

.1 on individual cargo tanks, the gas outlet pipe, if fitted, shall be positioned as far as practicable from the inert gas/air inlet and in accordance with paragraph 5.3 and

---

*   Refer to the Regulation for inert gas systems on chemical tankers adopted by the Organization by resolution A.567(14).

regulation 11.6. The inlet of such outlet pipes may be located either at deck level or at not more than 1 m above the bottom of the tank;

.2 *the cross-sectional area of such gas outlet pipe referred to in paragraph 5.6.3.1 shall be such that an exit velocity of at least 20 m/s can be maintained when any three tanks are being simultaneously supplied with inert gas. Their outlets shall extend not less than 2 m above deck level; and*

.3 *each gas outlet referred to in paragraph 5.6.3.2 shall be fitted with suitable blanking arrangements.*

5.7   Gas measurement

5.7.1   *Portable instrument*

Tankers shall be equipped with at least one portable instrument for measuring flammable vapour concentrations, together with a sufficient set of spares. Suitable means shall be provided for the calibration of such instruments.

5.7.2   Arrangements for gas measurement in double hull spaces and double bottom spaces

5.7.2.1 Suitable portable instruments for measuring oxygen and flammable vapour concentrations shall be provided. In selecting these instruments, due attention shall be given to their use in combination with the fixed gas sampling line systems referred to in paragraph 5.7.2.2.

5.7.2.2 Where the atmosphere in double hull spaces cannot be reliably measured using flexible gas sampling hoses, such spaces shall be fitted with permanent gas sampling lines. The configuration of gas sampling lines shall be adapted to the design of such spaces.

5.7.2.3 The materials of construction and the dimensions of gas sampling lines shall be such as to prevent restriction. Where plastic materials are used, they shall be electrically conductive.

5.8   Air supply to double hull spaces and double bottom spaces

Double hull spaces and double bottom spaces shall be fitted with suitable connections for the supply of air.

5.9   Protection of cargo area

Drip pans for collecting cargo residues in cargo lines and hoses shall be provided in the area of pipe and hose connections under the manifold area. Cargo hoses and tank washing hoses shall have electrical continuity over their entire lengths including couplings and flanges (except shore connections), and shall be earthed for removal of electrostatic charges.

5.10   Protection of cargo pump-rooms

5.10.1 *In tankers:*

.1 *cargo pumps, ballast pumps and stripping pumps, installed in cargo pump-rooms and driven by shafts passing through pump-room bulkheads shall be fitted with temperature sensing devices for bulkhead shaft glands, bearings and pump casings. A continuous audible and visual alarm signal shall be automatically effected in the cargo control room or the pump control station;*

.2 *lighting in cargo pump-rooms, except emergency lighting, shall be interlocked with ventilation such that the ventilation shall be in operation when switching on the lighting. Failure of the ventilation system shall not cause the lighting to go out;*

.3 *a system for continuous monitoring of the concentration of hydrocarbon gases shall be fitted. Sampling points or detector heads shall be located in suitable positions in order that potentially dangerous leakages are readily detected. When the hydrocarbon gas concentration reaches a pre-set level, which shall not be higher than 10% of the lower flammable limit, a continuous audible and visual alarm signal shall be automatically effected in the pump-room, engine control room, cargo control room and navigation bridge to alert personnel to the potential hazard; and*

.4 *all pump-rooms shall be provided with bilge level monitoring devices together with appropriately located alarms.*

Guidance 4

G4   Openings

G4.1   The 4% of the length of the ship, referred to in paragraph 5.2.1, should be measured from the line at which the superstructure or deckhouse ceases to have any forward projection when the superstructure or deckhouse is situated aft of the cargo area as illustrated in figure 9.8 in guidance to regulation 9.2 insulation of exterior boundaries of tankers. When the superstructure or deckhouse is situated forward of the cargo area, the method of measurement should be a 'mirror image' of that used for a superstructure or deckhouse situated aft of the cargo area.

G5   Doors

G5.1   Paragraph 5.2.2 does not permit doors to be fitted in the exterior boundaries of superstructures or deckhouses indicated in paragraph 5.2.1, to which the previous paragraph refers, except doors giving access to cargo control stations, provision rooms or store rooms provided that such a space does not give access to accommodation spaces, service spaces or control stations. The Regulation further indicates that when such a door gives access to any such space situated aft of the cargo area, the boundaries of the space, including the deckhead, but excluding the boundary facing the cargo area, should be insulated with an A–60 insulation. This requirement should also apply to any such door giving access to cargo control stations, provision rooms or store rooms situated forward of the cargo area in a superstructure or deckhouse enclosing accommodation, even though paragraph 5.2.2 may be interpreted as implying that the boundaries of such a space situated forward of the cargo area need not be insulated. The boundaries of such a space situated forward of the cargo area need not be insulated when it is in a superstructure or deckhouse which does not enclose accommodation and the space does not give access to any service space or control station. Furthermore, the requirement to insulate the boundaries of a cargo control station, provision room or store room with an A–60 insulation as indicated in paragraph 5.2.2 is illogical if applied literally to such spaces situated at the corners or sides of a superstructure or deckhouse and such spaces should be insulated as illustrated in figure 9.10 in guidance to regulation 9.2 on insulation of exterior boundaries of tankers.

G5.2   Surveyors should ensure that when bolted plates for the removal of machinery are fitted in the portions of the exterior boundaries of superstructures and deckhouses referred to in paragraph 5.2.1, the plates are insulated with an A–60 insulation in such a manner that the insulation is not likely to be damaged when the plates are removed and replaced. In the circumstances a board type insulation approved for A–60 general application may be less susceptible to damage than any other type of insulation, particularly if it were faced with sheet steel and its edges protected by flats welded to the plates.

G6   Gastightness test for the navigation bridge external doors and windows

G6.1   The navigation bridge external doors and windows which are located within the limits stated in paragraph 5.2.1 should be tested for gastightness. If a water hose test is to be used, then the following may be taken as a guide:

   .1   nozzle diameter, 12mm;

   .2   water pressure just before the nozzle, not less than 2 bar; and

   .3   distance between the nozzle and the doors or windows; maximum 1.5m.

G7   Windows and sidescuttles

G7.1   The frames of windows and sidescuttles situated in the portions of the exterior boundaries of superstructures and deckhouses referred to in paragraph 5.2.1 should be constructed of steel and such windows should be fitted with an approved fire resisting glass except that such glass should not be fitted in windows situated in the boundaries of the wheelhouse. The fire resisting glass should be fitted in accordance with the conditions in the approval certificate. Note, the maximum size of window which may be used in association with a fire resisting glass is also stipulated in the approval certificate.

G7.2   The fire resisting glass should be of a type which has been accepted for use in A60 divisions.

G7.3   Such glass or glass assemblies should be toughened safety glass as required by British Standard MA24: 1974.

G8   Lighting enclosures for illuminating cargo pump rooms.

G8.1   When light enclosures are intended to be fitted in boundary bulkheads and decks of cargo pump rooms as allowed in paragraph 5.2.5 details of their construction should be submitted to MCA Headquarters for consideration and approval.

G8.2   Electric cable transits which have been approved for use in watertight 'A' Class divisions should be used when the cables to the light enclosures pass through such boundary bulkheads and decks. See guidance G9.48.2 on electric cables penetrating watertight 'A' class divisions.

Fire growth potential

1.   Purpose

The purpose of this regulation is to limit the fire growth potential in every space of the ship. For this purpose, the following functional requirements shall be met:

> *.1 means of control for the air supply to the space shall be provided;*
>
> *.2 means of control for flammable liquids in the space shall be provided; and*
>
> *.3 the use of combustible materials shall be restricted.*

2   Control of air supply and flammable liquid to the space

2.1   Closing appliances and stopping devices of ventilation

2.1.1   The main inlets and outlets of all ventilation systems shall be capable of being closed from outside the spaces being ventilated. The means of closing shall be easily accessible as well as prominently and permanently marked and shall indicate whether the shut-off is open or closed.

2.1.2   Power ventilation of accommodation spaces, service spaces, cargo spaces, control stations and machinery spaces shall be capable of being stopped from an easily accessible position outside the space being served. This position shall not be readily cut off in the event of a fire in the spaces served.

2.1.3   In passenger ships carrying more than 36 passengers, power ventilation, except machinery space and cargo space ventilation and any alternative system which may be required under regulation 8.2, shall be fitted with controls so grouped that all fans may be stopped from either of two separate positions which shall be situated as far apart as practicable. Fans serving power ventilation systems to cargo spaces shall be capable of being stopped from a safe position outside such spaces.

2.2   Means of control in machinery spaces

2.2.1   Means of control shall be provided for opening and closure of skylights, closure of openings in funnels which normally allow exhaust ventilation and closure of ventilator dampers.

2.2.2   Means of control shall be provided for stopping ventilating fans. Controls provided for the power ventilation serving machinery spaces shall be grouped so as to be operable from two positions, one of which shall be outside such spaces. The means provided for stopping the power ventilation of the machinery spaces shall be entirely separate from the means provided for stopping ventilation of other spaces.

2.2.3   Means of control shall be provided for stopping forced and induced draught fans, oil fuel transfer pumps, oil fuel unit pumps, lubricating oil service pumps, thermal oil circulating pumps and oil separators (purifiers). However, paragraphs 2.2.4 and 2.2.5 need not apply to oily water separators.

2.2.4   The controls required in paragraphs 2.2.1 to 2.2.3 and in regulation 4.2.2.3.4 shall be located outside the space concerned so they will not be cut off in the event of fire in the space they serve.

2.2.5   In passenger ships, the controls required in paragraphs 2.2.1 to 2.2.4 and in regulations 8.3.3 and 9.5.2.3 and the controls for any required fire-extinguishing system shall be situated at one control position or grouped in as few positions as possible to the satisfaction of the Administration. Such positions shall have a safe access from the open deck.

2.3   Additional requirements for means of control in periodically unattended machinery spaces

2.3.1   For periodically unattended machinery spaces, the Administration shall give special consideration to maintaining the fire integrity of the machinery spaces, the location and centralization of the fire-extinguishing system controls, the required shutdown arrangements (e.g., ventilation, fuel pumps, etc.) and that additional fire-extinguishing appliances and other fire-fighting equipment and breathing apparatus may be required.

2.3.2   In passenger ships, these requirements shall be at least equivalent to those of machinery spaces normally attended.

Guidance 5

G1   Remote means of control

G1.1 Controls required for the closure of certain oil fuel suction valves, closing of openings, stopping of ventilation and forced draft fans etc., should be centralised as far as is reasonable and practicable. In respect of oil fuel suction valves, means should be provided at the remote station to show when the closure of the valve has been initiated. Where the means for the remote closing of oil valves is by extended spindle, no special fire protection need be fitted, provided no low melting point materials are used. Otherwise and where the means of closing is electric, pneumatic or hydraulic, the operating system should be capable of withstanding the appropriate fire test. The source of power to effect the closure of such power operated systems should be located outside the space in which the valves are situated.

G1.2 Power operated means for the closure of openings should, if they are the only means, be treated in a similar manner to power operated means provided for the closure of oil fuel. With regard to the remote means provided for stopping oil fuel pressure pumps, surveyors should ensure that such a facility is not merely part of a remote control system, i.e. designed to stop and start the said pumps, unless a manual reset is provided which must be operated before starting can be effected.

G1.3 The remote controls for stopping ventilation fans serving accommodation spaces should be extended to include remote stops for fans used in conjunction with air conditioning units. Any controls for operating the re-circulation of air should be capable of being rapidly put into the non-recirculation mode. This is to enable the units to be rapidly stopped from the centralised position to prevent circulation of smoke throughout the accommodation.

3   Fire protection materials

3.1   Use of non-combustible materials

3.1.1   Insulating materials

Insulating materials shall be non-combustible, except in cargo spaces, mail rooms, baggage rooms and refrigerated compartments of service spaces. Vapour barriers and adhesives used in conjunction with insulation, as well as the insulation of pipe fittings for cold service systems, need not be of non-combustible materials, but they shall be kept to the minimum quantity practicable and their exposed surfaces shall have low flame-spread characteristics.

3.1.2   Ceilings and linings

3.1.2.1   In passenger ships, except in cargo spaces, all linings, grounds, draught stops and ceilings shall be of non-combustible material except in mail rooms, baggage rooms, saunas or refrigerated compartments of service spaces. Partial bulkheads or decks used to subdivide a space for utility or artistic treatment shall also be of non-combustible materials.

3.1.2.2 In cargo ships, all linings, ceilings, draught stops and their associated grounds shall be of non-combustible materials in the following spaces:

.1 in accommodation and service spaces and control stations for ships where method IC is specified as referred to in regulation 9.2.3.1; and

.2 in corridors and stairway enclosures serving accommodation and service spaces and control stations for ships where method IIC and IIIC are specified as referred to in regulation 9.2.3.1.

3.2 Use of combustible materials

3.2.1 General

3.2.1.1 In passenger ships, "A", "B" or "C" class divisions in accommodation and service spaces which are faced with combustible materials, facings, mouldings, decorations and veneers shall comply with the provisions of paragraphs 3.2.2 to 3.2.4 and regulation 6. However, traditional wooden benches and wooden linings on bulkheads and ceilings are permitted in saunas and such materials need not be subject to the calculations prescribed in paragraphs 3.2.2 and 3.2.3.

3.2.1.2 In cargo ships, non-combustible bulkheads, ceilings and linings fitted in accommodation and service spaces may be faced with combustible materials, facings, mouldings, decorations and veneers provided such spaces are bounded by non-combustible bulkheads, ceilings and linings in accordance with the provisions of paragraphs 3.2.2 to 3.2.4 and regulation 6.

3.2.2 Maximum calorific value of combustible materials

Combustible materials used on the surfaces and linings specified in paragraph 3.2.1 shall have a calorific value* not exceeding 45 MJ/m^2 of the area for the thickness used. The requirements of this paragraph are not applicable to the surfaces of furniture fixed to linings or bulkheads.

3.2.3 Total volume of combustible materials

Where combustible materials are used in accordance with paragraph 3.2.1, they shall comply with the following requirements:

.1 The total volume of combustible facings, mouldings, decorations and veneers in accommodation and service spaces shall not exceed a volume equivalent to 2.5 mm veneer on the combined area of the walls and ceiling linings. Furniture fixed to linings, bulkheads or decks need not be included in the calculation of the total volume of combustible materials; and

.2 In the case of ships fitted with an automatic sprinkler system complying with the provisions of the Fire Safety Systems Code, the above volume may include some combustible material used for erection of "C" class divisions.

---

* Refer to the recommendations published by the International Organization for Standardization, in particular publication ISO 1716:2002, Determination of calorific potential.

3.2.4   Low flame-spread characteristics of exposed surfaces

The following surfaces shall have low flame-spread characteristics in accordance with the Fire Test Procedures Code:

> *3.2.4.1 In passenger ships:*
>
> *.1   exposed surfaces in corridors and stairway enclosures and of bulkhead and ceiling linings in accommodation and service spaces (except saunas) and control stations; and*
>
> *.2   surfaces and grounds in concealed or inaccessible spaces in accommodation and service spaces and control stations.*
>
> *3.2.4.2 In cargo ships:*
>
> *.1   exposed surfaces in corridors and stairway enclosures and of ceilings in accommodation and service spaces (except saunas) and control stations; and*
>
> *.2   surfaces and grounds in concealed or inaccessible spaces in accommodation and service spaces and control stations.*

3.3   Furniture in stairway enclosures of passenger ships

Furniture in stairway enclosures shall be limited to seating. It shall be fixed, limited to six seats on each deck in each stairway enclosure, be of restricted fire risk determined in accordance with the Fire Test Procedure Code, and shall not restrict the passenger escape route. The Administration may permit additional seating in the main reception area within a stairway enclosure if it is fixed, non-combustible and does not restrict the passenger escape route. Furniture shall not be permitted in passenger and crew corridors forming escape routes in cabin areas. In addition to the above, lockers of non-combustible material, providing storage for non-hazardous safety equipment required by these regulations, may be permitted. Drinking water dispensers and ice cube machines may be permitted in corridors provided they are fixed and do not restrict the width of the escape routes. This applies as well to decorative flower or plant arrangements, statues or other objects of art such as paintings and tapestries in corridors and stairways.

Guidance 5

G2   Insulating materials

G2.1   The 'exception' referred to in paragraph 3.1.1 regarding insulation of pipe fittings for cold service systems, may include the refrigerating machinery. When considering exposed surfaces in connection with insulating materials such surfaces should include the substrate insulation in the thickness used, or the greatest thickness permitted by the test method for the specimen construction, whichever is greatest.

G2.2   Where organic foam, cork or other highly flammable materials or materials known to readily emit toxic products when decomposing are used to insulate refrigerated compartments, the compartments should be located as remotely as practicable from the accommodation spaces. However when such spaces are adjacent to accommodation spaces the bulkheads and their supporting decks separating the compartments from the accommodation should be of gastight construction and any door in such bulkheads should be of gastight construction in compliance with the Merchant Shipping (Crew Accommodation) Regulations 1997 (Regulation 31 refers).

G3   Ceilings, linings etc

G3.1 In paragraph 3.1.2 a ceiling which is the insulating medium for an 'A' Class deck should not be penetrated by bulkheads and linings which are 'B' Class or 'C' Class divisions or combustible divisions nor should it rely on support afforded by such bulkheads and linings. The ceiling should be supported in accordance with the approved drawing at the ships side, deckhouse side or 'A' Class bulkheads and also from the deckhead by steel hangers and/or on the flanges of the top channel profiles of bulkheads and linings, the profiles being supported by steel hangers from the deckhead. Such top channel profiles should be unperforated as indicated in the guidance G9.2.5.5.

G3.2 Any material which is required by paragraph 3.1 to be non-combustible should be of an approved type except where such materials are not required to be tested as indicated in regulation 3.33 by the Fire Test Procedures Code.

G3.3 Combustible primary deck coverings should not be laid under 'A' Class insulations 'B' Class bulkheads or linings and 'C' Class bulkheads or linings.

G3.4 The ceilings and linings within accommodation spaces, service spaces, control stations and machinery spaces except in mail rooms, baggage rooms and refrigerated compartments, required by this regulation to be constructed of non-combustible materials may be the insulating media for 'A' Class divisions and/or 'B' Class divisions or 'C' Class divisions depending on the arrangements of the ship.

G4   Window and sidescuttle boxes

G4.1 Linings at the ships side, deck side or end in the way of windows or side scuttle openings should be boxed in. The boxes should generally be of the same material and thickness as the adjacent lining, except that where this is a B–0 or 'C' Class division, sheet steel may be used.

G4.2 The construction of the boxes should be similar to that of the lining as shown on the approved drawing relating to the boards or panels used and to the satisfaction of the surveyor.

G4.3 Notwithstanding the above comments when the structure is of steel the non-combustible boxes may be dispensed with for:

    .1 a space not exceeding 6m in length measured along the lining at the ships side or deckhouse side; or

    .2 a space of any length containing furniture and furnishings of restricted fire risk provided that in either case the bulkheads and ceilings bounding the space are carried to the ships side or deckhouse side.

G4.4 Draught stops should be fitted when spaces behind the linings exceed 14m in length.

G4.5 GRP window or sidescuttle boxes may be fitted in addition to, but not instead of, the non-combustible boxes and in the case of a passenger ship the GRP boxes should be included in the total volume of combustible facings, mouldings etc. referred to in paragraph 3.2.3.

G4.6 However GRP window and sidescuttle boxes should not be fitted on tankers around windows and sidescuttles in the exterior boundaries of superstructures and deckhouses referred to in regulation 9.2.4.2.5.

G5   Surface floor coverings

G5.1 In addition to the surfaces referred to in paragraph 3.2.4.1 surface floor coverings including carpets and carpet underlays, which are to be used in rooms containing furniture and furnishings of restricted fire risk, should be of an approved type having low flame spread characteristics determined in accordance with the Fire Test Procedure Code.

G5.2 Surface floor coverings should not be laid under 'A' Class insulation, 'B' Class bulkheads or and 'C' Class divisions.

G5.3 See regulation 4.4.3 for further information relating to surface deck coverings.

G6 Organic foams in furniture

G6.1 Organic foams should not be used in the construction of furniture other than in upholstered parts and mattresses. It is recommended that Combustion Modified High Resilient (CMHR) foams are used in the upholstered parts of furniture and mattresses on United Kingdom registered ships but, in any case, the upholstered parts of furniture in rooms on passenger ships containing 'furniture and furnishings of restricted fire risk' and in stairway enclosures of passenger ships, should be of restricted fire risk as referred to in regulation 3.40.6 and paragraph 3.3 respectively.

G6.2 Approved non-combustible materials which are used without any surface finishes may be accepted as having low flame spread characteristics without having been subjected to a test.

G7 Total volume of combustibles

G7.1 The total volume of combustibles from which the thickness of equivalent veneer is obtained should include laminates, wallcoverings, veneers, paints or any other finishes; skirtings; architraves and covings; mouldings and frames around mirrors, pictures and light fittings; window boxes and any other combustibles used for decorative or other purposes on the bulkheads, ceilings and linings of a space. Any wood dance floors should also be included. See guidance G11.2.1 to regulation 11.2.

G7.2 The total volume of combustibles should not include any textile materials, floor coverings or any part of built-in or free-standing furniture including any wood or chipboard backing board separating adjacent built-in seats provided that the board does not extend more than 300mm above the upholstery on the seat backs. In no case should a 'B' Class or 'C' Class bulkhead, ceiling or linings, or a lining or ceiling used respectively as the insulating medium for an 'A' Class bulkhead or deck be dispensed with in way of built-in furniture or any feature referred to in the previous paragraph.

G7.3 In the case of a ship protected by a sprinkler system where it is not possible to incorporate a decorative feature in a 'C' Class division using non-combustible materials e.g. a radiused corner or shaped portion, the decorative feature may be constructed of wood or composite wood products. This is provided that it is of minimum dimensions compatible with the design and is included in the total volume of combustibles.

G7.4 Each partial bulkhead or partition of any height or partial deck used to divide a space for utility or artistic purposes excluding any backing board referred to in the second paragraph, should be constructed as 'C' Class divisions and any of the features referred to in the first paragraph which are on the divisions should be included in the total volume of combustibles. In the case of a sprinkler protected ship any such divider, partial bulkhead or partition of full height may be included in the combined area of bulkheads, ceilings and linings for the purpose of obtaining the thickness of veneer equivalent to the total volume of combustibles.

G8 Surface finishes – gross calorific potential

G8.1 For the purpose of paragraph 3.2.2 veneers shall include laminates, wallcoverings or any other surface finishes. Approved surface finishes will satisfy this requirement.

G9 Adhesives

G9.1 Combustible adhesives are not required to be tested individually or approved. The type of adhesive which is used in practice to bond the surface finish materials referred to in paragraphs 3.2.4.1 and 3.2.4.2 to substrates is required to be the same as that used to bond the samples of the finish materials subjected to the low flame spread tests in the Fire Test Procedures Code.

G10 Details of construction for cargo ships and tankers

G10.1 Method IC

G10.1.1 Note: Regulation 9.2.4.1 states only method IC shall be used on tankers

G10.1.2 Paragraph 3.1.2.2.1 requires ceilings, linings, draught stops and their associated grounds in accommodation spaces, service spaces and control stations to be non-combustible. Consequently any ceiling or lining which is neither the insulating medium for an 'A' Class division nor a 'B' Class division, should be of 'C' Class standard i.e. constructed of non-combustible materials but having no fire integrity and insulation standards. 'C' Class divisions should be constructed as indicated in the guidance G9.3.

G10.1.3 Window and sidescuttle boxes should be constructed as indicated in the guidance G9.56

G10.1.4 The construction of window and sidescuttle boxes on tankers should be compatible with the standards of the linings in which they are fitted. See paragraph and guidance G9.43 and G9.56 on exterior boundaries of tankers after Regulations 9.2 and 9.4.

G10.2 Methods IIC and IIIC

G10.2.1 Paragraph 3.1.2.2.2 requires ceilings, linings, draught stops and their associated grounds in corridors and stairway enclosures serving accommodation spaces, service spaces and control stations to be non-combustible. Consequently any such ceiling or lining which is neither the insulating medium for an 'A' Class division nor a 'B' Class division, should be of 'C' Class standard i.e. constructed of non-combustible materials but having no fire integrity and insulation standards. 'C' Class divisions should be constructed as indicated in the guidance G9.3.

G10.2.2 Ceilings, linings, draught stops and their associated grounds, other than those fitted in corridors and stairway enclosures serving accommodation spaces, service spaces and control stations, may be combustible except when such ceilings and linings are either the insulating media for 'A' Class divisions or continuous 'B' Class divisions. There are no restrictions applied to combustible ceilings and linings subject to compliance with the Merchant Shipping (Crew Accommodation) Regulations 1997 and provided that:

.1 ceilings and linings are not constructed of organic foams, cork or other highly flammable materials capable of producing large quantities of smoke or toxic products; and

.2 ceilings are not constructed of sheets of polyvinyl chloride or similar materials which will soften at relatively low elevated temperatures and may collapse on sleeping cabin occupants during the early stages of a fire situation. Such materials may not necessarily contain highly flammable base products.

G10.2.3 However, these provisions do not apply to ceilings constructed of plywood, chipboard, steel or aluminium alloy either unfaced or faced with decorative laminates, paints or other surface finishes.

G11 Application of surface finish

G11.1 In no case should a surface flammability test pass be accepted if the surface finish is applied to a different non-combustible substrate from that on which it was tested, unless the non-combustible substrate has a similar or higher density or is of greater thickness if the density is more than 400kg/m^3 (as per MSC/Circ.1004).

G12 Approved paint schemes

G12.1 An approved paint scheme may be subsequently overcoated with paints from the same scheme or any other approved paint scheme, provided that:

.1 the paints are compatible when the paint scheme is to be over-coated with a different approved paint scheme; and

.2 the surface of the original scheme is properly prepared before overcoating e.g. flaking paint to be removed; grease, dirt and oil to be removed etc.

Smoke generation potential and toxicity

1. *Purpose*

The purpose of this regulation is to reduce the hazard to life from smoke and toxic products generated during a fire in spaces where persons normally work or live. For this purpose, the quantity of smoke and toxic products released from combustible materials, including surface finishes, during fire shall be limited.

Guidance 6

G1   Regulation 5 does not indicate that low flame spread rating applies to the surfaces of furniture, furnishings, machinery and similar items. However furniture, other than any upholstered parts, should not be constructed of organic foams, cork or any other highly flammable materials or other materials capable of producing large quantities of smoke or toxic products. This does not apply to wood or wood products, surface finishes such as laminates and veneers and plastic trim, skirtings etc. Also whilst regulation 5.3.3 permits decorative flower or plant arrangements in corridors it is recommended that any such items and their supports be not readily ignitable to a suitable standard.

2 *Paints, varnishes and other finishes*

Paints, varnishes and other finishes used on exposed interior surfaces shall not be capable of producing excessive quantities of smoke and toxic products, this being determined in accordance with the Fire Test Procedures Code.

Guidance 6

G2   Smoke and toxicity rating of finishes

G2.1   This requirement applies to the finishes of bulkheads, linings, ceilings and the surface deck coverings in corridors, stairway enclosures and rooms containing furniture and furnishings of restricted fire risk.

3 *Primary deck coverings*

Primary deck coverings, if applied within accommodation and service spaces and control stations, shall be of approved material which will not give rise to smoke or toxic or explosive hazards at elevated temperatures, this being determined in accordance with the Fire Test Procedures Code.

Guidance 6

G3   A primary deck covering is to be regarded as the first layer of a floor construction which is applied directly on top of the deck plating and is inclusive of any priming coat, anti-corrosive compound or adhesive which is necessary to provide protection or adhesion to the deck plating. This is the definition of a primary deck covering in Annex 1 Part 5.3.2.2 of the Fire Test Procedures Code.

G4   Every primary deck covering used in accommodation spaces, service spaces and control stations is to be of an approved type and should be laid in accordance with the conditions in the approval certificate. Also see regulation 4.4.4 referring to not readily ignitable.

REGULATION

7 Part C – Suppression of fire

Detection and Alarm

1   Purpose

The purpose of this regulation is to detect a fire in the space of origin and to provide for alarm for safe escape and fire-fighting activity. For this purpose, the following functional requirements shall be met:

> *.1 fixed fire detection and fire alarm system installations shall be suitable for the nature of the space, fire growth potential and potential generation of smoke and gases;*
>
> *.2 manually operated call points shall be placed effectively to ensure a readily accessible means of notification; and*
>
> *.3 fire patrols shall provide an effective means of detecting and locating fires and alerting the navigation bridge and fire teams.*

2   General requirements

2.1   A fixed fire detection and fire alarm system shall be provided in accordance with the provisions of this regulation.

2.2   A fixed fire detection and fire alarm system and a sample extraction smoke detection system required in this regulation and other regulations in this part shall be of an approved type and comply with the Fire Safety Systems Code.

2.3   Where a fixed fire detection and fire alarm system is required for the protection of spaces other than those specified in paragraph 5.1, at least one detector complying with the Fire Safety Systems Code shall be installed in each such space.

Guidance 7

G1   A section is defined as a group of detectors and manually operated call points as reported in the required indicating unit(s).

G2   A detector loop is defined as an electrical circuit linking detectors of various sections in a sequence and connected (input and output) to the indicating unit(s). Zone address identification capability is a system with individually identifiable fire detectors.

G3   Acceptable activating arrangements; the fire control panel may be permitted to:

.1   activate a paging system;

.2   activate the fan stops;

.3   activate the closure of fire doors;

.4   activate the closure of fire dampers;

.5   activate the sprinkler system;

.6   activate the smoke extraction system; and

.7   activate the low-location lighting system.

G4   Fire detection systems with a zone address identification capability. Shall comply with:

.1   Detectors installed within cold spaces such as refrigerated compartments should be tested according to IEC 68–2–1 (1990) – Section one – Test Aa. The temperature of operation of heat detectors in spaces covered by this Regulation may be 130°C, in saunas up to 140°C.

G5   Cargo spaces

G5.1 All spaces in a passenger ship except cargo spaces, baggage and store rooms may, as a general rule, be regarded as accessible to the fire patrol. In ships engaged on voyages not exceeding 10 hours, if the cargo holds are opened within that time to discharge or receive cargo etc. the holds may be deemed accessible to the patrol and an automatic fire detecting system need not be fitted. Applications for exemption should be submitted to MCA Headquarters in writing giving reasons why it would be unreasonable to comply with the requirements.

G5.2 Where a fire detecting system of the sample extraction smoke detection type is combined with a fixed gas fire extinguishing system, the arrangement should be such that gas cannot be admitted to the detecting cabinet.

G6   Fire detectors

G6.1 All fire detectors must be of approved types for the area in which they are to be used. In general the functional performance and sensitivity of detectors should be in accordance with the appropriate parts of BS 5445.

G7   Control and indicating units

G7.1 In general, control and indicating units should be designed and constructed in accordance with BS 5839: Part 4: 1988, but full compliance with the detail of that Standard is not necessary provided the equipment carries out the functions specified satisfactorily. A second battery reserved solely for fire detection purposes need not be provided if a second satisfactory source of power is available. However where such a second battery is provided its capacity should be sufficient for the maximum load of the system for the period stipulated for the emergency source of power on the ship.

G8   Ancillary equipment

G8.1 Ancillary equipment such as manual call points, sounders and power packs should, in general, be designed and constructed to the relevant British Standard where one is published. Where no relevant standard exists each case will be assessed individually on its merits.

G9   Environmental tests

G9.1 Environmental tests as specified in the various relevant standards are not adequate to prove equipment is suitable for use in the marine environment. In order to be considered suitable for this use the type approval certificate should specify that the appropriate tests have been carried out.

G10   Sample extraction smoke detection systems.

G10.1 Sequential scanning intervals, the interval (I) should depend on the number of scanning points (N) and the overall response time (T) of the fans. With a 20 per cent allowance:

$$I = 1.2 \times T \times N$$

However, the maximum allowable interval should not exceed 120 sec ($I_{max} = 120$ s) the maximum response time for the fans should be around 15 sec.

G11   Smoke detectors above ceilings – spacing

G11.1 The spacing of smoke detectors above ceilings should be in accordance with the table as follows (paragraph 2(e) of Schedule 5 of MSN 1666(M)) unless the presence of draught stops requires closer spacing.

3   Initial and periodical tests

3.1   The function of fixed fire detection and fire alarm systems required by the relevant regulations of this chapter shall be tested under varying conditions of ventilation after installation.

3.2   The function of fixed fire detection and fire alarm systems shall be periodically tested to the satisfaction of the Administration by means of equipment producing hot air at the appropriate temperature, or smoke or aerosol particles having the appropriate range of density or particle size, or other phenomena associated with incipient fires to which the detector is designed to respond.

Guidance 7

G12   Every vessel shall have developed a regular routine to ensure that detectors are functioning correctly, the test interval will take into account the degree of self-monitoring provided by the system. Addressable detectors should be tested every year and non addressable detectors every 3 months.

4   Protection of machinery spaces

4.1   Installation

A fixed fire detection and fire alarm system shall be installed in:

.1   periodically unattended machinery spaces; and

.2   machinery spaces where:

.2.1   the installation of automatic and remote control systems and equipment has been approved in lieu of continuous manning of the space; and

.2.2   the main propulsion and associated machinery including sources of the main sources of electrical power, are provided with various degrees of automatic or remote control and are under continuous manned supervision from a control room.

4.2   Design

The fixed fire detection and fire alarm system required in paragraph 4.1.1 shall be so designed and the detectors so positioned as to detect rapidly the onset of fire in any part of those spaces and under any normal conditions of operation of the machinery and variations of ventilation as required by the possible range of ambient temperatures. Except in spaces of restricted height and where their use is specially appropriate, detection systems using only thermal detectors shall not be permitted. The detection system shall initiate audible and visual alarms distinct in both respects from the alarms of any other system not indicating fire, in sufficient places to ensure that the alarms are heard and observed on the navigation bridge and by a responsible engineer officer. When the navigation bridge is unmanned, the alarm shall sound in a place where a responsible member of the crew is on duty.

REGULATION

7

5   *Protection of accommodation and service spaces and control stations*

5.1   Smoke detectors in accommodation spaces

Smoke detectors shall be installed in all stairways, corridors and escape routes within accommodation spaces as provided in paragraphs 5.2, 5.3 and 5.4. Consideration shall be given to the installation of special purpose smoke detectors within ventilation ducting.

5.2   Requirements for passenger ships carrying more than 36 passengers

A fixed fire detection and fire alarm system shall be installed and arranged as to provide smoke detection in service spaces, control stations and accommodation spaces, including corridors, stairways and escape routes within accommodation spaces. Smoke detectors need not be fitted in private bathrooms and galleys. Spaces having little or no fire risk such as voids, public toilets, carbon dioxide rooms and similar spaces need not be fitted with a fixed fire detection and alarm system.

5.3   Requirements for passenger ships carrying not more than 36 passengers

There shall be installed throughout each separate zone, whether vertical or horizontal, in all accommodation and service spaces and, where it is considered necessary by the Administration, in control stations, except spaces which afford no substantial fire risk such as void spaces, sanitary spaces, etc., either:

> *.1 a fixed fire detection and fire alarm system so installed and arranged as to detect the presence of fire in such spaces and providing smoke detection in corridors, stairways and escape routes within accommodation spaces; or*

> *.2 an automatic sprinkler, fire detection and fire alarm system of an approved type complying with the relevant requirements of the Fire Safety Systems Code and so installed and arranged as to protect such spaces and, in addition, a fixed fire detection and fire alarm system and so installed and arranged as to provide smoke detection in corridors, stairways and escape routes within accommodation spaces.*

5.4   Protection of atriums in passenger ships

The entire main vertical zone containing the atrium shall be protected throughout with a smoke detection system.

5.5   Cargo ships

Accommodation and service spaces and control stations of cargo ships shall be protected by a fixed fire detection and fire alarm system and/or an automatic sprinkler, fire detection and fire alarm system as follows depending on a protection method adopted in accordance with regulation 9.2.3.1.

5.5.1   Method IC – A fixed fire detection and fire alarm system shall be so installed and arranged as to provide smoke detection in all corridors, stairways and escape routes within accommodation spaces.

5.5.2   Method IIC – An automatic sprinkler, fire detection and fire alarm system of an approved type complying with the relevant requirements of the Fire Safety Systems Code shall be so installed and arranged as to protect accommodation spaces, galleys and other service spaces, except spaces which afford no substantial fire risk such as void spaces, sanitary spaces, etc. In addition, a fixed fire detection and fire alarm system shall be so installed and arranged as to provide smoke detection in all corridors, stairways and escape routes within accommodation spaces.

5.5.3   Method IIIC – A fixed fire detection and fire alarm system shall be so installed and arranged as to detect the presence of fire in all accommodation spaces and service spaces, providing smoke detection in corridors, stairways and escape routes within accommodation spaces, except spaces which afford no substantial fire risk such as void spaces, sanitary spaces, etc. In addition, a fixed fire detection and fire alarm system shall be so installed and arranged as to provide smoke detection in all corridors, stairways and escape routes within accommodation spaces.

Guidance 7

G13   Method IIC

G13.1 In a ship in which Method IIC has been adopted the following applies:

G13.2 The sprinkler system is required to be fitted in all accommodation spaces and service spaces in which fire may be expected to originate. Sprinklers need not be fitted in either private and communal sanitary accommodation not fitted with electric space heaters or void spaces. Surveyors should note that the Regulations do not require sprinklers to be fitted in fire control stations.

G14   Method IIIC

G14.1 In a ship in which Method IIIC has been adopted the following applies:

G14.2 The fire detection system is required to be fitted in all accommodation spaces and service spaces in which fire may be expected to originate except that smoke detection and manually operated call points are required to be fitted in corridors, stairway enclosures and escape routes within accommodation spaces. Fire detectors need not be fitted in either private and communal sanitary accommodation not fitted with electric space heaters or void spaces. Surveyors should note that the Regulations do not require fire detectors to be fitted in control stations.

6   Protection of cargo spaces in passenger ships

A fixed fire detection and fire alarm system or a sample extraction smoke detection system shall be provided in any cargo space which, in the opinion of the Administration, is not accessible, except where it is shown to the satisfaction of the Administration that the ship is engaged on voyages of such short duration that it would be unreasonable to apply this requirement.

7   Manually operated call points

Manually operated call points complying with the Fire Safety Systems Code shall be installed throughout the accommodation spaces, service spaces and control stations. One manually operated call point shall be located at each exit. Manually operated call points shall be readily accessible in the corridors of each deck such that no part of the corridor is more than 20 m from a manually operated call point.

Guidance 7

G15   Manual fire alarm systems may be combined with an automatic fire detection and alarm system and should be so arranged that a fire alarm can be raised, even though a zone or zones in the automatic detection system have been disconnected for maintenance or repair.

8   *Fire patrols in passenger ships*

8.1   *Fire patrols*

For ships carrying more than 36 passengers an efficient patrol system shall be maintained so that an outbreak of fire may be promptly detected. Each member of the fire patrol shall be trained to be familiar with the arrangements of the ship as well as the location and operation of any equipment he may be called upon to use.

8.2   *Inspection hatches*

The construction of ceilings and bulkheads shall be such that it will be possible, without impairing the efficiency of the fire protection, for the fire patrols to detect any smoke originating in concealed and inaccessible places, except where in the opinion of the Administration there is no risk of fire originating in such places.

Guidance 7

G16 See Regulation 8.G2

8.3   *Two-way portable radiotelephone apparatus*

Each member of the fire patrol shall be provided with a two-way portable radiotelephone apparatus.

9   *Fire alarm signalling systems in passenger ships**

9.1   *Passenger ships shall at all times when at sea, or in port (except when out of service), be so manned or equipped as to ensure that any initial fire alarm is immediately received by a responsible member of the crew.*

9.2   *The control panel of fixed fire detection and fire alarm systems shall be designed on the fail-safe principle (e.g., an open detector circuit shall cause an alarm condition).*

9.3   *Passenger ships carrying more than 36 passengers shall have the fire detection alarms for the systems required by paragraph 5.2 centralized in a continuously manned central control station. In addition, controls for remote closing of the fire doors and shutting down the ventilation fans shall be centralized in the same location. The ventilation fans shall be capable of reactivation by the crew at the continuously manned control station. The control panels in the central control station shall be capable of indicating open or closed positions of fire doors and closed or off status of the detectors, alarms and fans. The control panel shall*

---

*   Refer to the Code on Alarms and Indicators adopted by the Organization by resolution A.830(19).

be continuously powered and shall have an automatic change-over to standby power supply in case of loss of normal power supply. The control panel shall be powered from the main source of electrical power and the emergency source of electrical power defined by regulation II–1/42 unless other arrangements are permitted by the regulations, as applicable.

9.4   A special alarm, operated from the navigation bridge or fire control station, shall be fitted to summon the crew. This alarm may be part of the ship's general alarm system and shall be capable of being sounded independently of the alarm to the passenger spaces.

REGULATION 8

Control of smoke spread

1 Purpose

The purpose of this regulation is to control the spread of smoke in order to minimize the hazards from smoke. For this purpose, means for controlling smoke in atriums, control stations, machinery spaces and concealed spaces shall be provided.

2 Protection of control stations outside machinery spaces

Practicable measures shall be taken for control stations outside machinery spaces in order to ensure that ventilation, visibility and freedom from smoke are maintained so that, in the event of fire, the machinery and equipment contained therein may be supervised and continue to function effectively. Alternative and separate means of air supply shall be provided and air inlets of the two sources of supply shall be so disposed that the risk of both inlets drawing in smoke simultaneously is minimized. At the discretion of the Administration, such requirements need not apply to control stations situated on, and opening on to, an open deck or where local closing arrangements would be equally effective.

Guidance 8

G1   Air supply to control stations

G1.1 The two entirely separate means of supplying air to control stations referred to in paragraph 2 may serve other spaces but in no case should they serve the same spaces. However it would be preferable for at least one of the means of supplying air to be independent of any other space. Local closing arrangements mean, in the case of ventilation trunks, fire or smoke dampers capable of being closed manually from within the station.

G2   Detection of smoke by fire patrols

G2.1 Regulation 7.8.2 does not apply to enclosed spaces which do not contain electrical wiring or combustible fittings.

3 Release of smoke from machinery spaces

3.1 The provisions of this paragraph shall apply to machinery spaces of category A and, where the Administration considers desirable, to other machinery spaces.

3.2 Suitable arrangements shall be made to permit the release of smoke, in the event of fire, from the space to be protected, subject to the provisions of regulation 9.5.2.1. The normal ventilation systems may be acceptable for this purpose.

3.3 Means of control shall be provided for permitting the release of smoke and such controls shall be located outside the space concerned so that they will not be cut off from the space they serve.

3.4 In passenger ships, the controls required by paragraph 3.3 shall be situated at one control position or grouped in as few positions as possible to the satisfaction of the Administration. Such positions shall have a safe access from the open deck.

4   Draught stops

Air spaces enclosed behind ceilings, panelling or linings shall be divided by close-fitting draught stops spaced not more than 14m apart. In the vertical direction, such enclosed air spaces, including those behind linings of stairways, trunks, etc., shall be closed at each deck.

Guidance 8

G3   Draught stops – extent

G3.1   Care should be taken to ensure that where 'C' and 'B' Class ceilings and linings are not extended respectively to the ship's side and deckhead, the combined length of the air spaces behind the ceiling and lining is used to determine the spacing of draught stops.

G3.2   Draught stops should generally be fitted in the air space behind ceilings which are perforated or slatted when the air space exceeds 14m in length or breadth because a fire could quite rapidly develop in such a space and would nearly be as difficult to control as a fire behind an unperforated ceiling.

G4   Closure of decks

G4.1   Paragraph 4 requires air spaces behind ceilings and linings to be closed at each deck. The integrity and insulation standards of decks (as specified in tables 9.2, 9.4, 9.6 and 9.8) are to be maintained in the air spaces behind ceilings and linings as though such air spaces are part of the accommodation spaces, service spaces or control stations, as appropriate, from which they are separated. The air spaces behind ceilings and linings cannot be regarded as void spaces because the ceilings and linings separating the air spaces from the accommodation spaces, service spaces and control stations would have to be 'A' Class divisions in compliance with respective tables.

G4.2   Any draught stop fitted in the corridors or stairway enclosures should be constructed as indicated in G8.5 of this guidance.

G4.3   Draught stops on cargo ships using method IIc or IIIc, other than in corridors and stairway enclosures may be constructed of combustible board type materials such as plywood or chipboard of not less than 6mm thickness supported by steel or wooden grounds attached to the ships structure, bulkheads, ceilings or linings and fitted tightly to such structure and divisions subject to compliance with regulation 5.3.2.4.2.2.

G5   Draught stops – construction

G5.1   Where draught stops are required by regulation 5.3.1.2 to be constructed of non-combustible materials any of the following methods of construction may be used to form draught stops:

.1   the extension of 'B' Class bulkheads, ceilings or linings the details of which are shown on the appropriate approved drawings;

.2   the extension of 'C' Class bulkheads, ceilings or linings;

.3   steel curtain plates, stringers or webs intermittently welded to the structure, stiffened where necessary and attached to the top profiles of bulkheads or fitted tightly to ceilings or linings. Any lightening holes in ships structure which is used as part of a draught stop should be plated over;

.4   approved non-combustible board type materials supported by steel flat bars or steel angle or channel profiles attached to the ships structure, bulkheads, ceilings or linings and fitted tightly to such structure or divisions;

.5   approved 'A' Class mineral wool insulation faced on each side with expanded steel or weldmesh (50mm maximum mesh size), the sheets of expanded steel or weldmesh being tied together through the insulation by galvanised wire at not more than 450mm spacing. The expanded steel or weldmesh on one side of the insulation should be attached to the ships structure, bulkheads, ceilings or linings. Wire netting may be substituted for expanded steel or weldmesh on one side, but not on both sides of the draught stop; in such cases the securing ties should be spaced not more than 300mm apart. Adjacent slabs of insulation should be fitted tightly together and slabs adjacent to the structure, bulkheads, ceilings or linings should be fitted tightly to such structure or divisions. The insulation should not be less than 35mm in thickness.

G5.2   The construction of the draught stops should be to the satisfaction of the surveyor. However in no case should draught stops be wedged in place without any attachment to structure, bulkheads, ceilings or linings. The draught stops should form a close fit round pipes, cables, ducts or any other penetrations.

> 5   *Smoke extraction systems in atriums of passenger ships*
>
> *Atriums shall be equipped with a smoke extraction system. The smoke extraction system shall be activated by the required smoke detection system and be capable of manual control. The fans shall be sized such that the entire volume within the space can be exhausted in 10 min or less.*

Guidance 8

G6   Arrangement of exhaust fans for smoke extracting systems

G6.1   The application of paragraph 5 does not imply the need for additional exhaust fans other than those normally dedicated to the space considered, provided these latter fans are of sufficient size to meet the required capacity.

REGULATION
9
Containment of fire

1   Purpose

The purpose of this regulation is to contain a fire in the space of origin. For this purpose, the following functional requirements shall be met:

> *.1 the ship shall be subdivided by thermal and structural boundaries;*
>
> *.2 thermal insulation of boundaries shall have due regard to the fire risk of the space and adjacent spaces; and*
>
> *.3 the fire integrity of the divisions shall be maintained at openings and penetrations.*

Guidance 9

G1   Insulation of 'A' Class divisions

G1.1   Bulkhead and deck insulations - extent

G1.1.1   Bulkheads

G1.1.1.1 An insulation for an 'A' Class bulkhead should cover the whole area of the division and adjacent structures as indicated in paragraph 3.4 except that it may terminate on top of the expanded metal or equivalent fitted over the insulation incorporated in an 'A' Class deck covering of the same or higher 'A' Class standard provided the 'A' Class deck insulation is fitted tightly to the bulkhead plating. However when an 'A' Class bulkhead is connected to the double bottom plating or bottom shell plating, the insulation should terminate 400mm above the double bottom or bottom shell in order to reduce the risk of the insulation absorbing any oil or water which may be on the double bottom or shell plating. The lower edge of the insulation should terminate at a flat bar welded to the bulkhead.

G1.1.1.2 Any pipe penetrations situated in the bulkheads below the flat bar need not be insulated provided the penetrations are constructed in accordance with guidance G9.47.1 or G9.47.2.

G1.1.1.3 Any cable penetrations situated in the bulkheads below the flat bar need not be insulated except for those which are constructed of heat sensitive materials which should be insulated with approved materials fitted in accordance with the conditions specified in the approval certificate. The insulation should be protected by an oil and oil vapour barrier.

G1.1.2   Decks

G1.1.2.1 An insulation for an 'A' Class deck should cover the whole area of the division and adjacent structures as indicated in paragraph 3.4. It should not terminate at a ships side lining or a bulkhead lining except that a ceiling which is the insulating medium for an 'A' Class deck may terminate at a lining fitted deck to deck which is the insulating medium for an 'A' Class bulkhead.

G1.1.3   Insulations to be approved

G1.1.3.1 Steel 'A' Class divisions A–60, A–30 or A–15 standard or aluminium alloy 'A' Class divisions A–60, A–30 or A–15 standard are required to be insulated with non-combustible materials which have been formally approved for that particular standard. The method of applying each such insulation to an 'A' Class division should be strictly in accordance with the conditions stated in the certificate of approval.

G1.2   Continuous 'B' Class ceilings or linings as 'A' Class insulations

G1.2.1   A continuous 'B' Class ceiling or lining should only be used respectively as the insulating medium for 'A' Class decks or bulkheads when the boards or panels from which the ceiling or lining is constructed have been approved for such use and a certificate issued. The ceiling or lining should be constructed in accordance with the conditions indicated on the approval certificate.

G1.2.2   When used for this purpose, ceilings should terminate on or be continued to adjacent 'A' Class bulkheads, ship side or deckhouse side. Such divisions will therefore define the horizontal extent of the insulation 'A' Class deck. Where the ceiling void is bounded by A–0 bulkheads, the portions of these bulkheads above ceiling level should be insulated to the same standard as the ceiling.

G1.3   Mineral wool insulations

G1.3.1   For the purpose of this Guidance mineral wool insulations include ceramic fibre insulations. Mineral wool insulations should be stored in dry conditions before use and should be dry when attached to the ship's structure.

G1.4   Density

G1.4.1   The density of a mineral wool insulation is required to be within the range of ± 10% of the density specified by the manufacturer. Surveyors should occasionally check from the mass and volume of several slabs or rolls that the density of an insulation lies within this range.

G1.5   Securing insulations to steel structure

G1.5.1   Mineral wool insulations used for fire protection purposes should be secured mechanically to the steel structure by means of welded steel pins, normally spaced not more than 300mm apart, galvanised wire netting having a maximum mesh size of 25mm and spring steel washers, the steel pins being at least 12mm longer than the thickness of the insulation. As an alternative, surveyors may accept the insulation being secured by means of welded steel pins bent at right angles over the galvanised wire netting, the spring washers being dispensed with provided that the pins are at least 40mm longer than the thickness of the insulation and pins in adjacent rows are bent over in opposite directions. On no account should the pins be bent in the same direction because this may result in the wire netting becoming detached from the insulation. The pins should be bent over at the exposed surfaces of the insulation in order to maintain its thickness and prevent a 'quilted effect' occurring. Other retention systems will be specially considered.

G1.6   Securing insulations to aluminium alloy structure

G1.6.1   Mineral wool insulations used for fire protection purposes must be secured mechanically to the aluminium alloy structure by means of stainless steel pins screwed into aluminium alloy bosses welded to the structure, normally spaced not more than 300mm apart, galvanised wire netting having a maximum mesh size of 25mm and spring steel washers, the stainless steel pins being at least 12mm longer than the thickness of the insulation. The steel pins should not be bent over at right angles as an alternative method of securing the insulation because the thread in the bosses may be damaged in the process of bending the pins. Other retention systems will be specially considered.

G1.7   The effect of water in insulation

G1.7.1   Although water does not normally affect the insulating properties of 'A' Class mineral wool insulations it could seriously corrode the steel pins and galvanised wire netting which secure the insulations to the structure. Therefore surveyors should examine insulation which has been soaked with water and if there are any signs of deterioration in the pins and wire netting then the insulation should be removed, the pins renewed as necessary, the insulation replaced when dry if still in good condition or new insulation fitted, and new wire netting and spring steel washers fitted over the pins.

G1.7.2   Insulation fitted in boiler rooms should be examined regularly because similar deterioration may occur due to the high humidity in such spaces.

G1.8   Board insulations

G1.8.1   For the purpose of this Guidance, board insulations include panels consisting of mineral wool insulations faced with steel sheets.

G1.9 Density

G1.9.1 The density of a board insulation or the core insulation in the case of a panel consisting of mineral wool insulations faced with steel sheets is required to be within the range of ± 10% of the density specified by the manufacturer. Surveyors should occasionally check from the mass and volume of the boards or panels that the density of the board or insulation lies within this range.

G1.10 The extent of insulation

G1.10.1 Each board insulation which has been approved as the insulating medium for 'A' Class bulkheads should be fitted deck to deck except that it may terminate on top of the insulating component of an 'A' Class deck covering as indicated in the guidance G9.51.

G1.10.2 In no case should the board insulation terminate on any other type of deck covering or any combustible surface material on an 'A' Class deck covering.

G1.11 Insulation surfaces

G1.11.1 The boards may be faced on their exposed and concealed surfaces with a combustible material having low flame spread characteristics.

G1.12 Electrical fittings on 'A' Class linings

G1.12.1 Lighting switches, power sockets and other electrical fittings and cables leading to such fittings may be surface mounted on the unconcealed side of linings which are the insulating media for 'A' Class bulkheads in order to ensure that the insulation standards of the bulkheads are not impaired. The cables may be uncovered or fitted in conduits or covered by omega profiles of steel or other materials having low flame spread characteristics.

G1.13 Ceilings which are insulations for 'A' Class decks

G1.13.1 Ceilings which have been accepted as the insulating media for 'A' Class decks should not be fitted closer to the deck plating than the distance used when the test sample was fire tested. The panels from which a ceiling is constructed may be faced on their exposed and concealed surfaces with a combustible material having a surface spread of flame rating in accordance with regulation 5.3.2.4.

G1.14 Access panels

G1.14.1 Hinged panels may be fitted in an 'A' Class ceiling in order to provide access for the control and maintenance of fire dampers in ventilation ducting positioned above the ceiling provided that the integrity and insulation standard of the ceiling are not impaired, particularly when the ceiling incorporates an overlay of mineral wool insulation.

G1.15 Sprayed insulations

G1.15.1 Preparation

G1.15.1.1 The surfaces of the structure are to be prepared and coated in accordance with the manufacturer's instructions and any other conditions stated on the approval certificate for the insulation. Any retention clips or pins should be welded to the structure before the application of any coating. The sprayed insulation should be applied by trained and skilled operators.

G1.15.2 Density

G1.15.2.1 The density of a sprayed insulation in its dried-out condition is required to be within the range of ± 15% of the density specified by the manufacturer. It is very difficult to check the density of a sprayed insulation because it takes several weeks for it to achieve its dried-out condition and it cannot be known for certain when it has reached this condition. The density could then only be checked by removing a specific volume of insulation and weighing it and surveyors are not expected to resort to such measures. A crude method has been devised which enables a surveyor to check the density of an insulation immediately after it has been sprayed. Each manufacturer should indicate the number of bags of dry mix of the insulation which when mixed with water will cover a square metre of plating to the correct thickness at the specified density allowing for normal wastage. This coverage rate is stated in the approval certificate for the insulation. The number of bags of dry mix which should have been used to insulate the division can be obtained by dividing the area of the division by the manufacturers coverage rate and this can be compared with the number of bags of dry mix which have actually been used. When the stiffened side of a bulkhead or the deckhead is being insulated the area of each stiffener or beam should be obtained by multiplying its length by twice its depth. Some allowance may also need to be made for other structure such as stringers, brackets etc.

G1.15.3 Thickness

G1.15.3.1 The thickness of a sprayed insulation indicated in the approval certificate is a minimum thickness. Surveyors should use their discretion when checking the thickness of a sprayed insulation and may accept small areas in which the minimum thickness has not been achieved provided that the insulation in these areas is deficient by no more than 3mm and the thickness over the division is generally in excess of the minimum thickness.

G1.16 Bulkheads and linings fitted on overdeck insulations

G1.16.1 Linings which are the insulating media for 'A' Class bulkheads and bulkheads and linings which are 'B' Class or 'C' Class divisions or are combustible should not penetrate an 'A' Class overdeck insulation. In each case the bottom profile should be fitted to the top of the 'A' Class insulation as shown on the appropriate approved drawing. Any combustible surface covering on an 'A' Class insulation should not be laid under any bulkheads or linings except those which are combustible.

G2 Construction of 'B' Class divisions

G2.1 Method of erecting the divisions

G2.1.1 'B' Class bulkheads, ceilings and linings are required by the Regulations to be constructed of approved non-combustible materials which have been fire tested as a bulkhead, ceiling or lining respectively and satisfied the appropriate 'B' Class standard. The methods of erecting each such division should be in accordance with the conditions indicated in the approval certificate.

G2.2 Termination of divisions

G2.2.1 A 'B' Class division should not normally terminate at another 'B' Class division of lower standard, or 'C' Class division or a combustible division, but see paragraphs 2.2.2.2 and 2.2.2.3.

G2.3 Bottom profiles

G2.3.1 The steel angle or channel profiles which support the bottom edges of the boards or panels from which a 'B' Class bulkhead or lining is constructed, should be welded to the deck plating or connected to the expanded metal or equivalent fitted over an 'A' Class deck covering by welding or steel fastenings. In no case should a 'B' Class bulkhead or lining penetrate an 'A' Class insulation incorporated in an approved deck covering.

G2.4 Deck coverings

G2.4.1 Primary or surface deck coverings which are combustible should not be laid under 'B' Class bulkheads or linings.

G2.5 Top profiles

G2.5.1 The top edges of the boards or panels from which a 'B' Class bulkhead or lining is constructed should be housed in steel channel profiles with a gap between the top edges of the boards or panels and the inside of the webs of the channels in order to prevent the boards or panels being affected by any movement in the ships structure due to pitching and rolling and reduce the effects of vibration and structure-borne noise.

G2.5.2 The channel profiles supporting the top edges of the boards or panels should be welded to either:

.1 the deckhead;

.2 the bottom edges of the beams, the gaps between the beams being plated-in or filled-in using the same boards or panels from which the bulkhead or lining is constructed;

.3 the bottom edge of a continuous steel curtain plate having a minimum thickness of 3mm. When the depth of a curtain plate exceeds 450mm its lower edge should be flanged and it should be stiffened to the satisfaction of the surveyor. When the bulkhead or lining is of B–15 standard the curtain plate should be insulated on one side with an 'A' Class mineral wool insulation of A–15 standard attached to the curtain plate by means of welded steel pins, wire netting and spring steel washers; or

.4 steel hangers welded to the deckhead of rectangular section 3mm x width of top profile and fitted at 1000mm centres approximately, or some equivalent arrangement. When the distance between the top channel profile and the deckhead is in excess of 500mm, the surveyor should consider whether or not it is necessary to increase the scantlings of the steel hangers in order to maintain the stability of the bulkhead or lining particularly in a direction at right angles to the division. The hangers may be omitted in the case of a lining which terminates at a continuous 'B' Class ceiling provided that the top channel profile of the lining is welded to the steel stringer and flats which connect the ceiling to the ships side or deckhouse side and 'A' Class bulkheads respectively as shown on the approved drawing for the ceiling panels.

G2.5.3 In no case should the top channel profile be laid directly on top of the boards or panels from which a 'B' Class bulkhead or lining is constructed i.e. without an air gap.

G2.5.4 When a shipbuilder wishes to construct a 'B' Class bulkhead or lining by erecting the boards or panels before the steel hangers and channel profile, the gap between the top edge of the boards or panels and the inside of the profile should be maintained by bonding strips of 'A' Class mineral wool insulation to the top edge of the boards or panels at approximately 600mm spacing before fitting the top channel profile. The strips of insulation should be bonded in place with their fibres positioned vertically and their length should be 100mm, their width equal to that of the boards or panels and their depth equal to the gap above the top edge of the boards or panels as indicated on the approved drawing.

G2.5.5 The top channel profiles of 'B' Class bulkheads should be unperforated when they support ceilings which are the insulating media for 'A' Class decks of A–60 standard except for holes which are permitted for the passage of electrical cables.

G2.6 Combustible inserts

G2.6.1 Combustible inserts which are designed to reduce noise and/or vibration should only be used in the construction of 'B' Class divisions as follows:

.1 in the top and bottom profiles housing the boards or panels which form 'B' Class bulkheads or linings provided that the inserts do not exceed 1.5mm in thickness; and

.2 in association with particular boards or panels, when they have been incorporated in a fire test specimen and the test has shown they have no effect on the fire performance of the division constructed of the boards or panels.

G2.7 Access panels

G2.7.1 Hinged panels may be fitted in a 'B' Class ceiling or lining in order to provide access for the control and maintenance of fire dampers in ventilation ducting positioned behind the ceiling or lining provided that the integrity and insulation standards of the ceiling or lining are not impaired particularly in the case of a ceiling overlaid with a mineral wool insulation. Each panel should be provided with a bolt or catch to keep it in the closed position. Bayonet type catches should not be used.

G3 Construction of 'C' Class divisions

G3.1 Construction

G3.1.1 Although the MCA does not require approval certificates for 'C' Class divisions they should always be constructed of approved non-combustible materials except that combustible materials may be used to the extent referred to in the guidance G5.7 to regulation 5. Profiles used in the construction of 'C' Class divisions should be of steel or aluminium alloy. The divisions may be faced with approved combustible materials as permitted by regulations 5.3.2.1 and 5.3.2.2.

G3.1.2 Shipbuilders and shipowners should be advised that the use of glass in 'C' Class bulkheads or partitions should be kept to a minimum because of the hazards which could be created if such bulkheads or partitions were to collapse or shatter during a fire or other emergency situation.

G3.1.3 'C' Class bulkheads or linings and their method of attachment on Ro-Ro passenger ships must be capable of supporting the handrail and other loadings specified in regulation 13.7.3.1 and 13.7.3.2. This should be checked on installation.

G3.2 'A' Class overdeck insulations (under 'C' Class divisions)

G3.2.1 A 'C' Class bulkhead or lining should not penetrate an 'A' Class overdeck insulation incorporated in an approved deck covering. The bottom profile of the bulkhead or lining should be attached to the expanded metal or equivalent fitted over the insulation by means of welding or steel fastenings whichever is applicable as shown on the approved drawing for the 'A' Class deck covering.

G3.3 Deck coverings (under 'C' Class divisions)

G3.3.1 Primary or surface deck coverings which are combustible should not be laid under 'C' Class bulkheads or linings.

2   Thermal and structural boundaries

2.1   Thermal and structural subdivision

Ships of all types shall be subdivided into spaces by thermal and structural divisions having regard to the fire risks of the space.

2.2   Passenger ships

2.2.1   Main vertical zones and horizontal zones

2.2.1.1.1 In ships carrying more than 36 passengers, the hull, superstructure and deckhouses shall be subdivided into main vertical zones by "A–60" class divisions.

Steps and recesses shall be kept to a minimum, but where they are necessary they shall also be "A–60" class divisions. Where a category (5), (9) or (10) space defined in paragraph 2.2.3.2.2 is on one side or where fuel oil tanks are on both sides of the division the standard may be reduced to "A–0".

2.2.1.1.2 In ships carrying not more than 36 passengers, the hull, superstructure and deckhouses in way of accommodation and service spaces shall be subdivided into main vertical zones by "A" class divisions. These divisions shall have insulation values in accordance with tables in paragraph 2.2.4.

2.2.1.2 As far as practicable, the bulkheads forming the boundaries of the main vertical zones above the bulkhead deck shall be in line with watertight subdivision bulkheads situated immediately below the bulkhead deck. The length and width of main vertical zones may be extended to a maximum of 48 m in order to bring the ends of main vertical zones to coincide with watertight subdivision bulkheads or in order to accommodate a large public space extending for the whole length of the main vertical zone provided that the total area of the main vertical zone is not greater than 1,600 m² on any deck. The length or width of a main vertical zone is the maximum distance between the furthermost points of the bulkheads bounding it.

2.2.1.3 Such bulkheads shall extend from deck to deck and to the shell or other boundaries.

2.2.1.4 Where a main vertical zone is subdivided by horizontal "A" class divisions into horizontal zones for the purpose of providing an appropriate barrier between a zone with sprinklers and a zone without sprinklers, the divisions shall extend between adjacent main vertical zone bulkheads and to the shell or exterior boundaries of the ship and shall be insulated in accordance with the fire insulation and integrity values given in table 9.4.

2.2.1.5.1 On ships designed for special purposes, such as automobile or railroad car ferries, where the provision of main vertical zone bulkheads would defeat the purpose for which the ship is intended, equivalent means for controlling and limiting a fire shall be substituted and specifically approved by the Administration. Service spaces and ship stores shall not be located on ro-ro decks unless protected in accordance with the applicable regulations.

2.2.1.5.2 However, in a ship with special category spaces, such spaces shall comply with the applicable provisions of regulation 20 and, where such compliance would be inconsistent with other requirements for passenger ships specified in this chapter, the requirements of regulation 20 shall prevail.

2.2.2 Bulkheads within a main vertical zone

2.2.2.1 For ships carrying more than 36 passengers, bulkheads which are not required to be "A" class divisions shall be at least "B" class or "C" class divisions as prescribed in the tables in paragraph 2.2.3.

2.2.2.2 For ships carrying not more than 36 passengers, bulkheads within accommodation and service spaces which are not required to be "A" class divisions shall be at least "B" class or "C" class divisions as prescribed in the tables in paragraph 2.2.4. In addition, corridor bulkheads, where not required to be "A" class, shall be "B" class divisions which shall extend from deck to deck except:

.1 *when continuous "B" class ceilings or linings are fitted on both sides of the bulkhead, the portion of the bulkhead behind the continuous ceiling or lining shall be of material which, in thickness and composition, is acceptable in the construction of "B" class divisions, but which shall be required to meet "B" class integrity standards only in so far as is reasonable and practicable in the opinion of the Administration; and*

.2 *in the case of a ship protected by an automatic sprinkler system complying with the provisions of the Fire Safety Systems Code, the corridor bulkheads may terminate at a ceiling in the corridor provided such bulkheads and ceilings are of "B" class standard in compliance with paragraph 2.2.4. All doors and frames in such bulkheads shall be of non-combustible materials and shall have the same fire integrity as the bulkhead in which they are fitted.*

2.2.2.3 Bulkheads required to be "B" class divisions, except corridor bulkheads as prescribed in paragraph 2.2.2.2, shall extend from deck to deck and to the shell or other boundaries. However, where a continuous "B" class ceiling or lining is fitted on both sides of a bulkhead which is at least of the same fire resistance as the adjoining bulkhead, the bulkhead may terminate at the continuous ceiling or lining.

2.2.3 *Fire integrity of bulkheads and decks in ships carrying more than 36 passengers*

2.2.3.1 In addition to complying with the specific provisions for fire integrity of bulkheads and decks of passenger ships, the minimum fire integrity of all bulkheads and decks shall be as prescribed in tables 9.1 and 9.2. Where, due to any particular structural arrangements in the ship, difficulty is experienced in determining from the tables the minimum fire integrity value of any divisions, such values shall be determined to the satisfaction of the Administration.

2.2.3.2 The following requirements shall govern application of the tables:

.1 *Table 9.1 shall apply to bulkheads not bounding either main vertical zones or horizontal zones. Table 9.2 shall apply to decks not forming steps in main vertical zones nor bounding horizontal zones.*

.2 *For determining the appropriate fire integrity standards to be applied to boundaries between adjacent spaces, such spaces are classified according to their fire risk as shown in categories (1) to (14) below. Where the contents and use of a space are such that there is a doubt as to its classification for the purpose of this regulation, or where it is possible to assign two or more classifications to a space, it shall be treated as a space within the relevant category having the most stringent boundary requirements. Smaller, enclosed rooms within a space that have less than 30% communicating openings to that space are considered separate spaces. The fire integrity of the boundary bulkheads and decks of such smaller rooms shall be as prescribed in tables 9.1 and 9.2. The title of each category is intended to be typical rather than restrictive. The number in parentheses preceding each category refers to the applicable column or row in the tables.*

(1)   Control stations

Spaces containing emergency sources of power and lighting.

Wheelhouse and chartroom.

Spaces containing the ship's radio equipment.

Fire control stations

Control room for propulsion machinery when located outside the propulsion machinery space.

Spaces containing centralized fire alarm equipment.

Spaces containing centralized emergency public address system stations and equipment.

(2)   Stairways

Interior stairways, lifts, totally enclosed emergency escape trunks, and escalators (other than those wholly contained within the machinery spaces) for passengers and crew and enclosures thereto.

In this connection, a stairway which is enclosed at only one level shall be regarded as part of the space from which it is not separated by a fire door.

(3)   Corridors

Passenger and crew corridors and lobbies.

(4)   Evacuation stations and external escape routes

Survival craft stowage area.

Open deck spaces and enclosed promenades forming lifeboat and liferaft embarkation and lowering stations.

Assembly stations, internal and external.

External stairs and open decks used for escape routes.

The ship's side to the waterline in the lightest seagoing condition, superstructure and deckhouse sides situated below and adjacent to the liferaft and evacuation slide embarkation areas.

(5)   Open deck spaces

Open deck spaces and enclosed promenades clear of lifeboat and liferaft embarkation and lowering stations. To be considered in this category, enclosed promenades shall have no significant fire risk, meaning that furnishings shall be restricted to deck furniture. In addition, such spaces shall be naturally ventilated by permanent openings.

Air spaces (the space outside superstructures and deckhouses).

(6)   Accommodation spaces of minor fire risk

Cabins containing furniture and furnishings of restricted fire risk.

Offices and dispensaries containing furniture and furnishings of restricted fire risk.

Public spaces containing furniture and furnishings of restricted fire risk and having a deck area of less than 50 m².

(7)   Accommodation spaces of moderate fire risk

Spaces as in category (6) above but containing furniture and furnishings of other than restricted fire risk.

Public spaces containing furniture and furnishings of restricted fire risk and having a deck area of 50 m² or more.

Isolated lockers and small store-rooms in accommodation spaces having areas less than 4 m² (in which flammable liquids are not stowed).

Sale shops. Motion picture projection and film stowage rooms. Diet kitchens (containing no open flame).

Cleaning gear lockers (in which flammable liquids are not stowed).

Laboratories (in which flammable liquids are not stowed).

Pharmacies.

Small drying rooms (having a deck area of 4 m² or less).

Specie rooms.

Operating rooms.

(8)   Accommodation spaces of greater fire risk

Public spaces containing furniture and furnishings of other than restricted fire risk and having a deck area of 50 m² or more.

Barber shops and beauty parlours.

Saunas.

(9)   Sanitary and similar spaces

Communal sanitary facilities, showers, baths, water closets, etc.

Small laundry rooms.

Indoor swimming pool area.

Isolated pantries containing no cooking appliances in accommodation spaces.

Private sanitary facilities shall be considered a portion of the space in which they are located.

(10)   Tanks, voids and auxiliary machinery spaces having little or no fire risk

Water tanks forming part of the ship's structure.

Voids and cofferdams.

Auxiliary machinery spaces which do not contain machinery having a pressure lubrication system and where storage of combustibles is prohibited, such as: ventilation and air-conditioning rooms; windlass room; steering gear room; stabiliser equipment room; electrical propulsion motor room; rooms containing section switchboards and purely electrical equipment other than oil-filled electrical transformers (above 10 kVA); shaft alleys and pipe tunnels; spaces for pumps and refrigeration machinery (not handling or using flammable liquids).

Closed trunks serving the spaces listed above.

Other closed trunks such as pipe and cable trunks.

(11)   Auxiliary machinery spaces, cargo spaces, cargo and other oil tanks and other similar spaces of moderate fire risk

Cargo oil tanks.

Cargo holds, trunkways and hatchways.

Refrigerated chambers.

Oil fuel tanks (where installed in a separate space with no machinery).

Shaft alleys and pipe tunnels allowing storage of combustibles.

Auxiliary machinery spaces as in category (10) which contain machinery having a pressure lubrication system or where storage of combustibles is permitted.

Oil fuel filling stations.

Spaces containing oil-filled electrical transformers (above 10 kVA).

Spaces containing turbine and reciprocating steam engine driven auxiliary generators and small internal combustion engines of power output up to 110 kW driving generators, sprinkler, drencher or fire pumps, bilge pumps, etc.

Closed trunks serving the spaces listed above.

(12) Machinery spaces and main galleys

Main propulsion machinery rooms (other than electric propulsion motor rooms) and boiler rooms.

Auxiliary machinery spaces other than those in categories (10) and (11) which contain internal combustion machinery or other oil-burning, heating or pumping units.

Main galleys and annexes.

Trunks and casings to the spaces listed above.

(13) Store-rooms, workshops, pantries, etc.

Main pantries not annexed to galleys.

Main laundry.

Large drying rooms (having a deck area of more than 4 m²)

Miscellaneous stores.

Mail and baggage rooms.

Garbage rooms.

Workshops (not part of machinery spaces, galleys, etc.).

Lockers and store-rooms having areas greater than 4 m², other than those spaces that have provisions for the storage of flammable liquids.

(14) Other spaces in which flammable liquids are stowed

Paint lockers.

Store-rooms containing flammable liquids (including dyes, medicines, etc.).

Laboratories (in which flammable liquids are stowed);

.3 *Where a single value is shown for the fire integrity of a boundary between two spaces, that value shall apply in all cases.*

.4 *Notwithstanding the provisions of paragraph 2.2.2 there are no special requirements for material or integrity of boundaries where only a dash appears in the tables.*

.5 *The Administration shall determine in respect of category (5) spaces whether the insulation values in table 9.1 shall apply to ends of deckhouses and superstructures, and whether the insulation values in table 9.2 shall apply to weather decks. In no case shall the requirements of category (5) of tables 9.1 or 9.2 necessitate enclosure of spaces which in the opinion of the Administration need not be enclosed.*

TABLE 9.1 Bulkheads not bounding either main vertical zones or horizontal zones

Spaces		(1)	(2)	(3)	(4)	(5)	(6)	(7)	(8)	(9)	(10)	(11)	(12)	(13)	(14)
Control stations	(1)	B-0[a]	A-0	A-0	A-0	A-0	A-60	A-60	A-60	A-0	A-0	A-60	A-60	A-60	A-60
Stairways	(2)		A-0[a]	A-0	A-0	A-0	A-0	A-15	A-15	A-0[c]	A-0	A-15	A-30	A-15	A-30
Corridors	(3)			B-15	A-60	A-0	B-15	B-15	B-15	B-15	A-0	A-15	A-30	A-0	A-30
Evacuation stations and external escape routes	(4)					A-0	A-60[b,d]	A-60[b,d]	A-60[b,d]	A-0[d]	A-0	A-60[b]	A-60[b]	A-60[b]	A-60[b]
Open deck spaces	(5)						A-0	A-0	A-0	A-0	A-0	A-0	A-0	A-0	A-0
Accommodation spaces of minor fire risk	(6)						B-0	B-0	B-0	C	A-0	A-0	A-30	A-0	A-30
Accommodation spaces of moderate fire risk	(7)							B-0	B-0	C	A-0	A-15	A-60	A-15	A-60
Accommodation spaces of greater fire risk	(8)								B-0	C	A-0	A-30	A-60	A-15	A-60
Sanitary and similar spaces	(9)									C	A-0	A-0	A-0	A-0	A-0
Tanks, voids and auxiliary machinery spaces having little or no fire risk	(10)										A-0[a]	A-0	A-0	A-0	A-0
Auxiliary machinery spaces, cargo spaces, cargo and other oil tanks and similar spaces of moderate fire risk	(11)											A-0[a]	A-0	A-0	A-15
Machinery spaces and main galleys	(12)												A-0[a]	A-0	A-60
Store-rooms, workshops, pantries, etc.	(13)													A-0[a]	A-0
Other spaces in which flammable liquids are stowed	(14)														A-30

See notes following table 9.2

TABLE 9.2

Decks not forming steps in main vertical zones nor bounding horizontal zones

Space below ↓ / Space above →		(1)	(2)	(3)	(4)	(5)	(6)	(7)	(8)	(9)	(10)	(11)	(12)	(13)	(14)
Control stations	(1)	A-30	A-30	A-15	A-0	A-0	A-0	A-15	A-30	A-0	A-0	A-0	A-60	A-0	A-60
Stairways	(2)	A-0	A-0	A-0	A-0	A-0	A-0	A-0	A-0	A-0	A-0	A-0	A-30	A-0	A-30
Corridors	(3)	A-15	A-0	A-0ᵃ	A-60	A-0	A-0	A-15	A-15	A-0	A-0	A-0	A-30	A-0	A-30
Evacuation stations and external escape routes	(4)	A-0	A-0	A-0	A-0	–	A-0	A-0	A-0	A-0	A-0	A-0	A-0	A-0	A-0
Open deck spaces	(5)	A-0	A-0	A-0	A-0	–	A-0	A-0	A-0	A-0	A-0	A-0	A-0	A-0	A-0
Accommodation spaces of minor fire risk	(6)	A-60	A-15	A-0	A-60	A-0	A-0	A-0	A-0	A-0	A-0	A-0	A-0	A-0	A-0
Accommodation spaces of moderate fire risk	(7)	A-60	A-15	A-15	A-60	A-0	A-0	A-15	A-15	A-0	A-0	A-0	A-0	A-0	A-0
Accommodation spaces of greater fire risk	(8)	A-60	A-15	A-15	A-60	A-0	A-15	A-15	A-30	A-0	A-0	A-0	A-0	A-0	A-0
Sanitary and similar spaces	(9)	A-0	A-0	A-0	A-0	A-0	A-0	A-0	A-0	A-0	A-0	A-0	A-0	A-0	A-0
Tanks, voids and auxiliary machinery spaces having little or no fire risk	(10)	A-0	A-0	A-0	A-0	A-0	A-0	A-0	A-0	A-0	A-0ᵃ	A-0	A-0	A-0	A-0
Auxiliary machinery spaces, cargo spaces, cargo and other oil tanks and similar spaces of moderate fire risk	(11)	A-60	A-60	A-60	A-60	A-0	A-0	A-15	A-30	A-0	A-0	A-0ᵃ	A-0	A-0	A-30
Machinery spaces and main galleys	(12)	A-60	A-60	A-60	A-60	A-0	A-60	A-60	A-60	A-0	A-0	A-30	A-30ᵃ	A-0	A-60
Store-rooms, workshops, pantries, etc.	(13)	A-60	A-30	A-15	A-60	A-0	A-15	A-30	A-30	A-0	A-0	A-0	A-0	A-0	A-0
Other spaces in which flammable liquids are stowed	(14)	A-60	A-60	A-60	A-60	A-0	A-30	A-60	A-60	A-0	A-0	A-0	A-0	A-0	A-0

Notes: To be applied to tables 9.1 and 9.2., as appropriate.

a Where adjacent spaces are in the same numerical category and superscript "a" appears, a bulkhead or deck between such spaces need not be fitted if deemed unnecessary by the Administration. For example, in category (12) a bulkhead need not be required between a galley and its annexed pantries provided the pantry bulkhead and decks maintain the integrity of the galley boundaries. A bulkhead is, however, required between a galley and machinery space even though both spaces are in category (12).

b The ship's side, to the waterline in the lightest seagoing condition, superstructure and deckhouse sides situated below and adjacent to liferafts and evacuation slides may be reduced to "A-30".

c Where public toilets are installed completely within the stairway enclosure, the public toilet bulkhead within the stairway enclosure can be of "B" class integrity.

d Where spaces of categories (6), (7), (8) and (9) are located completely within the outer perimeter of the assembly station, the bulkheads of these spaces are allowed to be of "B-0" class integrity. Control positions for audio, video and light installations may be considered as part of the assembly station.

2.2.3.3 Continuous "B" class ceilings or linings, in association with the relevant decks or bulkheads, may be accepted as contributing, wholly or in part, to the required insulation and integrity of a division.

2.2.3.4 Construction and arrangement of saunas

2.2.3.4.1 The perimeter of the sauna shall be of "A" class boundaries and may include changing rooms, showers and toilets. The sauna shall be insulated to "A–60" standard against other spaces except those inside of the perimeter and spaces of categories (5), (9) and (10).

2.2.3.4.2 Bathrooms with direct access to saunas may be considered as part of them. In such cases, the door between sauna and the bathroom need not comply with fire safety requirements.

2.2.3.4.3 The traditional wooden lining on the bulkheads and ceiling are permitted in the sauna. The ceiling above the oven shall be lined with a non-combustible plate with an air gap of at least 30 mm. The distance from the hot surfaces to combustible materials shall be at least 500 mm or the combustible materials shall be protected (e.g., non-combustible plate with an air gap of at least 30 mm).

2.2.3.4.4 The traditional wooden benches are permitted to be used in the sauna.

2.2.3.4.5 The sauna door shall open outwards by pushing.

2.2.3.4.6 Electrically heated ovens shall be provided with a timer.

2.2.4 Fire integrity of bulkheads and decks in ships carrying not more than 36 passengers

2.2.4.1 In addition to complying with the specific provisions for fire integrity of bulkheads and decks of passenger ships, the minimum fire integrity of bulkheads and decks shall be as prescribed in tables 9.3 and 9.4.

2.2.4.2 The following requirements govern application of the tables:

.1 Tables 9.3 and 9.4 shall apply respectively to the bulkheads and decks separating adjacent spaces.

.2 For determining the appropriate fire integrity standards to be applied to divisions between adjacent spaces, such spaces are classified according to their fire risk as shown in categories (1) to (11) below. Where the contents and use of a space are such that there is a doubt as to its classification for the purpose of this regulation, or where it is possible to assign two or more classifications to a space, it shall be treated as a space within the relevant category having the most stringent boundary requirements. Smaller, enclosed rooms within a space that have less than 30% communicating openings to that space are considered separate spaces. The fire integrity of the boundary bulkheads and decks of such smaller rooms shall be as prescribed in tables 9.3 and 9.4. The title of each category is intended to be typical rather than restrictive. The number in parentheses preceding each category refers to the applicable column or row in the tables.

(1) Control stations

Spaces containing emergency sources of power and lighting.

Wheelhouse and chartroom.

Spaces containing the ship's radio equipment.

Fire control stations.

Control room for propulsion machinery when located outside the machinery space.

Spaces containing centralized fire alarm equipment.

(2) Corridors

Passenger and crew corridors and lobbies.

(3) Accommodation spaces

Spaces as defined in regulation 3.1 excluding corridors.

(4) Stairways

Interior stairways, lifts, totally enclosed emergency escape trunks, and escalators (other than those wholly contained within the machinery spaces) and enclosures thereto.

In this connection, a stairway which is enclosed only at one level shall be regarded as part of the space from which it is not separated by a fire door.

(5) Service spaces (low risk)

Lockers and store-rooms not having provisions for the storage of flammable liquids and having areas less than 4 m² and drying rooms and laundries.

(6) Machinery spaces of category A

Spaces as defined in regulation 3.31.

(7) Other machinery spaces

Electrical equipment rooms (auto-telephone exchange, air-conditioning duct spaces).

Spaces as defined in regulation 3.30 excluding machinery spaces of category A.

(8) Cargo spaces

All spaces used for cargo (including cargo oil tanks) and trunkways and hatchways to such spaces, other than special category spaces.

(9) Service spaces (high risk)

Galleys, pantries containing cooking appliances, paint lockers, lockers and store-rooms having areas of 4 m² or more, spaces for the storage of flammable liquids, saunas and workshops other than those forming part of the machinery spaces.

(10) Open decks

Open deck spaces and enclosed promenades having little or no fire risk. To be considered in this category enclosed promenades should have no significant fire risk, meaning that furnishing shall be restricted to deck furniture. In addition, such spaces shall be naturally ventilated by permanent openings. Air spaces (the space outside superstructures and deckhouses).

(11) Special category and ro-ro spaces
Spaces as defined in regulations 3.41 and 3.46.

.3 *In determining the applicable fire integrity standard of a boundary between two spaces within a main vertical zone or horizontal zone which is not protected by an automatic sprinkler system complying with the provisions of the Fire Safety Systems Code or between such zones neither of which is so protected, the higher of the two values given in the tables shall apply.*

.4 *In determining the applicable fire integrity standard of a boundary between two spaces within a main vertical zone or horizontal zone which is protected by an automatic sprinkler system complying with the provisions of the Fire Safety Systems Code or between such zones both of which are so protected, the lesser of the two values given in the tables shall apply. Where a zone with sprinklers and a zone without sprinklers meet within accommodation and service spaces, the higher of the two values given in the tables shall apply to the division between the zones.*

2.2.4.3 Continuous "B" class ceilings or linings, in association with the relevant decks or bulkheads, may be accepted as contributing, wholly or in part, to the required insulation and integrity of a division.

2.2.4.4 External boundaries which are required in regulation 11.2 to be of steel or other equivalent material may be pierced for the fitting of windows and sidescuttles provided that there is no requirement for such boundaries of passenger ships to have "A" class integrity. Similarly, in such boundaries which are not required to have "A" class integrity, doors may be constructed of materials which are to the satisfaction of the Administration.

2.2.4.5   Saunas shall comply with paragraph 2.2.3.4.

TABLE 9.3 Fire integrity of bulkheads separating adjacent spaces

Spaces		(1)	(2)	(3)	(4)	(5)	(6)	(7)	(8)	(9)	(10)	(11)
Control stations	(1)	A-0^c	A-0	A-60	A-0	A-15	A-60	A-15	A-60	A-60	*	A-60
Corridors	(2)		C^e	B-0^e	A-0^a B-0^e	B-0^e	A-60	A-0	A-0	A-15 A-0^d	*	A-15
Accommodation spaces	(3)			C^e	A-0^a B-0^e	B-0^e	A-60	A-0	A-0	A-15 A-0^d	*	A-30 A-0^d
Stairways	(4)				A-0^a B-0^e	A-0^a B-0^e	A-60	A-0	A-0	A-15 A-0^d	*	A-15 A-0^d
Service spaces (low risk)	(5)					C^e	A-60	A-0	A-0	A-0	*	A-0
Machinery spaces of category A	(6)						*	A-0	A-0	A-60	*	A-60
Other machinery spaces	(7)							A-0^b	A-0	A-0	*	A-0
Cargo spaces	(8)								*	A-0	*	A-0
Service spaces (high risk)	(9)									A-0^b	*	A-30
Open decks	(10)											A-0
Special category and ro-ro spaces	(11)											A-0

See notes following table 9.4

TABLE 9.4 Fire integrity of decks separating adjacent spaces

Space below↓ sp. above→	(1)	(2)	(3)	(4)	(5)	(6)	(7)	(8)	(9)	(10)	(11)
Control stations	(1)	A-0	A-0	A-0	A-0	A-0	A-60	A-0	A-0	A-0	*	A-30
Corridors	(2)	A-0	*	*	A-0	*	A-60	A-0	A-0	A-0	*	A-0
Accommodation spaces	(3)	A-60	A-0	*	A-0	*	A-60	A-0	A-0	A-0	*	A-30 A-0^d
Stairways	(4)	A-0	A-0	A-0	*	A-0	A-60	A-0	A-0	A-0	*	A-0
Service spaces (low risk)	(5)	A-15	A-0	A-0	A-0	*	A-60	A-0	A-0	A-0	*	A-0
Machinery spaces of category A	(6)	A-60	A-60	A-60	A-60	A-60	*	A-60^i	A-30	A-60	*	A-60
Other machinery spaces	(7)	A-15	A-0	A-0	A-0	A-0	A-0	*	A-0	A-0	*	A-0
Cargo spaces	(8)	A-60	A-0	A-0	A-0	A-0	A-0	A-0	*	A-0	*	A-0
Service spaces (high risk)	(9)	A-60	A-30 A-0^d	A-30 A-0^d	A-30 A-0^d	A-0	A-60	A-0	A-0	A-0	*	A-30
Open decks	(10)	*	*	*	*	*	*	*	*	*	-	A-0
Special category and ro-ro spaces	(11)	A-60	A-15	A-30 A-0^d	A-15	A-0	A-30	A-0	A-0	A-30	A-0	A-0

Notes: To be applied to both tables 9.3 and 9.4 as appropriate.

a For clarification as to which applies, see paragraphs 2.2.2 and 2.2.5.

b Where spaces are of the same numerical category and superscript "b" appears, a bulkhead or deck of the rating shown in the tables is only required when the adjacent spaces are for a different purpose, (e.g., in category (9)). A galley next to a galley does not require a bulkhead but a galley next to a paint room requires an "A-0" bulkhead.

c Bulkhead separating the wheelhouse and chartroom from each other may have a "B-0" rating.

d See paragraphs 2.2.4.2.3 and 2.2.4.2.4.

e For the application of paragraph 2.2.1.1.2, "B–0" and "C", where appearing in table 9.3, shall be read as "A–0".

f Fire insulation need not be fitted if the machinery space in category (7), in the opinion of the Administration, has little or no fire risk.

* Where an asterisk appears in the tables, the division is required to be of steel or other equivalent material, but is not required to be of "A" class standard. However, where a deck, except in a category (10) space, is penetrated for the passage of electric cables, pipes and vent ducts, such penetrations shall be made tight to prevent the passage of flame and smoke. Divisions between control stations (emergency generators) and open decks may have air intake openings without means for closure, unless a fixed gas fire-extinguishing system is fitted.

For the application of paragraph 2.2.1.1.2, an asterisk, where appearing in table 9.4, except for categories (8) and (10), shall be read as "A–0".

2.2.5   Protection of stairways and lifts in accommodation area

2.2.5.1 Stairways shall be within enclosures formed of "A" class divisions, with positive means of closure at all openings, except that:

.1 a stairway connecting only two decks need not be enclosed, provided the integrity of the deck is maintained by proper bulkheads or self-closing doors in one 'tween-deck space. When a stairway is closed in one 'tween-deck space, the stairway enclosure shall be protected in accordance with the tables for decks in paragraphs 2.2.3 or 2.2.4; and

.2 stairways may be fitted in the open in a public space, provided they lie wholly within the public space.

2.2.5.2 Lift trunks shall be so fitted as to prevent the passage of smoke and flame from one 'tween-deck to another and shall be provided with means of closing so as to permit the control of draught and smoke. Machinery for lifts located within stairway enclosures shall be arranged in a separate room, surrounded by steel boundaries, except that small passages for lift cables are permitted. Lifts which open into spaces other than corridors, public spaces, special category spaces, stairways and external areas shall not open into stairways included in the means of escape.

Guidance 9

G4   Continuity of bulkheads

G4.1   It should be ensured that the continuity of main vertical zone bulkheads above and below a horizontal zone is maintained through any casings or other spaces which are situated within the same 'tween-deck as the horizontal zone.

G5   Impairment of main zone bulkheads

G5.1   It should be ensured that stairway enclosures, lift trunks or trunks for any other purposes do not impair main vertical zone bulkheads when the bulkheads are stepped. See also guidance G9.28 in this section on "stairways" penetrating main fire zone steps.

G6   Spaces used for the carriage of trains

G6.1   For the purpose of compliance with paragraph 2.2.1.5.1 the boundary bulkheads and decks of any 'tween-deck which is used for the carriage of trains incorporating passenger carriages with or without freight rolling stock should be treated in the same manner as the boundary bulkheads and decks of a special category space.

G7   Corridor bulkheads

G7.1 As an alternative to the requirements of paragraph 2.2.2.2, corridor bulkheads may be fitted in accordance with the arrangements agreed internationally and shown in MSC/Circ.699, i.e. as illustrated in figures 9.1 and 9.2 (The adoption of these alternative arrangements does not in any way dispense with the need to fit the draught stops, required by regulation 8.4).

G8   Divisions within accommodation spaces, service spaces and control stations

G8.1   'B' Class divisions

G8.1.1 The 'other boundaries' referred to in paragraph 2.2.2.3, to which a 'B' Class bulkhead is required to extend, in addition to the ships side, are:

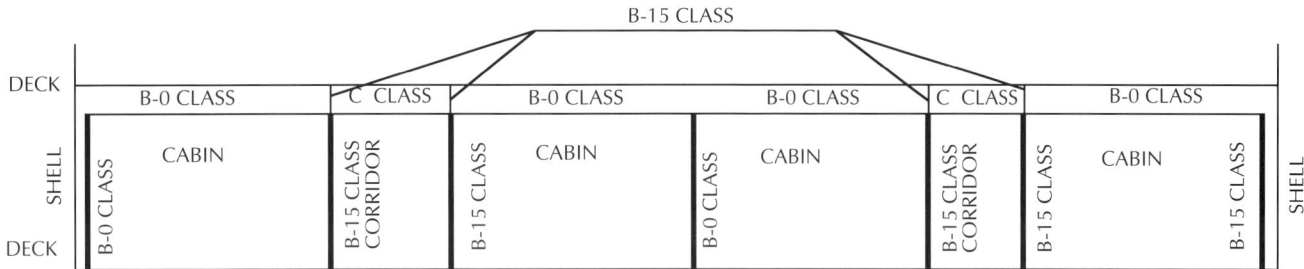

Figure 9.1 Fire integrity of bulkheads and ceilings in accommodation spaces

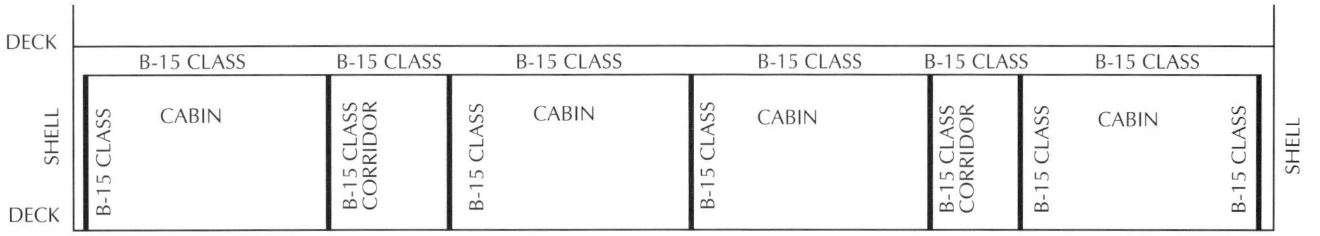

Figure 9.2 Fire integrity of bulkheads and ceilings in accommodation

.1 a deckhouse side;

.2 an 'A' Class bulkhead except that the 'B' Class bulkhead should not penetrate the 'A' Class insulation; and

.3 another 'B' Class bulkhead of the same or higher 'B' Class standard.

G8.1.2 When continuous 'B' Class ceilings and/or linings are fitted on both sides of a 'B' Class bulkhead, the bulkhead should only terminate at the ceilings or linings if they are of the same or higher 'B' Class standard.

G8.1.3 This Regulation is illustrated in figures 9.1 and 9.2.

G8.2 Continuous 'B' Class ceiling or lining

G8.2.1 Continuous 'B' class ceilings referred to in paragraph 2.2.2.3 are to be as follows:-

G8.2.2 A continuous 'B' Class ceiling should terminate at:

.1 an 'A' Class bulkhead except that it should not penetrate the 'A' Class insulation;

.2 the ship's side or deckhouse side;

.3 a 'B' Class bulkhead of the same or higher standard, fitted deck to deck; or

.4 a 'B' Class lining of the same or higher standard, fitted deck to deck.

G8.2.3 A continuous 'B' Class lining should be fitted deck to deck except that it may stop short of the deckhead at a continuous 'B' Class ceiling extending each side of the lining. A continuous 'B' Class lining should terminate in a horizontal direction at:

.1 an 'A' Class division, except that it should not penetrate the 'A' Class insulation;

.2 the ship's side or deckhouse side; or

.3 a 'B' Class bulkhead of the same or higher standard, extending each side of the lining.

G9   Modular cabins

G9.1   The approval of modular cabins is to be in accordance with the guidelines in MSC/Circ.917 – Guidelines on Fire Safety Construction in Accommodation Areas.

G9.2   Attention should be paid to panel connections and to penetrations, for services, which will not have been fire tested.

G10   Group of spaces

G10.1   A group of spaces which are used for different purposes should generally not be treated as a single space with its boundary divisions having the most stringent fire standards appropriate to the boundary divisions of any space within the group and apply no fire standards to the internal bulkheads separating the spaces within the group. This restriction does not apply to any groups of spaces specifically referred to in the Regulations such as galleys and their annexes, refrigerated chambers or a cabin and private sanitary facilities.

G11   Insulation values of spaces with special characters of two or more space categories.

G11.1   In cases where a space has the special characters of two or more space categories, the insulation values of the divisions of such a space should be the highest for the space categories concerned. For example the fire insulation values of the divisions of emergency generator rooms in passenger ships carrying more than 36 passengers should be the highest value for the space when the space is considered being a control station (Category (1)) and a machinery space (Category (11) or (12)).

G12   Spaces used for unrelated purposes

G12.1   A space should not be used for two or more unrelated purposes e.g. for stores and housing fans in which case the stores and fans should be located in a storeroom (Category (13)) and a ventilation room (Category (10) in tables 9.1 and 9.2). It is inappropriate to apply the category which provides the more stringent fire integrity and insulation standards to the boundary bulkheads and decks (in this case there are only minor differences) because the combined space may justify applying much more stringent standards and it would be impossible to compensate for the loss of the A-0 bulkhead which should separate the spaces.

G13   Spaces of more than one category

G13.1   When a space may be included in more than one category e.g. a space containing a diesel driven emergency generator (Categories (1) and (11) or (12) in tables 9.1 and 9.2) whichever is applicable, then the category which should be used is the one which requires the more stringent fire integrity and insulation standard for the bulkhead or deck which separates the space from an adjacent space.

G14   Stairways closed at one level and escape trunks

G14.1   A stairway or an escape trunk which is closed at only one level, other than one which forms a protected enclosure from the lower part of a machinery space referred to in regulation 13.4.1.1.1 or 13.4.2.1.1 should be regarded as part of the space from which it is not separated by a fire door i.e. it should not be regarded as a Category (2) or (4) space. The category of the trunk should not be changed in such a case when it is intended to fit a non-combustible door having no fire resisting properties to the 'open' end of the stairway or trunk.

G15   Sales shops

G15.1   For passenger ships carrying more than 36 passengers, sales shops are included in Category (7) in tables 9.1 and 9.2, and may be used for the sale of any commodities including those which have a flammable content such as spirits, perfumes, hair sprays, lighter fuel etc. However, sales shops should only have a daily supply on display in the shop of these highly inflammable items. All other stock of highly inflammables should be kept in a category (14) storeroom.

G15.2 Sale shops for passenger ships carrying not more than 36 passengers should be included in Category (3) in tables 9.3 and 9.4, and may be used for the sale of any commodities including those which have a flammable content such as spirits, perfumes, hair sprays, lighter fuel etc.

G15.3 The same proviso however, to that for passenger ships carrying more than 36 passengers applies i.e. other stock of highly inflammables should be kept in category (9) store room/s.

G16   Pantries containing no cooking appliances - on passenger ships

G16.1 A pantry in Category (9) (or (3) on passenger ships carrying not more than 36 passengers) may contain coffee automats, toasters, dish washers, microwave ovens, water boilers and similar appliances each with a maximum power of 5kW. They may also contain electrically heated cooking plates and hot plates for keeping food warm each with a maximum power of 2kW and a surface temperature not above 150°C. (Note: a dining room containing the appliances mentioned above should not be regarded as a pantry).

G16.2 The position of power sockets should be such that when heat producing appliances such as toasters are plugged into them the appliances are clear of curtains, towel rails etc.

G16.3 A microwave oven may be included in a pantry containing no cooking appliances subject to the following conditions:

  .1   the oven should comply with the latest relevant standards as indicated in the 'Survey of Crew Accommodation in Merchant Ships-Instructions for the Guidance of Surveyors';

  .2   the oven should be suitable for the maximum ambient temperature which will be encountered in the space in which it is to be fitted;

  .3   the oven should be fitted with a thermal protective device arranged to interrupt the electrical supply to the oven in the event of overheating e.g. should the timer fail to operate;

  .4   a permanent notice should be displayed adjacent to each oven stating that the oven must not be operated if the door interlock is not operating, the door is damaged or ill-fitting or the door seals are damaged; and

  .5   the oven should be tested periodically in service for radiation leakage to ensure that the leakage levels do not exceed those allowed by the standards referred to in (a) above. Such tests should be carried out by a person having the necessary specialist experience and equipment.

G17   Diet kitchens

G17.1 Diet kitchens (containing no open flame) should be in compliance with the interpretations for pantries of Category (9).

G18   Main pantries, pantries containing cooking appliances and galleys

G18.1 Main pantries and pantries containing cooking appliances may contain:

  .1   coffee automats, toasters, dish washers, microwave ovens, water boilers and similar appliances each of them with a power of more than 5 kW;

  .2   electrically heated cooking plates and hot plates for keeping food warm each of them with a maximum power of 5 kW.

G18.2 Spaces containing any electrically heated cooking plate or hot plates for keeping food warm with a maximum power of more than 5 kW should be regarded as galleys.

G19   Saunas

G19.1   A sauna is a hot room where the heat of that space is provided with a hot surface (e.g. an electrically heated oven). The term 'sauna' means here the space where the oven is located, and it may also include the bathroom. The temperature in the sauna is normally between 80–120°C.

G20   Separation of machinery spaces from other spaces

G20.1   Any insulated bulkhead or deck which separates any machinery space from any other space should not be substituted by a cofferdam formed by uninsulated bulkheads or decks even though the arrangement would theoretically satisfy the Regulations by treating the cofferdam as an intervening void space. A cofferdam does not provide the same degree of protection as an insulated division.

G20.2   This should also apply to any arrangement involving a false deck (see guidance G11.2 to regulation 11.2 defining a false deck).

G21   Auxiliary machinery spaces in which combustibles are stowed

G21.1   Category (11) in tables 9.1 and 9.2 includes auxiliary machinery spaces specified in Category (10) in which combustibles are permitted to be stowed. Such combustibles should only be those which are to be used in the machinery spaces and workshops such as boxed or crated spares, staging planks, wooden shores and wedges, cartons or boxes containing cleaning materials, rags and hand cleansers, tins or drums of grease etc.

G22   Superscription 'a' in the tables 9.1 and 9.2

G22.1   When adjacent spaces are in the same numerical category and a superscription 'a' appears in the table and the spaces are used for the same purpose, a bulkhead is fitted between two such spaces the bulkhead need only be of steel having no fire integrity standard or may be of expanded metal.

G23   Superscription 'b' and asterisk in the tables 9.3 and 9.4

G23.1   When adjacent spaces are in the same numerical category and a superscription 'b' appears in the table and the spaces are used for the same purpose, a bulkhead need not be fitted between the spaces e.g. in Category (7), two machinery space of other Category A adjacent to each other. If a bulkhead is fitted between two such spaces the bulkhead need only be of steel having no fire integrity standard or it may be of expanded metal.

G23.2   Although a paint room and a store room having an area of more than 2m^2 are in the same numerical category (Category (9) in table 9.3) they are used for different purposes and therefore a bulkhead of A-0 standard should be fitted between them as indicated in table 1.

G23.3   Similarly in Category (9) table 9.3, a bulkhead need not be fitted between two storerooms which are used for the same purpose or, if a bulkhead is fitted, it need have no fire integrity standard e.g. two linen storerooms. However the bulkhead separating two storerooms used for different purposes e.g. linen and provision storerooms should be of A-0 standard as specified in tables 9.3 and 9.4.

G23.4   Notwithstanding the provision of an asterisk in the tables, any of the following structure which is constructed of aluminium alloy should be an 'A' Class division of A-0 standard:

  .1   any part of the hull or side of a superstructure or deckhouse which does not support the lifeboat, liferaft and marine escape system embarkation, stowage, handling and lowering positions but is within 3m of such positions;

  .2   the ends and sides of any superstructure or deckhouses which overlook a deck used for transferring passengers or crew from a muster station to an embarkation deck, the superstructure or deckhouse not being one which supports the lifeboat, liferaft and marine escape system embarkation, stowage, handling and lowering positions; and

  .3   any deck which is used for transferring passengers or crew from a muster station to an embarkation deck.

G24   Spaces not included in any category

G24.1 Tanks, voids and similar spaces listed under Category (10) in paragraph 2.2.3.2.2, which are not listed under any category in paragraph 2.2.4.2.2, should be regarded as Category (7) spaces.

G24.2 Spaces behind ceiling and linings should not be regarded as voids (see guidance G8.5.1).

G24.3 Similarly spaces listed under Category (11) of tables 9.1 and 9.2 which are not listed under any category in tables 9.3 and 9.4 should be regarded as Category (9) spaces.

G25 Internal bulkheads of refrigerated chambers

G25.1 The internal bulkheads of refrigerated chambers (Category (11) or (9) for passenger ship carrying more than 36 passengers) including the bulkhead between the storerooms and the handling room need not meet any fire integrity standard provided that the handling room is included in the chambers when obtaining the fire integrity and insulation standards of the boundary divisions from the tables. See guidance G5.2.2 to regulation 5.3.1.2 for refrigerated chambers insulated with organic foams, cork or other flammable materials.

G26 Ends and sides of superstructures and deckhouses in table 9.1

G26.1 The A–0 standards specified in table 9.1 need not apply to the ends of superstructures or deckhouses constructed of steel which overlook open deck spaces (Category (5). This relaxation may also apply to the sides of superstructures and deckhouses constructed of steel which are at least 3m clear longitudinally of the lifeboat, liferaft and marine escape system embarkation, stowage, handling and lowering positions and similarly clear of any deck which is used for transferring passengers or crew from a muster station to an embarkation deck.

G26.2 The relaxation should not apply to the ends of sides of superstructures or deckhouses constructed of aluminium alloy.

G26.3 The sides of superstructures or deckhouses constructed of steel or aluminium alloy which are within 3m longitudinally of the lifeboat, liferaft and marine escape system embarkation, stowage, handling and lowering positions and are similarly in way of any deck which is used for transferring passengers or crew from a muster station to an embarkation deck should be treated as though they are overlooking Category (4) spaces.

G26.4 For passenger ships carrying not more than 36 passengers (Regulation 9.2.2.4.4 – external boundaries) see guidance G9.37.1.1 which applies to these ships in the same way as to cargo ships.

G27 Fire standards for weatherdecks in table 9.2

G27.1 The A–0 standards specified in table 9.2 need not apply to decks constructed of steel which have open deck spaces (Category (5)) above and/or below them.

G27.2 The relaxation should apply only to decks constructed of aluminium alloy which have open deck spaces (Category (5)) above and below them or only below them.

G27.3 Any deck which has only an open deck space above it and the deck is used for transferring passengers or crew from a muster station to an embarkation deck should be treated as a deck under a Category (4) space.

G28 Stairways penetrating main zone steps

G28.1 When a stairway enclosure penetrates a step in a main zone bulkhead, the bulkheads and decks forming the enclosure which project above or below the step should be regarded as main zone divisions and tables 9.1, 9.2, 9.3 and 9.4 used to determine their fire integrity and insulation standards and any penetrations through such bulkheads and decks should be treated accordingly.

G29 Stairways serving two decks

G29.1 The enclosure bulkheads surrounding a stairway serving only two decks should be insulated where necessary with an insulation approved for 'A' Class bulkheads having the same 'A' Class standard of the deck which is penetrated by the stairway.

G29.2 The boundaries and doors of a lift trunk which is situated within a stairway enclosure are not required to meet any 'A' Class standard provided that:

> .1 any boundary of the lift trunk which forms part of the stairway enclosure is an 'A' Class division of the appropriate standard specified in the tables 9.1, 9.2, 9.3 and 9.4; and

> .2 any opening in the lift trunk which gives direct access to any space situated outside the stairway enclosure is provided with an approved lift door of the same 'A' Class standard as the bulkhead in which it is fitted.

G29.3 A lift trunk which extends above or below a stairway enclosure may be treated in the same manner.

G30 Means of closure

G30.1 Door openings in lift trunks should be fitted with efficient doors. Where the opening occurs in an area of the trunk which forms an 'A' Class division, then the door should be of an approved type of the same 'A' Class standard or greater.

2.3 Cargo ships except tankers

2.3.1 Methods of protection in accommodation area

2.3.1.1 One of the following methods of protection shall be adopted in accommodation and service spaces and control stations:

> *.1 Method IC – The construction of internal divisional bulkheads of non-combustible "B" or "C" class divisions generally without the installation of an automatic sprinkler, fire detection and fire alarm system in the accommodation and service spaces, except as required by regulation 7.5.5.1; or*

> *.2 Method IIC – The fitting of an automatic sprinkler, fire detection and fire alarm system as required by regulation 7.5.5.2 for the detection and extinction of fire in all spaces in which fire might be expected to originate, generally with no restriction on the type of internal divisional bulkheads; or*

> *.3 Method IIIC – The fitting of a fixed fire detection and fire alarm system as required by regulation 7.5.5.3 in spaces in which a fire might be expected to originate, generally with no restriction on the type of internal divisional bulkheads, except that in no case shall the area of any accommodation space or spaces bounded by an "A" or "B" class division exceed 50 m². However, consideration may be given by the Administration to increasing this area for public spaces.*

2.3.1.2 The requirements for the use of non-combustible materials in the construction and insulation of boundary bulkheads of machinery spaces, control stations, service spaces, etc., and the protection of the above stairway enclosures and corridors will be common to all three methods outlined in paragraph 2.3.1.1.

2.3.2 Bulkheads within accommodation area

2.3.2.1 Bulkheads required to be "B" class divisions shall extend from deck to deck and to the shell or other boundaries. However, where a continuous "B" class ceiling or lining is fitted on both sides of the bulkhead, the bulkhead may terminate at the continuous ceiling or lining.

2.3.2.2 Method IC – Bulkheads not required by this or other regulations for cargo ships to be "A" or "B" class divisions, shall be of at least "C" class construction.

2.3.2.3 Method IIC – There shall be no restriction on the construction of bulkheads not required by this or other regulations for cargo ships to be "A" or "B" class divisions except in individual cases where "C" class bulkheads are required in accordance with table 9.5.

2.3.2.4 Method IIIC – There shall be no restriction on the construction of bulkheads not required for cargo ships to be "A" or "B" class divisions except that the area of any accommodation space or spaces bounded by a continuous "A" or "B" class division shall in no case exceed 50 m², except in individual cases where "C" class bulkheads are required in accordance with table 9.5. However, consideration may be given by the Administration to increasing this area for public spaces.

2.3.3 Fire integrity of bulkheads and decks

2.3.3.1 In addition to complying with the specific provisions for fire integrity of bulkheads and decks of cargo ships, the minimum fire integrity of bulkheads and decks shall be as prescribed in tables 9.5 and 9.6.

2.3.3.2 The following requirements shall govern application of the tables:

.1 Tables 9.5 and 9.6 shall apply respectively to the bulkheads and decks separating adjacent spaces.

.2 For determining the appropriate fire integrity standards to be applied to divisions between adjacent spaces, such spaces are classified according to their fire risk as shown in categories (1) to (11) below. Where the contents and use of a space are such that there is a doubt as to its classification for the purpose of this regulation, or where it is possible to assign two or more classifications to a space, it shall be treated as a space within the relevant category having the most stringent boundary requirements. Smaller, enclosed rooms within a space that have less than 30% communicating openings to that space are considered separate spaces. The fire integrity of the boundary bulkheads and decks of such smaller rooms shall be as prescribed in tables 9.5 and 9.6. The title of each category is intended to be typical rather than restrictive. The number in parentheses preceding each category refers to the applicable column or row in the tables;

(1) Control stations
 Spaces containing emergency sources of power and lighting.
 Wheelhouse and chartroom.
 Spaces containing the ship's radio equipment.
 Fire control stations.

Control room for propulsion machinery when located outside the machinery space.

Spaces containing centralized fire alarm equipment.

(2)   Corridors

Corridors and lobbies.

(3)   Accommodation spaces

Spaces as defined in regulation 3.1, excluding corridors.

(4)   Stairways

Interior stairway, lifts, totally enclosed emergency escape trunks, and escalators (other than those wholly contained within the machinery spaces) and enclosures thereto.

In this connection, a stairway which is enclosed only at one level shall be regarded as part of the space from which it is not separated by a fire door.

(5)   Service spaces (low risk)

Lockers and store-rooms not having provisions for the storage of flammable liquids and having areas less than 4 m² and drying rooms and laundries.

(6)   Machinery spaces of category A

Spaces as defined in regulation 3.31.

(7)   Other machinery spaces

Electrical equipment rooms (auto-telephone exchange, air-conditioning duct spaces).

Spaces as defined in regulation 3.30, excluding machinery spaces of category A.

(8)   Cargo spaces

All spaces used for cargo (including cargo oil tanks) and trunkways and hatchways to such spaces.

(9)   Service spaces (high risk)

Galleys, pantries containing cooking appliances, saunas, paint lockers and store-rooms having areas of 4 m² or more, spaces for the storage of flammable liquids, and workshops other than those forming part of the machinery spaces.

(10) Open decks

Open deck spaces and enclosed promenades having little or no fire risk. To be considered in this category, enclosed promenades shall have no significant fire risk, meaning that furnishings shall be restricted to deck furniture. In addition, such spaces shall be naturally ventilated by permanent openings.

Air spaces (the space outside superstructures and deckhouses).

(11) Ro-ro and vehicle spaces

Ro-ro spaces as defined in regulation 3.41.

Vehicle spaces as defined in regulation 3.49.

TABLE 9.5 Fire integrity of bulkheads separating adjacent spaces

Spaces		(1)	(2)	(3)	(4)	(5)	(6)	(7)	(8)	(9)	(10)	(11)
Control stations	(1)	A-0^e	A-0	A-60	A-0	A-15	A-60	A-15	A-60	A-60	*	A-60
Corridors	(2)		C	B-0	B-0 A-0^c	B-0	A-60	A-0	A-0	A-0	*	A-30
Accommodation spaces	(3)			C$^{a,\,b}$	B-0 A-0^c	B-0	A-60	A-0	A-0	A-0	*	A-30
Stairways	(4)				B-0 A-0^c	B-0 A-0^c	A-60	A-0	A-0	A-0	*	A-30
Service spaces (low risk)	(5)					C	A-60	A-0	A-0	A-0	*	A-0
Machinery spaces of category A	(6)						*	A-0	A-0^g	A-60	*	A-60^f
Other machinery spaces	(7)							A-0^d	A-0	A-0	*	A-0
Cargo spaces	(8)								*	A-0	*	A-0
Service spaces (high risk)	(9)									A-0^d	*	A-30
Open decks	(10)										—	A-0
Ro-ro and vehicle spaces	(11)											*^{h}

See notes following table 9.6

TABLE 9.6 Fire integrity of decks separating adjacent spaces

Space below ↓ Sp. above →	(1)	(2)	(3)	(4)	(5)	(6)	(7)	(8)	(9)	(10)	(11)
Control stations (1)	A-0	A-0	A-0	A-0	A-0	A-60	A-0	A-0	A-0	*	A-60
Corridors (2)	A-0	*	*	A-0	*	A-60	A-0	A-0	A-0	*	A-30
Accommodation spaces (3)	A-60	A-0	*	A-0	*	A-60	A-0	A-0	A-0	*	A-30
Stairways (4)	A-0	A-0	A-0	*	A-0	A-60	A-0	A-0	A-0	*	A-30
Service spaces (low risk) (5)	A-15	A-0	A-0	A-0	*	A-60	A-0	A-0	A-0	*	A-0
Machinery spaces of category A (6)	A-60	A-60	A-60	A-60	A-60	*	A-60i	A-30	A-60	*	A-60
Other machinery spaces (7)	A-15	A-0	A-0	A-0	A-0	A-0	*	A-0	A-0	*	A-0
Cargo spaces (8)	A-60	A-0	A-0	A-0	A-0	A-0	A-0	*	A-0	*	A-0
Service spaces (high risk) (9)	A-60	A-0	A-0	A-0	A-0	A-60	A-0	A-0	A-0d	*	A-30
Open decks (10)	*	*	*	*	*	*	*	*	*	–	*
Ro-ro and vehicle spaces (11)	A-60	A-30	A-30	A-30	A-0	A-60	A-0	A-0	A-30	*	*h

Note: To be applied to tables 9.5 and 9.6, as appropriate.

a   No special requirements are imposed upon bulkheads in methods IIC and IIIC fire protection.

b   In case of method IIIC, "B" class bulkheads of "B–0" rating shall be provided between spaces or groups of spaces of 50 m^2 and over in area.

c   For clarification as to which applies, see paragraphs 2.3.2 and 2.3.4.

d   Where spaces are of the same numerical category and superscript d appears, a bulkhead or deck of the rating shown in the tables is only required when the adjacent spaces are for a different purpose (e.g., in category (9)). A galley next to a galley does not require a bulkhead, but a galley next to a paint room requires an "A–0" bulkhead.

e   Bulkheads separating the wheelhouse, chartroom and radio room from each other may have a "B–0" rating.

f   An "A–0" rating may be used if no dangerous goods are intended to be carried or if such goods are stowed not less than 3 m horizontally from such a bulkhead.

g   For cargo spaces in which dangerous goods are intended to be carried, regulation 19.3.8 applies.

h   Bulkheads and decks separating ro-ro spaces shall be capable of being closed reasonably gastight and such divisions shall have "A" class integrity in so far as reasonable and practicable, if in the opinion of the Administration it has little or no fire risk.

i   Fire insulation need not be fitted in the machinery space in category (7) if, in the opinion of the Administration, it has little or no fire risk.

*   Where an asterisk appears in the tables, the division is required to be of steel or other equivalent material but is not required to be of "A" class standard. However, where a deck, except an open deck, is penetrated for the passage of electric cables, pipes and vent ducts, such penetrations should be made tight to prevent the passage of flame and smoke. Divisions between control stations (emergency generators) and open decks may have air intake openings without means for closure, unless a fixed gas fire-extinguishing system is fitted.

2.3.3.3 Continuous "B" class ceilings or linings, in association with the relevant decks or bulkheads, may be accepted as contributing, wholly or in part, to the required insulation and integrity of a division.

2.3.3.4 External boundaries which are required in regulation 11.2 to be of steel or other equivalent material may be pierced for the fitting of windows and sidescuttles provided that there is no requirement for such boundaries of cargo ships to have "A" class integrity. Similarly, in such boundaries which are not required to have "A" class integrity, doors may be constructed of materials which are to the satisfaction of the Administration.

2.3.3.5 Saunas shall comply with paragraph 2.2.3.4.

2.3.4   Protection of stairways and lift trunks in accommodation spaces, service spaces and control stations

2.3.4.1 Stairways which penetrate only a single deck shall be protected, at a minimum, at one level by at least "B–0" class divisions and self-closing doors. Lifts which penetrate only a single deck shall be surrounded by "A–0" class divisions with steel doors at both levels. Stairways and lift trunks which penetrate more than a single deck shall be surrounded by at least "A–0" class divisions and be protected by self-closing doors at all levels.

2.3.4.2 On ships having accommodation for 12 persons or less, where stairways penetrate more than a single deck and where there are at least two escape routes direct to the open deck at every accommodation level, the "A–0" requirements of paragraph 2.3.4.1 may be reduced to "B–0".

Guidance 9

G31   Cargo Ships – Method of fire protection in accommodation.

G31.1 General.

G31.1.1 The provision, or otherwise of a fire detection and/or sprinkler system in accordance with regulation 7.5 determines whether method IC, IIC or IIIC can be adopted.

G31.1.2 Also guidance G9.8.1 and G9.8.2 in respect of:

.1   'B' Class divisions, and

.2   continuous 'B' Class ceiling or lining applies in a similar manner.

G32.1 Bulkheads in ships in which Method IC has been adopted

G32.1.1 All bulkheads within accommodation spaces, service spaces and control stations in ships in which Method IC has been adopted are required to be 'A' Class, 'B' Class or 'C' Class divisions as indicated in table 9.5. These divisions should be constructed and insulated as indicated in guidance G9.1, G9.2 and G9.3.

G32.2 Bulkheads in ships in which Method IIC has been adopted

G32.2.1 There are no restrictions on the construction of bulkheads within accommodation spaces, service spaces and control stations in ships in which Method IIC has been adopted i.e. the bulkheads may be combustible subject to the following guidance, or non-combustible with no restrictions on the methods of their erection except where bulkheads are required to be:

.1   'A' Class or 'B' Class divisions; or

.2   'C' Class divisions as indicated by a letter 'C' with no superscription 'a' in table 9.5 e.g. a bulkhead separating two service spaces of low fire risk.

G32.2.2 In no case should a bulkhead which is permitted by the Regulations to be combustible penetrate an 'A' Class insulation or a 'B' Class division.

G32.3 Bulkheads in ships in which Method IIIC has been adopted

G32.3.1 There are no restrictions on the construction of bulkheads within accommodation spaces, service spaces and control stations in ships in which Method IIIC has been adopted i.e. the bulkheads may be combustible subject to the following guidance or non-combustible with no restriction on the methods of their erection except where bulkheads are required to be:

.1   'A' Class or 'B' Class divisions; or

.2   'C' Class divisions as indicated by a letter 'C' with no superscription 'b' in table 9.5 e.g. a bulkhead separating two service spaces of low fire risk.

G32.3.2 When the public space referred to in paragraph 2.3.1.1.3 and 2.3.2.4 is bounded by 'A' class and 'B' class divisions or by 'B' class divisions only the area may be increased to a maximum of 75m^2.

G33   Combustible Bulkheads

G33.1 In no case should a bulkhead which is permitted by the Regulations to be combustible penetrate an 'A' Class insulation or a 'B' Class division.

G33.2 Combustible bulkheads should comply with the Merchant Shipping (Crew Accommodation) Regulations 1997 and should not be constructed of organic foams, cork and other highly flammable materials, or other materials capable of producing large quantities of smoke or toxic products. This does not apply to wood products and surface finish materials referred to in regulation 6.2.

G34   Cargo ships – fire integrity of bulkheads and decks

G34.1 Minimum standards and categories

G34.1.1 Each space throughout the ship should be allocated a category from the list of categories (1) to (11) inclusive for tables 9.5 and 9.6. The minimum fire integrity and insulation standards of the bulkheads or decks separating adjacent spaces should be determined by cross referencing the categories of the spaces in the appropriate table.

G34.1.2 In respect of the following items the referred guidance should be applied in a similar manner:

.1   Group of spaces (G9.10)

.2   Insulation values of spaces with special characters of two or more space categories. (G9.11)

.3   Spaces used for unrelated purposes (G9.12)

.4   Spaces of more than one category (G9.13)

.5   Stairways closed at one level and escape trunks (G9.14)

.6   Separation of machinery spaces from other spaces (G9.20)

G35   Weather decks used for cargo stowage

G35.1 Weather decks used for cargo stowage should be considered as Category (8) in tables 9.5 and 9.6, except for cargoes which constitute a low fire risk.

G36   Pantries not containing cooking appliances

G36.1 Pantries not containing cooking appliances should be included in Category (3) in tables 9.5 and 9.6. See guidance G9.16.1 on these pantries on passenger ships for the definition of such a pantry and the conditions under which a microwave oven may be fitted in such a pantry.

G37   Cargo ships – external boundaries (Regulation 9.2.3.3.4)

G37.1 Windows and sidescuttle

G37.1.1 The outer boundaries of the hull, superstructures and deckhouses may be pierced by windows and sidescuttles which are not required by the Regulations to meet any 'A' Class or 'B' Class standard. Surveyors should however recommend to shipbuilders and owners that any windows which are fitted in such boundaries within 3m of the lifeboat and liferaft embarkation, stowage, handling and lowering positions should be fitted with an approved fire resisting glass. The glass to be fitted in accordance with the conditions stated in the approval certificate. This recommendation does not apply to windows fitted in a superstructure or deckhouse situated on any deck above the highest deck on which the lifeboat, liferaft or marine escape system positions are situated. Any fire rated glass fitted to the above windows should be of an approved type and fitted in accordance with the conditions stated in the certificate of approval.

G37.2 Doors

G37.2.1 Doors in the outer boundaries of superstructures and deckhouses may be of any material or construction subject to compliance with any of the Load Line requirements. However, any such doors which are within 3m of the lifeboat and liferaft embarkation, stowage, handling and lowering positions should be of substantial steel construction except that any such door giving access to accommodation spaces may be of solid wood construction.

G37.2.2 'A' Class door assemblies designed for interior use may not be suitable for use in external positions exposed to the weather, because of their light construction and susceptibility to corrosion.

G38   Superscriptions in tables 9.5 and 9.6

G38.1 Superscription 'a'

G38.1.1 Where superscription 'a' appears in table 9.5 the bulkheads, for which there are no special requirements, may be constructed of combustible or non-combustible materials and erected as the shipbuilder chooses subject to guidance G9.32.2 concerning method IIC.

G38.2 Superscription 'b'

G38.2.1 Where superscription 'b' appears in table 9.5 there are no special requirements applicable to the construction and erection of bulkheads separating accommodation spaces in a ship in which Method IIIC has been adopted i.e. bulkheads may be constructed of combustible or non-combustible materials and erected as the shipbuilder chooses subject to guidance G9.32.3 concerning method IIIC.

G38.3 Superscription 'c'

G38.3.1 Where superscription 'c' appears in table 9.5 the A–0 standard or B–0 standard applies to the bulkheads which are required to enclose stairways and lifts as indicated in paragraph 2.3.4. See also guidance G39.

G38.4 Superscription 'd'

G38.4.1 Where superscription 'd' appears in tables 9.5 and 9.6 the A–0 standard only applies to bulkheads and decks separating spaces which are used for different purposes e.g. in Category (9) in table 9.5, a bulkhead separating a galley and a paint room. A bulkhead or deck need not be fitted between two spaces used for the same or similar purposes e.g. two machinery spaces of other than Category A. However, if a shipbuilder decides to fit a bulkhead between two such spaces, the bulkhead need only be of steel having no fire integrity standard or may be of expanded metal.

G38.4.2 Similarly in Category (9) in table 9.5, a bulkhead need not be fitted between two storerooms having areas in excess of 2m² which are used for the same purpose or, if a bulkhead is fitted, it need have no fire integrity standard e.g. two provision storerooms. However the bulkhead separating two storerooms used for different purposes e.g. linen and provision storerooms should be of A–0 standard as specified in table 9.5.

G38.5 Superscription 'e'

G38.5.1 Bulkheads separating control stations are required by table 9.5 to be of A–0 standard except that bulkheads separating the wheelhouse, chartroom and radio office may be of B–0 standard.

G38.6 Superscription 'f'

G38.6.1 When dangerous goods other than dangerous goods of Class 1 are intended to be carried in a cargo space, any bulkheads and decks separating the cargo space from a machinery space of Category A are required by regulation 19.3.8 to be insulated to A–60 standard except that the A–60 insulation on the bulkheads may be dispensed with if the dangerous goods are stowed at least 3m clear of such bulkheads including stepped or recessed portions. Figures 9.3 and 9.4 illustrate this paragraph.

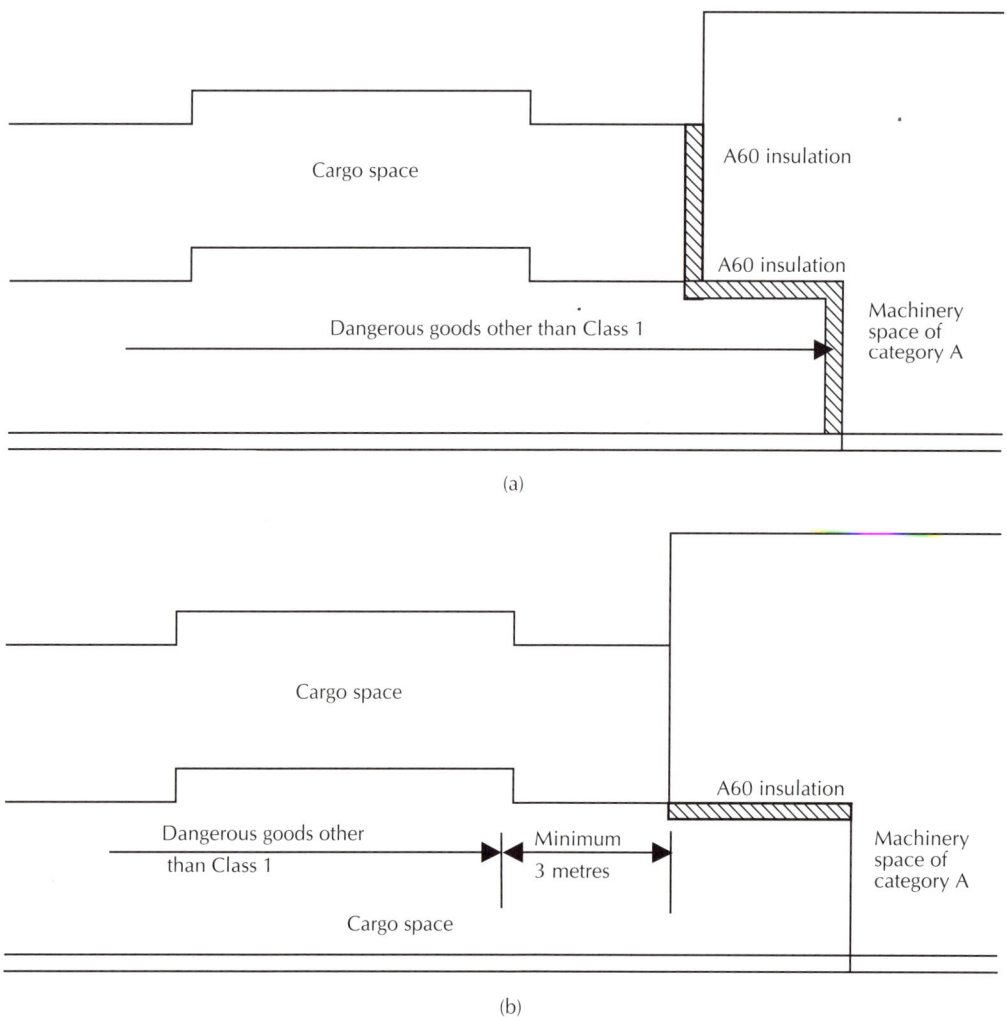

Figure 9.3 Dangerous goods other than those of Class 1

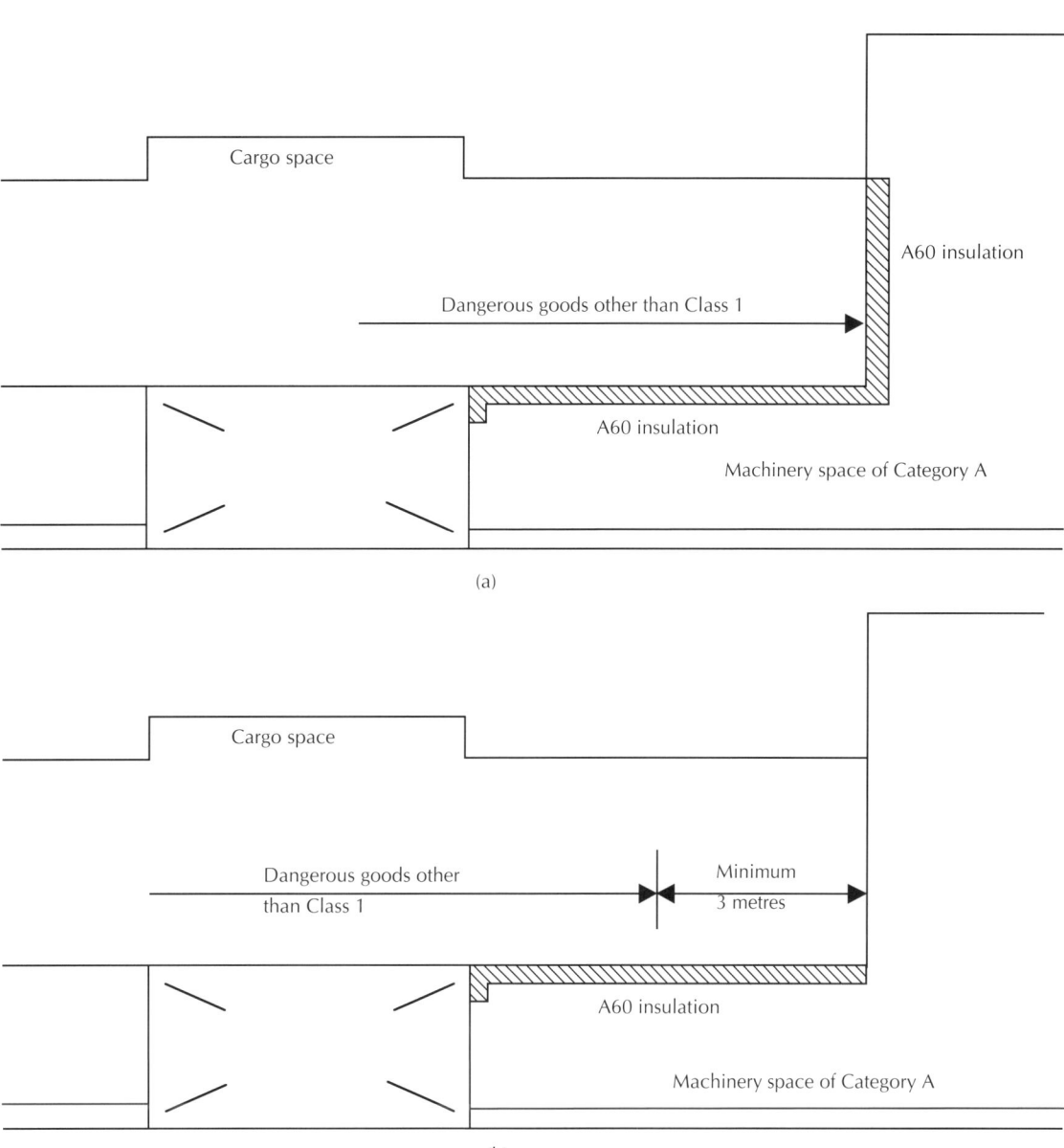

Figure 9.4 Dangerous goods other than those of Class 1

G38.7 Superscription 'g'

G38.7.1 When dangerous goods of Class 1 are intended to be carried in a cargo space, any bulkheads and decks separating the cargo space from a machinery space of Category A are required by regulation 19.3.8 to be insulated to A–60 standard including any stepped or recessed portions of such a bulkhead and the dangerous goods are to be stowed at least 3m clear of such bulkheads including any stepped or recessed portions. Figure 9.5 on page 90 illustrates this paragraph.

G38.8 Superscription 'h'

G38.8.1 Decks separating Ro-Ro spaces should be gastight. However any opening between such spaces, other than an opening required by the Load Line Regulations to be fitted with a watertight closing device, should be fitted with a steel door or cover which should be gas tight as far as is reasonably practicable to the satisfaction of the surveyor. In addition any such opening which is used for access should be fitted with a self closing steel door or cover which should not be capable of being held in the open position.

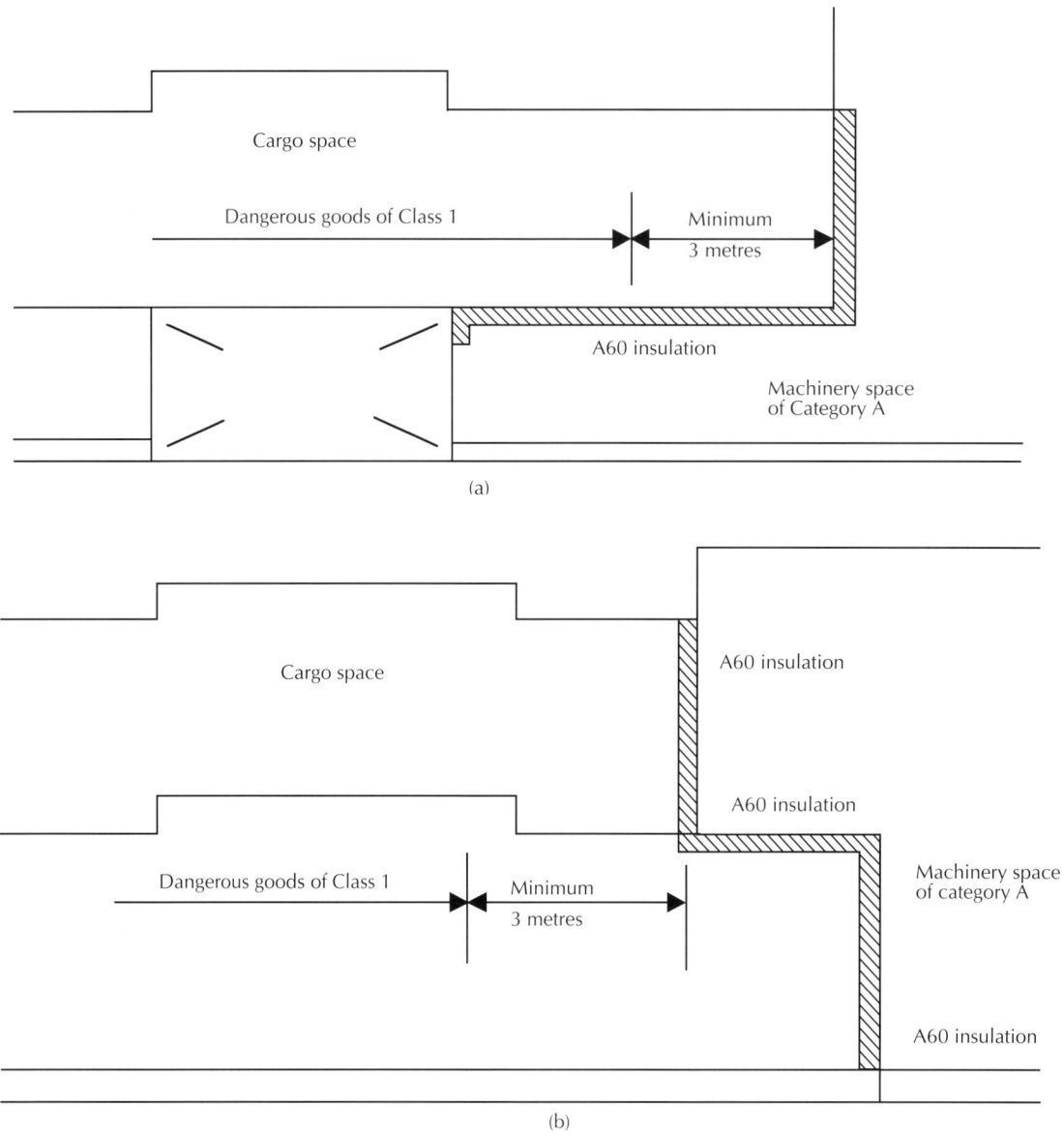

Figure 9.5 Dangerous goods of Class 1

G38.9 Superscription 'i'

G38.9.1 Where a superscription 'i' appears in table 9.6 the A–60 insulation need not be fitted to a deck separating a machinery space of Category A and a space containing either:

.1 auxiliary machinery not having a pressure lubricating system and not having any combustibles stowed in the space;

.2 ventilation and air conditioning machinery; or

.3 switchboards and major electrical equipment except oil-filled electrical transformers above 10 kVA and switchboards and electrical equipment used for emergency purposes.

G38.9.2 This relaxation does not apply to spaces containing minor electrical equipment such as section switchboards, fuse boxes and junction boxes.

G38.10   An asterisk in the tables

G38.10.1 Where an asterisk appears in tables 9.5 and 9.6, the bulkheads and decks are required to be of steel or equivalent material but need to have no 'A' Class standard except that the crowns and casings of machinery spaces of Category A are required by regulation 11.4.1 to be constructed only of steel. However, where such a deck, except an open deck, is penetrated for the passage of electric cables, pipes and vent ducts, such penetrations should be made tight to prevent the passage of flame and smoke. When such bulkheads and decks are constructed of aluminium alloy, then regulation 11.3 should apply.

G38.10.2 Notwithstanding the provision of an asterisk in the tables, any of the following structure which is constructed of aluminium alloy should be an 'A' Class division of A–0 standard:

.1   any part of the hull or sides of a superstructure or deckhouse which does not support the lifeboat and liferaft embarkation, stowage, handling and lowering positions but is within 3m of such positions; and

.2   the ends and sides of any superstructure or deckhouse which overlook a deck, walkway or stairway which may be used as an escape route from accommodation spaces, service spaces, control stations or machinery spaces to the lifeboat or liferaft embarkation deck, the superstructure or deckhouse not being one which supports the lifeboat and liferaft embarkation, stowage, handling and lowering positions.

2.4   Tankers

2.4.1   Application

For tankers, only method IC as defined in paragraph 2.3.1.1 shall be used.

2.4.2   Fire integrity of bulkheads and decks

2.4.2.1 In lieu of paragraph 2.3 and in addition to complying with the specific provisions for fire integrity of bulkheads and decks of tankers, the minimum fire integrity of bulkheads and decks shall be as prescribed in tables 9.7 and 9.8.

2.4.2.2 The following requirements shall govern application of the tables:

.1   Tables 9.7 and 9.8 shall apply respectively to the bulkhead and decks separating adjacent spaces.

.2   For determining the appropriate fire integrity standards to be applied to divisions between adjacent spaces, such spaces are classified according to their fire risk as shown in categories (1) to (10) below. Where the contents and use of a space are such that there is a doubt as to its classification for the purpose of this regulation, or where it is possible to assign two or more classifications to a space, it shall be treated as a space within the relevant category having the most stringent boundary requirements. Smaller, enclosed areas within a space that have less than 30% communicating openings to that space are considered separate areas. The fire integrity of the boundary bulkheads and decks of such smaller spaces shall be as prescribed in tables 9.7 and 9.8. The title of each category is intended to be typical rather than restrictive. The number in parentheses preceding each category refers to the applicable column or row in the tables.

(1)   Control stations

Spaces containing emergency sources of power and lighting.

Wheelhouse and chartroom.

Spaces containing the ship's radio equipment.

Fire control stations.

Control room for propulsion machinery when located outside the machinery space.

Spaces containing centralized fire alarm equipment.

(2)   Corridors

Corridors and lobbies.

(3)   Accommodation spaces

Spaces as defined in regulation 3.1, excluding corridors.

(4)   Stairways

Interior stairways, lifts, totally enclosed emergency escape trunks, and escalators (other than those wholly contained within the machinery spaces) and enclosures thereto.

In this connection, a stairway which is enclosed only at one level shall be regarded as part of the space from which it is not separated by a fire door.

(5)   Service spaces (low risk)

Lockers and store-rooms not having provisions for the storage of flammable liquids and having areas less than 4 m² and drying rooms and laundries.

(6)   Machinery spaces of category A

Spaces as defined in regulation 3.31.

(7)   Other machinery spaces

Electrical equipment rooms (auto-telephone exchange and air-conditioning duct spaces).

Spaces as defined in regulation 3.30 excluding machinery spaces of category A.

(8)   Cargo pump-rooms

Spaces containing cargo pumps and entrances and trunks to such spaces.

(9)   Service spaces (high risk)

Galleys, pantries containing cooking appliances, saunas, paint lockers and store-rooms having areas of 4 m² or more, spaces for the storage of flammable liquids and workshops other than those forming part of the machinery spaces.

(10)   Open decks

Open deck spaces and enclosed promenades having little or no fire risk. To be considered in this category, enclosed promenades shall have no significant fire risk, meaning that furnishings shall be restricted to deck furniture. In addition, such spaces shall be naturally ventilated by permanent openings.

Air spaces (the space outside superstructures and deckhouses).

TABLE 9.7

Fire integrity of bulkheads separating adjacent spaces

Spaces	(1)	(2)	(3)	(4)	(5)	(6)	(7)	(8)	(9)	(10)
Control stations (1)	A-0[c]	A-0	A-60	A-0	A-15	A-60	A-15	A-60	A-60	*
Corridors (2)		C	B-0	B-0 A-0[a]	B-0	A-60	A-0	A-60	A-0	*
Accommodation spaces (3)			C	B-0 A-0[a]	B-0	A-60	A-0	A-60	A-0	*
Stairways (4)				B-0 A-0[a]	B-0 A-0[a]	A-60	A-0	A-60	A-0	*
Service spaces (low risk) (5)					C	A-60	A-0	A-60	A-0	*
Machinery spaces of category A (6)						*	A-0	A-0[d]	A-60	*
Other machinery spaces (7)							A-0[b]	A-0	A-0	*
Cargo pump-rooms (8)								*	A-60	*
Service spaces (high risk) (9)									A-0[b]	*
Open decks (10)										—

See notes following table 9.8

TABLE 9.8 Fire integrity of decks separating adjacent spaces

Space below ↓ Space above →	(1)	(2)	(3)	(4)	(5)	(6)	(7)	(8)	(9)	(10)
Control stations	(1)	A-0	A-0	A-0	A-0	A-0	A-60	A-0	—	A-0	*
Corridors	(2)	A-0	*	*	A-0	*	A-60	A-0	—	A-0	*
Accommodation spaces	(3)	A-60	A-0	*	A-0	*	A-60	A-0	—	A-0	*
Stairways	(4)	A-0	A-0	A-0	*	A-0	A-60	A-0	—	A-0	*
Service spaces (low risk)	(5)	A-15	A-0	A-0	A-0	*	A-60	A-0	—	A-0	*
Machinery spaces of category A	(6)	A-60	A-60	A-60	A-60	A-60	*	A-60[e]	A-0	A-60	*
Other machinery spaces	(7)	A-15	A-0	A-0	A-0	A-0	A-0	*	A-0	A-0	*
Cargo pump-rooms	(8)	—	—	—	—	—	A-0[d]	A-0	*	—	*
Service spaces (high risk)	(9)	A-60	A-0	A-0	A-0	A-0	A-60	A-0	—	A-0[b]	*
Open decks	(10)	*	*	*	*	*	*	*	*	*	—

Notes: To be applied to tables 9.7 and 9.8 as appropriate.

a For clarification as to which applies, see paragraphs 2.3.2 and 2.3.4.

b Where spaces are of the same numerical category and superscript 'b' appears, a bulkhead or deck of the rating shown in the tables is only required when the adjacent spaces are for a different purpose (e.g., in category (9)). A galley next to a galley does not require a bulkhead but a galley next to a paint room requires an "A–0" bulkhead.

c Bulkheads separating the wheelhouse, chartroom and radio room from each other may have a "B–0" rating.

d Bulkheads and decks between cargo pump-rooms and machinery spaces of category A may be penetrated by cargo pump shaft glands and similar gland penetrations, provided that gas tight seals with efficient lubrication or other means of ensuring the permanence of the gas seal are fitted in way of the bulkheads or deck.

e Fire insulation need not be fitted if the machinery space in category (7) if, in the opinion of the Administration, it has little or no fire risk.

* Where an asterisk appears in the table, the division is required to be of steel or other equivalent material, but is not required to be of "A" class standard. However, where a deck, except an open deck, is penetrated for the passage of electric cables, pipes and vent ducts, such penetrations shall be made tight to prevent the passage of flame and smoke. Divisions between control stations (emergency generators) and open decks may have air intake openings without means for closure, unless a fixed gas fire-extinguishing system is fitted.

2.4.2.3 Continuous "B" class ceilings or linings, in association with the relevant decks or bulkheads, may be accepted as contributing, wholly or in part, to the required insulation and integrity of a division.

2.4.2.4 External boundaries which are required in regulation 11.2 to be of steel or other equivalent material may be pierced for the fitting of windows and sidescuttles provided that there is no requirement for such boundaries of tankers to have "A" class integrity. Similarly, in such boundaries which are not required to have "A" class integrity, doors may be constructed of materials which are to the satisfaction of the Administration.

2.4.2.5 Exterior boundaries of superstructures and deckhouses enclosing accommodation and including any overhanging decks which support such accommodation, shall be constructed of steel and insulated to "A–60" standard for the whole of the portions which face the cargo area and on the outward sides for a distance of 3 m from the end boundary facing the cargo area. The distance of 3 m shall be measured horizontally and parallel to the middle line of the ship from the boundary which faces the cargo area at each deck level. In the case of the sides of those superstructures and deckhouses, such insulation shall be carried up to the underside of the deck of the navigation bridge.

2.4.2.6 Skylights to cargo pump-rooms shall be of steel, shall not contain any glass and shall be capable of being closed from outside the pump-room.

2.4.2.7 Construction and arrangement of saunas shall comply with paragraph 2.2.3.4.

Guidance 9

G39   Cargo ships – Protection of stairways and lifts

G39.1 Construction and insulation

G39.1.1 The stiles, treads, and if fitted backing plates, of stairways should be constructed of steel except that they may be constructed of aluminium alloy suitably insulated when the structure is of aluminium alloy.

G39.1.2 Every stairway and lift is required by paragraph 2.3.4 to lie within an enclosure or trunk constructed of 'A' Class divisions of A–0 standard, except that a stairway serving only two decks need only be enclosed at one level by 'A' Class divisions of A–0 standard or 'B' Class divisions of B–0 standard. However when a stairway abuts a machinery space of Category A or a Ro-Ro space, the bulkhead or deck separating the stairway from the machinery space or Ro-Ro space is to be determined respectively by reference to table 9.5 or 9.6.

G39.1.3 Figure 9.6, on page 96, shows three acceptable methods of enclosing stairways on cargo ships and tankers when the stairways serve more than two decks.

.1   It should be noted however that the arrangement shown in figure 9.6(a) provides a much safer means of escape and access for fire parties than the arrangements in figures 9.6(b) and (c) should the corridors become filled with smoke. Furthermore, the arrangement shown in figure 9.6(a) imposes no more restrictions on the accommodation layout than the other two arrangements as can be seen by comparing the plan views in figure 9.7 (see page 97).

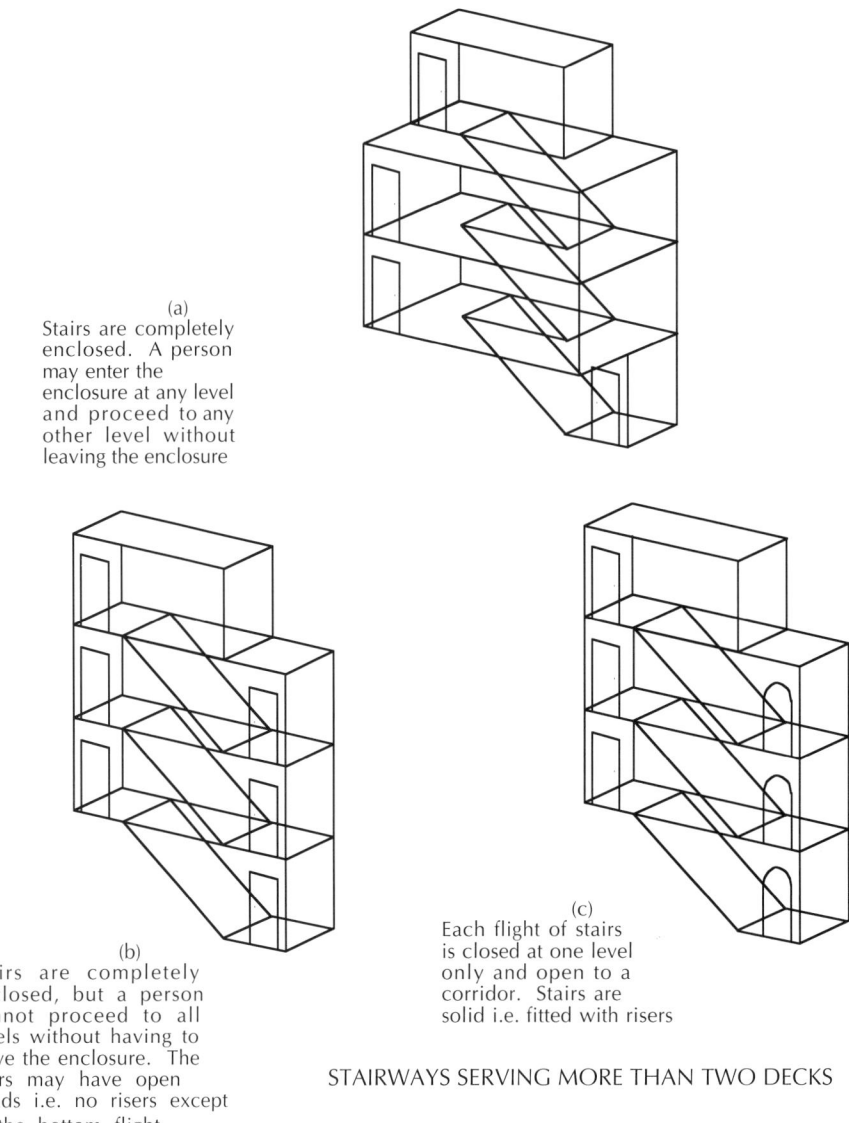

(a)
Stairs are completely enclosed. A person may enter the enclosure at any level and proceed to any other level without leaving the enclosure

(b)
Stairs are completely enclosed, but a person cannot proceed to all levels without having to leave the enclosure. The stairs may have open treads i.e. no risers except in the bottom flight

(c)
Each flight of stairs is closed at one level only and open to a corridor. Stairs are solid i.e. fitted with risers

STAIRWAYS SERVING MORE THAN TWO DECKS

Figure 9.6

.2 Shipbuilders and shipowners should be recommended by surveyors to incorporate the arrangement shown in figure 9.6(a) in accommodation layouts whenever possible.

.3 When it is not possible to arrange a stairway enclosure as indicated in figure 9.6(a) then the arrangement shown in figure 9.6(b) is preferred to that shown in figure 9.6(c).

G39.1.4 Stairway enclosures and lift trunks constructed of steel which are required by the tables to be insulated, may be insulated on either side, but in any case measures should be taken to prevent heat transmission through divisions in way of decks, landings etc.

G39.2 Openings in stairway enclosures

G39.2.1 Openings in stairway enclosures should be fitted with approved doors of the same 'A' Class or 'B' Class standard as the bulkhead in which they are fitted except that approved drop rolling shutters may be fitted in lieu of a door to an opening in an enclosure bulkhead of A–0 standard.

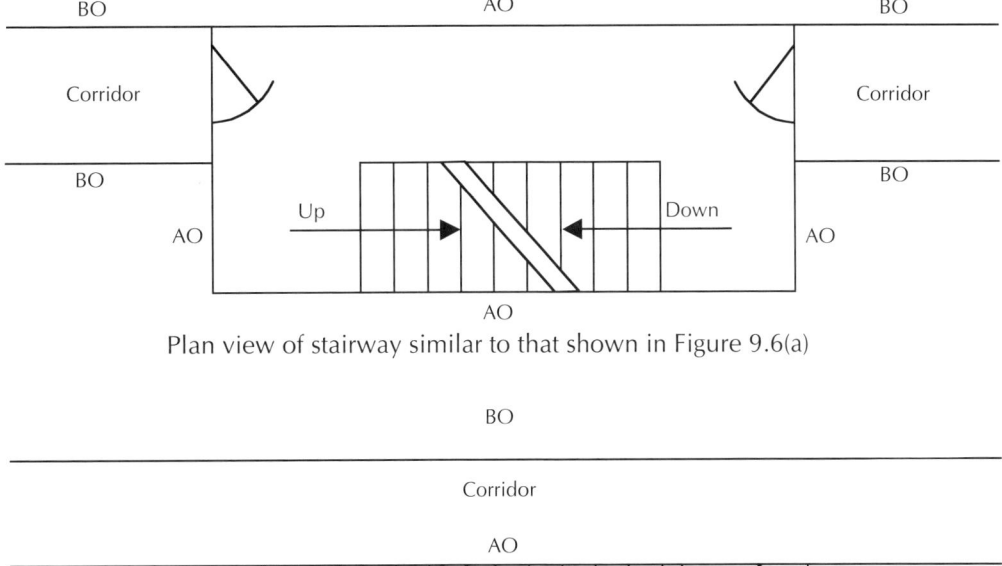

Plan view of stairway similar to that shown in Figure 9.6(a)

Plan view of stairway similar to that shown in Figure 9.6(b)

Figure 9.7

G39.3 Access into stairway enclosures

G39.3.1 Stairway enclosures should be connected to corridors. As far as is reasonably practicable spaces containing combustibles such as cabins, offices, storerooms, lockers etc. should not be situated in a stairway enclosure or have direct access into the enclosure.

G39.4 Lift trunks in stairway enclosures

G39.4.1 The boundaries and doors of a lift trunk which is situated within a stairway enclosure are not required to meet any 'A' Class standard provided that:

.1 any boundary of the lift trunk which forms part of the stairway enclosure is an 'A' Class division of the appropriate standard specified in tables 9.5 and 9.6; and

.2 any opening in the lift trunk which gives direct access to any space situated outside the stairway enclosure is provided with an approved lift door of the same 'A' Class standard as the bulkhead in which it is fitted.

G39.4.2 A lift trunk extending above or below a stairway enclosure may be treated in the same manner.

G39.5 Means of closure of lift trunks

G39.5.1 Each opening in a lift trunk should be provided with an approved lift door of the same 'A' Class standard as the bulkhead in which it is fitted, except for any opening provided with a door which is not required to meet any 'A' Class standard as indicated earlier, i.e. when the lift trunk is in a stairway enclosure.

G40   Tankers – Method of fire protection in accommodation

G40.1   General

G40.1.1 For tankers only method IC can be adopted:

G40.2   Bulkheads within accommodation spaces, service spaces and control stations on tankers

G40.2.1 All bulkheads within accommodation spaces, service spaces and control stations are required to be 'A' Class, 'B' Class or 'C' Class divisions as indicated in table 9.7. These divisions should be constructed and insulated as indicated in guidance G9.1, G9.2 and G9.3.

G41   Tanker fire integrity of bulkheads and decks

G41.1   Minimum standards and categories

G41.1.1 Each space throughout the ship should be allocated a category from the list of categories ((1) to (10) inclusive) indicated in tables 9.7 and 9.8. The minimum fire integrity and insulation standards of the bulkheads or decks separating adjacent spaces should be determined by cross referencing the categories of the spaces in the appropriate table.

G41.1.2 In respect of the following items the referred guidance should be applied in a similar manner:

.1   Group of spaces (G9.10)

.2   Insulation values of spaces with special characters of two of more space categories. (G9.11)

.3   Spaces used for unrelated purposes (G9.12)

.4   Spaces of more than one category (G9.13)

.5   Stairways closed at one level and escape trunks (G9.14)

.6   Separation of machinery spaces from other spaces (G9.20)

G42   Pantries containing no cooking appliances

G42.1   Pantries containing no cooking appliances should be included in category (3) in tables 9.7 and 9.8. See guidance G9.16.1 on these pantries on passenger ships for the definition of such a pantry and the condition under which a microwave oven may be fitted in such a pantry.

G43   Tankers – external boundaries

G43.1   Windows and sidescuttles

G43.1.1 The outer boundaries of the hull, superstructure and deckhouses may be pierced by windows and sidescuttles which are not required to meet any 'A' Class or 'B' Class standard except that windows and sidescuttles situated in the portions of exterior boundaries of superstructures and deckhouses referred to in regulation 4.5.2.1 should comply with the guidance G4.7 to regulation 4.5.2.3. Furthermore surveyors should recommend to shipbuilders and owners that any windows which are fitted in superstructures or deckhouses within 3m of the lifeboat and liferaft embarkation, stowage, handling and lowering positions should be fitted with an approved fire resisting glass. The glass to be fitted in accordance with the conditions stated in the approval certificate. This recommendation does not apply to windows fitted in a superstructure or deckhouse situated on any deck above the highest deck on which the lifeboat, liferaft or marine escape system positions are situated.

G43.2 Doors

G43.2.1 Doors in the outer boundaries of superstructures and deckhouses may be of any material or construction subject to compliance with any load line requirements. However any such doors which are within 3m of the lifeboat and liferaft embarkation, stowage, handling and lowering positions should be of substantial steel construction except that any such door giving access to accommodation spaces may be of solid wood construction.

G43.2.2 See guidance G4.5, regarding the restrictions on the fitting of doors in the portions of the exterior boundaries of superstructures and deckhouses referred to in regulation 4.5.2.1.

G43.2.3 'A' Class door assemblies designed for interior use may not be suitable for use in external positions exposed to the weather because of their light construction and susceptibility to corrosion.

G44 Tankers – Exterior boundaries of superstructures and deckhouses

G44.1 Insulated boundaries

G44.1.1 Only the exterior boundaries of superstructures and/or deckhouses which enclose accommodation including any overhanging decks supporting such accommodation need be insulated with an A–60 insulation on the portions which face the cargo area and on the side portions for a distance of at least 3m from the portions which face the cargo area. This Regulation does not require the exterior boundaries of superstructures and/or deckhouses which do not enclose accommodation to be insulated. However the inclusion of one or more accommodation space in any position in a superstructure or deckhouse would necessitate it having to be insulated in compliance with that Regulation.

G44.1.2 Each 3m minimum length of insulated side portion of a superstructure or deckhouse is to be measured horizontally and parallel to the centre line of the ship from the line at which the superstructure or deckhouse ceases to have any forward or aft projection depending on whether the superstructure or deckhouse is aft or forward of the cargo area. This subparagraph as applicable to a deckhouse situated aft of the cargo area is illustrated in figure 9.8.

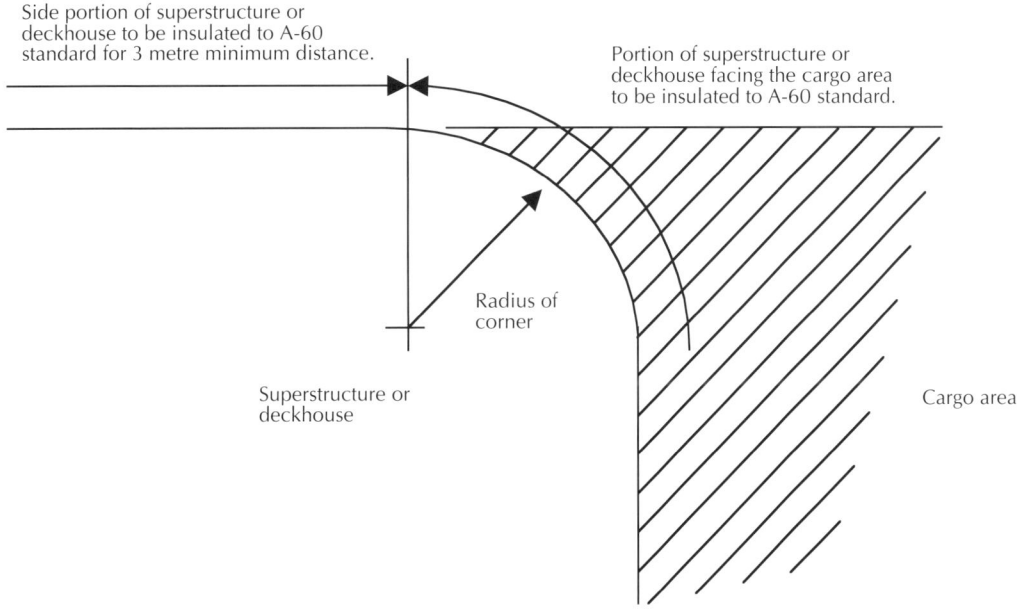

Figure 9.8 Insulated boundaries of superstructure and deckhouse

G44.1.3 The insulation used to insulate the exterior boundaries of superstructures and deckhouses in compliance with this regulation should be an insulation approved for general application in the construction of 'A' Class bulkheads of A–60 standard. The insulation should be fitted deck to deck in accordance with the conditions indicated in the approval certificate. The insulation need not however be extended for a distance of 450mm along the bulkheads, decks and other internal structure adjacent to the exterior boundaries.

G44.1.4 Any overhanging deck supporting accommodation should be insulated for the whole of its length. An overhanging deck would best be insulated on its upperside using an approved A–60 deck covering rather than apply insulation to the underside where it would be exposed to the weather.

G44.1.5 Any step in the exterior boundaries of superstructures or deckhouses situated aft of the cargo area which is not an overhanging deck, should be insulated from its end nearest the cargo area to at least 3m aft of the line at which the superstructure or deckhouse under the step ceases to have any forward projection. Any similar step in the exterior boundaries of superstructures and deckhouses which enclose accommodation and are situated forward of the cargo area should be treated as a 'mirror image' of the superstructures and deckhouses situated aft of the cargo area. This subparagraph as applicable to a step in the exterior boundaries of deckhouses situated aft of the cargo area is illustrated in figure 9.9.

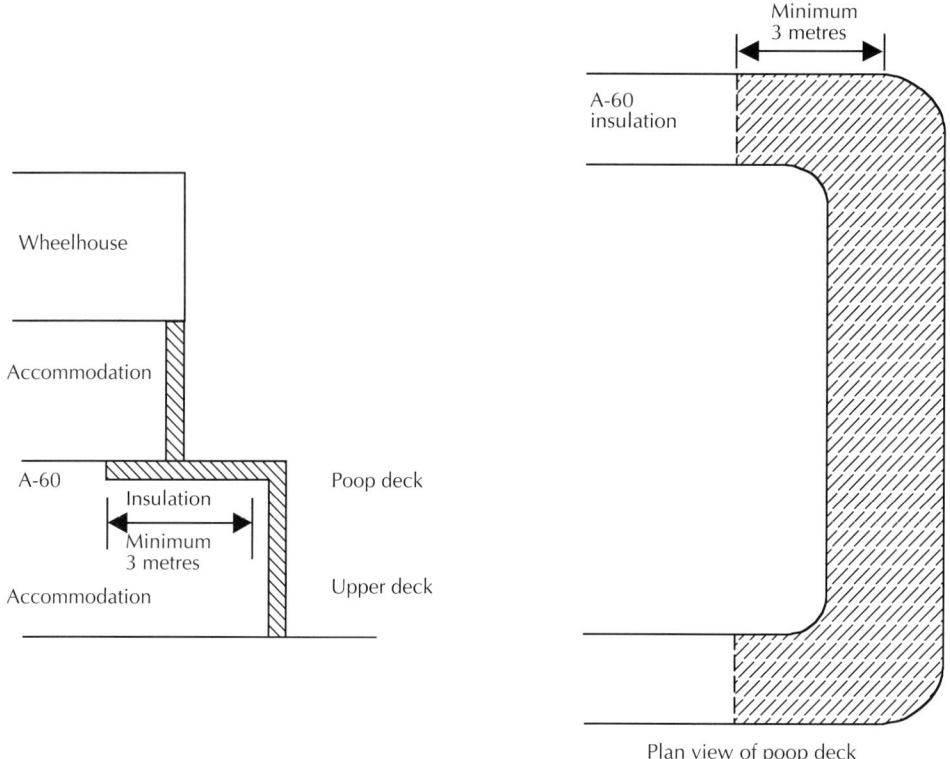

Figure 9.9 Extent of insulation applied to a deck which is not an overhanging deck

G45   Superscriptions in tables 9.7 and 9.8

G45.1 Superscription 'a'

G45.1.1 Where superscription 'a' appears in table 9.7, the A–0 standard or B–0 standard applies to the bulkheads which are required to enclose stairways and lifts as indicated in paragraph 2.3.4 which may also be applied to tankers. See also guidance G46.

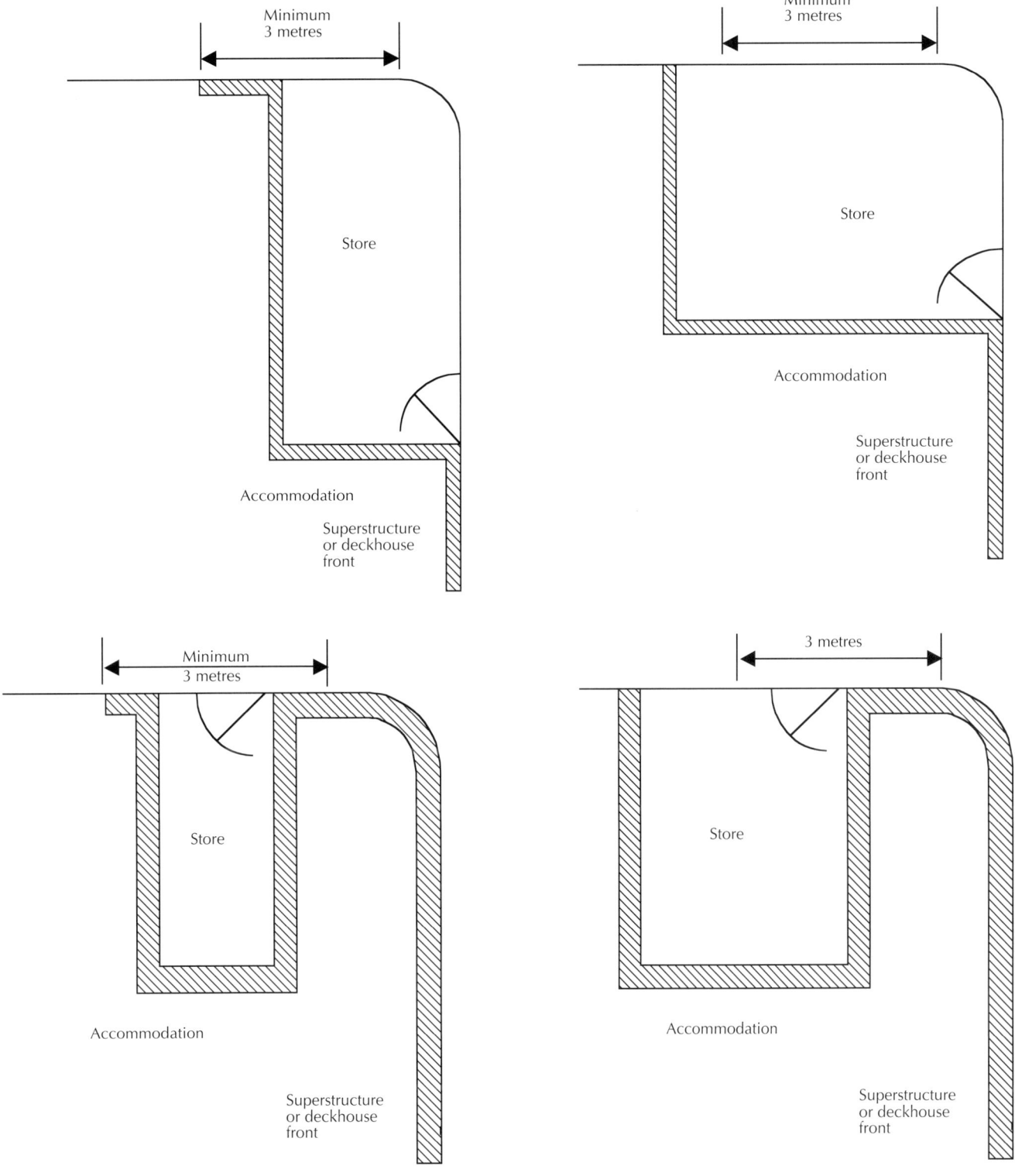

(In all cases the deckhead of the space should be insulated.)

Figure 9.10 Extent of A-60 insulation around a space having a door which is permitted by Regulation 4.5.2.2 to be fitted within the limits specified in Regulation 4.5.2.1

G45.2 Superscription 'b'

G45.2.1 Where superscription 'b' appears in tables 9.7 and 9.8, the A–0 standard only applies to bulkheads and decks separating spaces which are used for different purposes e.g. in Category (9) in table 9.7, a bulkhead separating a galley and a paint room. A bulkhead or deck need not be fitted between two spaces used for the same or similar purposes e.g. two machinery spaces of other than Category A. However, if a shipbuilder decides to fit a bulkhead between two such spaces, the bulkhead need only be of steel having no fire integrity standard or may be of expanded metal.

G45.2.2 Similarly in Category (9) in table 9.7, a bulkhead need not be fitted between two storerooms having areas in excess of 2m which are used for the same purpose or, if a bulkhead is fitted, it need have no fire integrity standard e.g. two provision storerooms. However the bulkhead separating two storerooms used for different purposes e.g. linen and provision storerooms should be of A–0 standard as specified in table 9.7.

G45.3 Superscription 'c'

G45.3.1 Bulkheads separating control stations are required by table 9.7 to be of A–0 standard except that bulkheads separating the wheelhouse, chartroom and radio office may be of B–0 standard.

G45.4 Superscription 'e'

G45.4.1 Where a superscription 'e' appears in table 9.8 the A–60 insulation need not be fitted to a deck separating a machinery space of Category A and a space containing either:

.1 auxiliary machinery not having a pressure lubricating system and not having any combustibles stowed in the space;

.2 ventilation and air conditioning machinery; or

.3 switchboards and major electrical equipment except oil-filled electrical transformers above 10 KVA and switchboards and electrical equipment used for emergency purposes.

G45.4.2 This relaxation does not apply to spaces containing minor electrical equipment such as section switchboards, fuse boxes and junction boxes.

G45.5 Asterisk in the tables

G45.5.1 Where an asterisk appears in tables 9.7 and 9.8, the bulkheads and decks are required to be of steel or equivalent material but need have no 'A' Class standard except that the crowns and casings of machinery spaces of Category A and the exterior boundaries of superstructures and deckhouses which are required to be insulated with an A–60 insulation in compliance with paragraph 2.4.2.5 are required by these Regulations to be constructed only of steel. When such bulkheads and decks are constructed of aluminium alloy then regulation 11.3 should apply.

G45.5.2 Notwithstanding the provision of an asterisk in the tables, any of the following structure which is constructed of aluminium alloy should be an 'A' Class division of A–0 standard:

.1 any part of the hull or sides of a superstructure or deckhouse which does not support the lifeboat and liferaft embarkation, stowage, handling and lowering positions but is within 3m of such positions; and

.2 the ends and sides of any superstructure or deckhouse which overlook a deck, walkway or stairway which may be used as an escape route from accommodation spaces, service spaces, control stations or machinery spaces to the lifeboat or liferaft embarkation deck, the superstructure or deckhouse not being one which supports the lifeboat and liferaft embarkation, stowage, handling and lowering positions.

G46   Tankers – Protection of stairways and lifts

G46.1 Guidance on items .1 to .5 below should follow the appropriate paragraphs of G9.39 with the following amendments:

.1   Construction and insulation – reference to Ro-Ro spaces are to Cargo pump rooms and to tables 9.5 and 9.6 are to tables 9.7 and 9.8

.2   Openings to stairway enclosures – applies fully

.3   Access into stairway enclosures – applies fully

.4   Lift trunks in stairway enclosures – reference to tables 9.5 and 9.6 are to tables 9.7 and 9.8

.5   Means of closure of lift trunks – applies fully

except that boundaries specified in .4 are those in tables 9.7 and 9.8.

G46.2 Every stairway and lift on a tanker is also required by paragraph 2.3.4 to lie within an enclosure or trunk constructed of 'A' Class divisions of A–0 standard except that an isolated stairway serving only two decks need only be enclosed at one level by 'A' Class divisions of A–0 standard or 'B' Class divisions of B–0 standard. However when a stairway abuts a machinery space of Category A or a cargo pump-room, the bulkhead or deck separating the stairway from the machinery space or cargo pump-room is to be determined respectively by reference to tables 9.7 or 9.8.

3   *Penetrations in fire-resisting divisions and prevention of heat transmission*

3.1   *Where "A" class divisions are penetrated, such penetrations shall be tested in accordance with the Fire Test Procedures Code, subject to the provisions of paragraph 4.1.1.5. In the case of ventilation ducts, paragraphs 7.1.2 and 7.3.1 apply. However, where a pipe penetration is made of steel or equivalent material having a thickness of 3mm or greater and a length of not less than 900 mm (preferably 450 mm on each side of the division), and there are no openings, testing is not required. Such penetrations shall be suitably insulated by extension of the insulation at the same level of the division.*

3.2   *Where "B" class divisions are penetrated for the passage of electric cables, pipes, trunks, ducts, etc., or for the fitting of ventilation terminals, lighting fixtures and similar devices, arrangements shall be made to ensure that the fire resistance is not impaired, subject to the provisions of paragraph 7.3.2. Pipes other than steel or copper that penetrate "B" class divisions shall be protected by either:*

.1   *a fire-tested penetration device suitable for the fire resistance of the division pierced and the type of pipe used; or*

.2   *a steel sleeve, having a thickness of not less than 1.8 mm and a length of not less than 900 mm for pipe diameters of 150 mm or more and not less than 600 mm for pipe diameters of less than 150 mm (preferably equally divided to each side of the division). The pipe shall be connected to the ends of the sleeve by flanges or couplings; or the clearance between the sleeve and the pipe shall not exceed 2.5 mm; or any clearance between pipe and sleeve shall be made tight by means of non-combustible or other suitable material.*

3.3   *Uninsulated metallic pipes penetrating "A" or "B" class divisions shall be of materials having a melting temperature which exceeds 950°C for "A–0" and 850°C for "B–0" class divisions.*

3.4   In approving structural fire protection details, the Administration shall have regard to the risk of heat transmission at intersections and terminal points of required thermal barriers. The insulation of a deck or bulkhead shall be carried past the penetration, intersection or terminal point for a distance of at least 450 mm in the case of steel and aluminium structures. If a space is divided with a deck or a bulkhead of "A" class standard having insulation of different values, the insulation with the higher value shall continue on the deck or bulkhead with the insulation of the lesser value for a distance of at least 450 mm.

Guidance 9

G47   Pipes Penetrating 'A' Class Divisions

G47.1 Approved manufactured systems for pipe penetrations

G47.1.1 Any approved manufactured system for pipe penetration may be used for pipes penetrating 'A' Class divisions subject to compliance with the conditions specified in the approval certificate.

G47.1.2 Bends in pipes should be arranged sufficiently clear of a bulkhead or deck so as not to interfere with a pipe penetration (pipe penetration systems are normally tested only on straight pipes).

G47.1.3 Alternatively the procedures outlined in the next paragraph may be adopted.

G47.2 Alternative acceptable systems for pipe penetrations

G47.2.1 Penetration with pipes having a high melting point

G47.2.1.1 When the piping is of steel or any other material having a melting point of 950°C or more, either .1 or .2 should apply.

.1   The pipe should be welded directly to the division or joined to a bulkhead or deck fitting of the same material which should be welded or bolted to the division as shown in figures 9.11 and 9.12. Where practicable in the case of an insulated division the bulkhead or deck fitting should be of sufficient length to ensure that bolted flanges are clear of the insulation which is to be continued along the fitting for a distance of 380mm from the division. When compression, push-in or similar joints are used the length of the portion of the piping or fitting which is welded or bolted to the division should not be less than 900mm with at least 400mm on the insulated side of an insulated division.

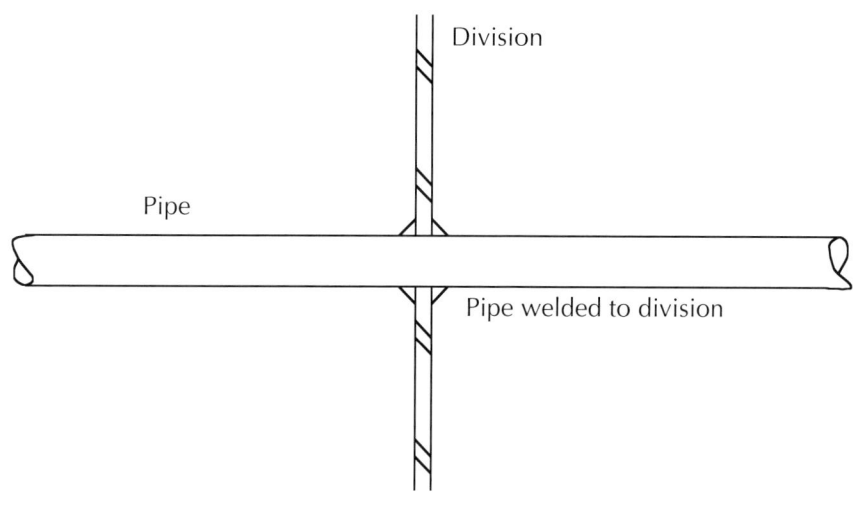

Figure 9.11

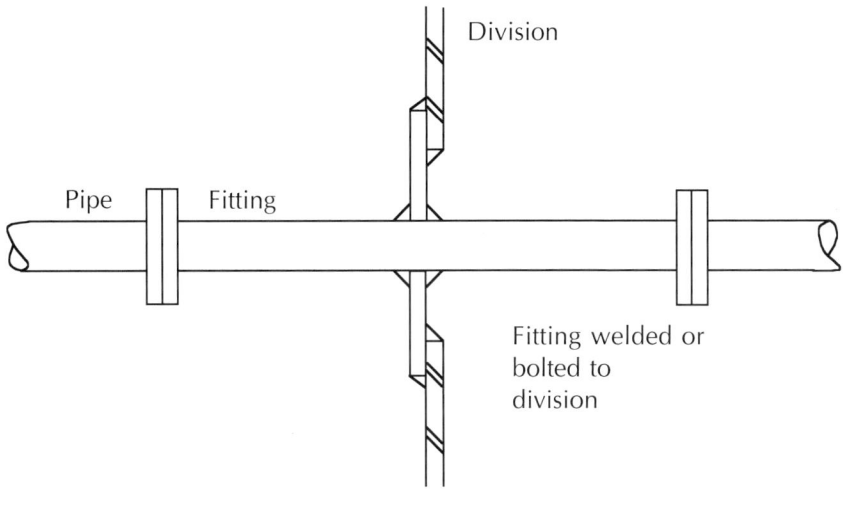

Figure 9.12

.2 When the pipe is not welded or bolted to the division as stated in sub-paragraph .1 then each pipe should be passed through a steel circular spigot, of 3mm minimum thickness and 400mm minimum length, which should be welded to the division. A nominal 20mm gap should be provided between the pipe and the spigot which should be packed tightly throughout its length with an approved A60 insulation and sealed at each end with a suitable flexible sealant. Where the outside diameter of the pipe is 150mm or more the spigot should not be less than 900mm in length. Compression, push-in or similar type of joints should not be positioned within the spigot and should not be less than 900mm apart. The spigot should be positioned such that at least 400mm of its length is on the insulated side of an insulated division. Figure 9.13 illustrates this sub-paragraph.

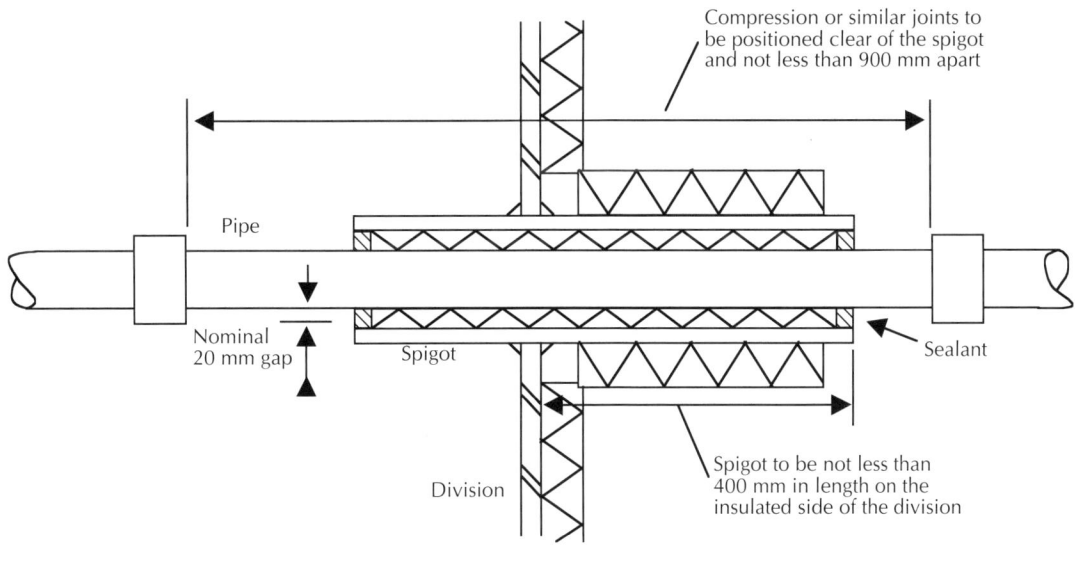

Figure 9.13

G47.3 Penetration of 'A' Class divisions with pipes having low melting points.

G47.3.1 When penetrations through 'A' Class divisions are made with small bore piping having a melting point less than 950°C then:

.1 each pipe should be passed individually through a 900mm long steel circular spigot of 5mm minimum thickness which should be welded to the division. A nominal 20mm gap should be provided between the pipe and the spigot which should be packed tightly throughout its length with an approved A–60 insulation and sealed at each end with a suitable flexible sealant. There should be no joints in the pipe within the length of the spigot. The spigot should be positioned such that at least 400mm of its length is on the insulated side of an insulated division; and

.2   pipes penetrating decks should be treated as indicated in sub-paragraph .1 except that when the piping extends vertically through more than one 'tween-deck, the vertical piping in alternate 'tween-decks should be of steel irrespective of whether or not the pipe is offset within its length.

G47.4   Piping penetrating watertight 'A' Class divisions

G47.4.1   The piping should be of steel or any other material having a melting point of 950°C or more and should be welded directly to the division or joined to a bulkhead or deck fitting of the same material which should be welded or bolted to the division as indicated in G9.47.2.1, 'pipes having high melting point'.

G47.4.2   Compression, push-in or similar joints should not be used in piping systems which penetrate watertight 'A' Class divisions.

G47.5   The insulation of pipe penetrations

G47.5.1   When the piping penetrations referred to in previous paragraphs pass through insulated 'A' Class divisions the insulation on the plating of the division should be continued along the piping or spigot for a distance of not less than 450mm. Where a pipe has a bend close to the division the 450mm should be measured along the insides of the bend. The insulation should be secured effectively in place by wire netting and steel wire. See also guidance to paragraph 1 for pipe penetration at bottom of bulkhead where bulkhead insulation is allowed to be omitted.

G48   Electric Cables Penetrating 'A' Class Divisions

G48.1   Electric cables penetrating non-watertight 'A' Class divisions

G48.1.1   Any approved manufactured cable transit may be used for electric cables penetrating non-watertight 'A' Class divisions subject to compliance with the conditions specified in the approval certificate. Alternatively the following procedures may be adopted.

G48.1.2   The cables should be passed through steel spigots having a minimum length of 450mm and a minimum thickness of 3mm which should be welded to the divisions. The internal cross sectional area of the spigots should not exceed $0.05m^2$. A nominal distance of 20mm should be maintained between the cables and between the cables and spigot. The space between the cable and between the cables and spigot should be packed tightly throughout the length of the spigot with an approved A–60 insulation and the ends of the spigot sealed with a suitable flexible sealant. When the division is insulated the spigot may project up to 400mm on the insulated side of the division but should not project more than 225mm on the uninsulated side of the division. The insulation on the division should be continued along the spigot and cables where applicable for a distance of not less than 450mm. The insulation should be secured effectively in place by wire netting and steel wire. When the division is uninsulated the spigot may project up to 400mm on either side of the division. Figure 9.14 illustrates this arrangement.

G48.2   Electric cables penetrating watertight 'A' Class divisions

G48.2.1   Electric cables which penetrate watertight 'A' Class divisions should only be passed through approved manufactured cable transits which have been approved for this purpose. Moreover, such penetrations should be located as high as practicable in order to reduce the risk of progressive flooding in the event of the compartment being breached.

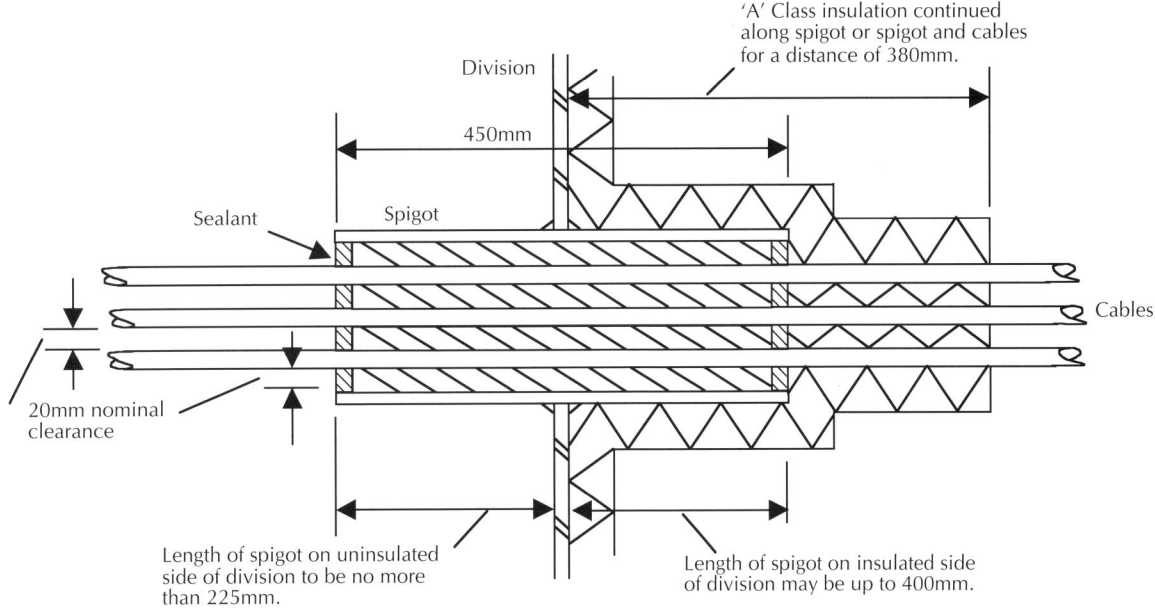

Figure 9.14

G49   Pipes Penetrating 'B' Class Divisions

G49.1 Penetrations with pipes having high melting points

G49.1.1 When pipes of steel or any other material having a melting point of 850°C or more pass through a 'B' Class division they should be fitted with collars made from the same material as that of the division. The collars should be fitted on one side of the division only and adequately screwed to the division. The collars should be a tight fit around the pipes in order to maintain the integrity of the division. When compression, push-in or similar joints are used the length of the portion of the pipe which is collared to the division should not be less than 900mm in order to ensure that the integrity of the division is not impaired if there is movement in the pipe and a joint separates adjacent to the division.

G49.2 Penetrations with pipes having low melting points

G49.2.1 When pipes of any material having a melting point of less than 850°C pass through a 'B' Class division they should be fitted individually in a steel circular spigot having a minimum thickness of 1.5mm. Each spigot should be a close fit in the hole in the division and should have a welded steel collar which is to be screwed to the division. A nominal 20mm gap should be provided between the pipe and the spigot which should be packed tightly throughout its length with an approved A–60 insulation and sealed at each end with a suitable flexible sealant. The length of the spigots should be as follows:

O/D of pipe	Minimum length of spigot
50mm or less	400mm
150mm or more	900mm

G49.2.2 Lengths of spigots for intermediate diameters of pipe should be obtained by interpolation. When a spigot is fitted in a 'B' Class division of B–15 standard it should be positioned such that at least 400mm of its length is on one side of the division. Compression, push-in or similar type of joints should not be positioned within the spigot and should not be less than 900mm apart.

G49.3 Support and insulation of pipes penetrating 'B' Class divisions

G49.3.1 The pipes referred to in these paragraphs should be supported from the deckhead or other structure to the satisfaction of the surveyor.

G49.3.2 When a pipe penetrates a 'B' Class division of B–15 standard the pipe or spigot where applicable should be insulated for a distance of 380mm from the division with an approved A–15 insulation. Where a pipe has a bend close to the division the 380mm should be measured along the inside of the bend. The insulation should be effectively secured by wire netting and steel wire.

G49.3.3 See guidance G9.55 to regulation 9.4 which deals specifically with the regulations referring to openings in 'B' Class divisions.

G50   Cables Penetrating 'B' Class Divisions

G50.1 Electric cables in conduit penetrating 'B' Class divisions

G50.1.1 Where up to three in number of cables for lighting and power in cabins and similar spaces penetrate 'B' Class divisions they may be fitted in steel conduit having a minimum length of 400mm and of such an internal diameter as to provide a close fit round the cables. The conduit should be passed through a hole in the division having the same diameter as the outside diameter of the conduit. The ends of the conduit should be glanded or sealed with a suitable flexible sealant except that the sealant need not be applied to the end of a conduit which is inside a switch or socket.

G50.2 Electric cables in transits penetrating 'B' Class divisions

G50.2.1 Where cables other than those referred to in the previous paragraph penetrate a 'B' Class division they may be passed through transits having a minimum length of 300mm and constructed from steel of 1.5mm thickness, 'B' Class bulkhead material or double steel spiroducting. The internal cross sectional area of the transits should not exceed 0.05m^2. The transits should be a close fit in the holes in the divisions and should be attached to the divisions by screwed steel angle or plate collars such that the integrity of the divisions are not impaired. A nominal distance of 20mm should be maintained between the cables and the cables and a transit. The space between the cables and between the cables and the transit should be packed tightly throughout the length of the transit with an approved A–60 insulation and the ends of the transit sealed with a suitable flexible sealant. Transits constructed of steel or spiroducting which are fitted in 'B' Class divisions of B–15 standard should be insulated for a distance of 380mm from the division with an approved A–15 insulation. The insulation should be effectively secured by wire netting and steel wire.

G51   Insulation at intersection and terminal points

G51.1 In order to meet paragraph 3.4 the thickness of the insulation used in the continuation ribands should be the same as that fitted over the plating of the division which is being insulated and not as that of the insulation fitted over the stiffeners and or beams. This should apply to all structures, except those referred to below, at which the division terminates or which abuts or intersects the division such as bulkheads or decks, ship's side or deckhouse side, webs or girders and beams or stiffeners. It may be necessary to fit ribands of insulation on the opposite side of the division to that on which the insulation is fitted. When a division is insulated by means of approved board or panels the continuation of the insulation may best be achieved by the use of an approved mineral wool insulation having a thickness corresponding to the same 'A' Class standard as that of the division which is being insulated. The continuation ribands may be omitted in the following instances:

.1   on the underside of a weather deck abutting a bulkhead which is being insulated; and

.2   on the upperside of a deck intersecting a bulkhead which is being insulated except when the bulkhead is a machinery casing.

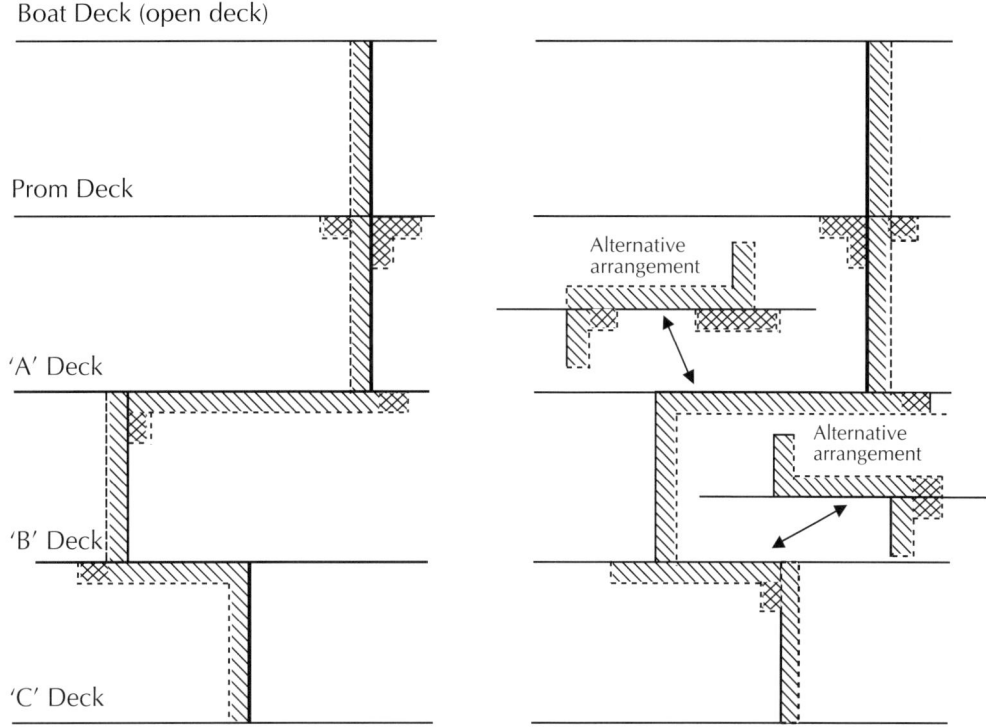

Boat Deck (open deck)

Prom Deck

Alternative arrangement

'A' Deck

Alternative arrangement

'B' Deck

'C' Deck

(The ribands of insulation at boundaries and intersections are shown double hatched.)

Figure 9.15 Two Profiles of a typical Main Zone Bulkhead insulated on the fore and after sides.

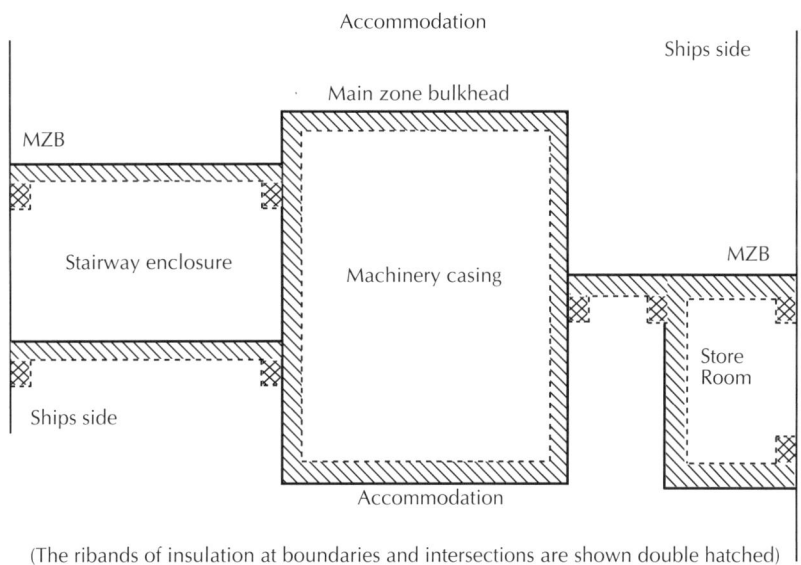

Accommodation

Ships side

Main zone bulkhead

MZB

Stairway enclosure

Machinery casing

MZB

Store Room

Ships side

Accommodation

(The ribands of insulation at boundaries and intersections are shown double hatched)

Figure 9.16 Plan view of a typical Main Zone Bulkhead in association with other 'A' Class Bulkheads.

(Figures 9.15, 9.16 and 9.17 (see page 110) illustrate typical examples of where continuation ribands of insulation are necessary.)

G52   Heat transmission of cable hangers, lighting fittings and cables inside 'B' Class divisions

G52.1 Cable-tray hangers

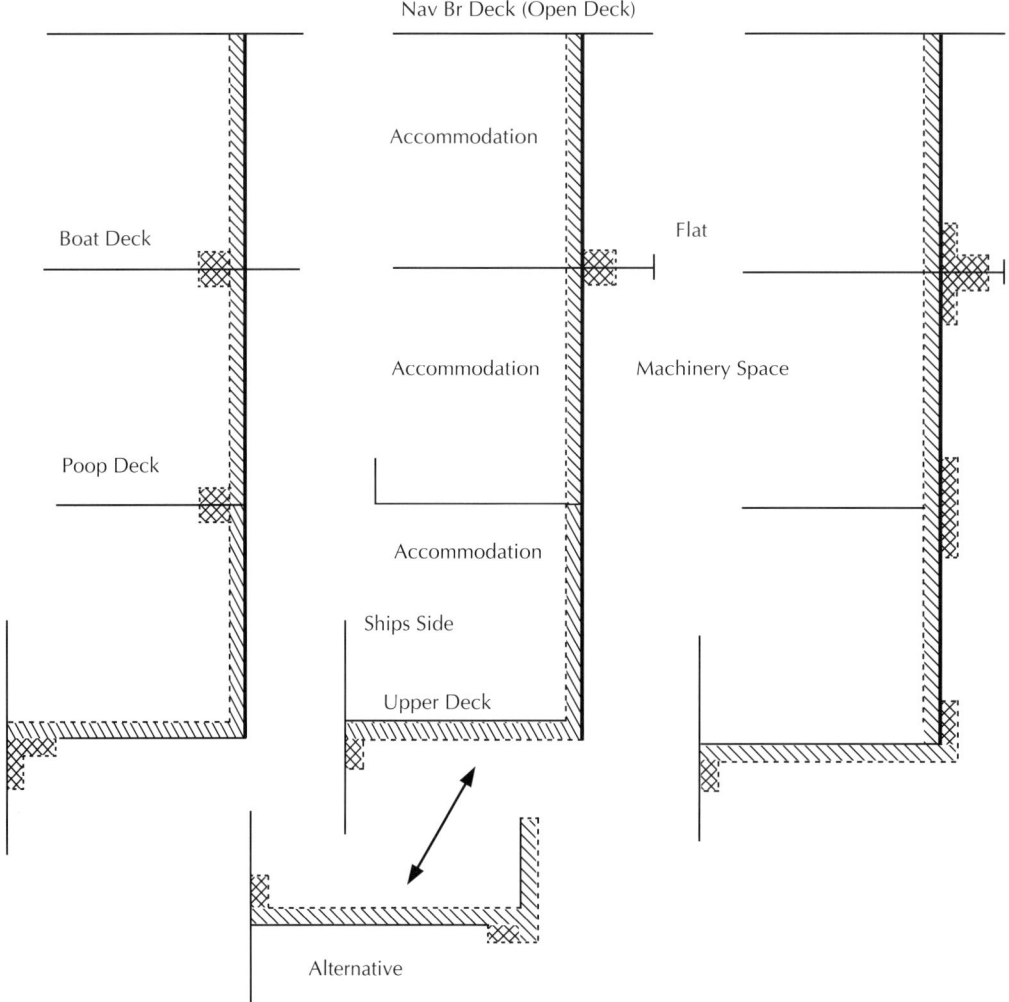

(The ribands of insulating at boundaries and intersections are shown double-hatched.)

Figure 9.17 Three methods of insulating a typical machinery casing

G52.1.1 Hangers used to support cable trays, suspended ceilings etc. and welded to deck beams or bulkhead frames should be insulated for a length of 450mm from the plating and to the same standard as the plating insulation. If the cross-sectional area of the hanger is less than 100mm² this requirement may be waived.

G52.2 Lighting fittings

G52.2.1 Lighting fittings should preferably be surface mounted on a 'B' Class ceiling, but when a fitting penetrates the ceiling it should be of steel or covered by a steel box and fastened effectively to the ceiling in order to maintain the integrity of the ceiling. When the ceiling is of B–15 standard the steel light fitting or steel cover should be covered by a mineral wool insulation which has been approved for A–15 standard, the insulation being effectively secured to the fitting or cover. Alternatively the light fitting may be boxed-in using a 'B' Class material having a thickness appropriate to B–15 standard.

G52.3 Electric cables inside boards, panels or jointing profiles

G52.3.1 Electric cables should not be fitted in ducts arranged in boards or panels from which 'B' Class bulkheads or linings are constructed or in the jointing profiles unless a bulkhead incorporating cables and switches has been successfully fire tested. Only cables from switches and/or power sockets situated on the same side of a bulkhead or lining should be led through a duct or profile.

4   Protection of openings in fire-resisting divisions

4.1   Openings in bulkheads and decks in passenger ships

4.1.1   Openings in "A" class divisions

4.1.1.1 Except for hatches between cargo, special category, store, and baggage spaces, and between such spaces and the weather decks, openings shall be provided with permanently attached means of closing which shall be at least as effective for resisting fires as the divisions in which they are fitted.

4.1.1.2 The construction of doors and door frames in "A" class divisions, with the means of securing them when closed, shall provide resistance to fire as well as to the passage of smoke and flame equivalent to that of the bulkheads in which the doors are situated, this being determined in accordance with the Fire Test Procedures Code. Such doors and door frames shall be constructed of steel or other equivalent material. Watertight doors need not be insulated.

4.1.1.3 It shall be possible for each door to be opened and closed from each side of the bulkhead by one person only.

4.1.1.4 Fire doors in main vertical zone bulkheads, galley boundaries and stairway enclosures other than power-operated watertight doors and those which are normally locked shall satisfy the following requirements:

.1   the doors shall be self-closing and be capable of closing with an angle of inclination of up to 3.5° opposing closure;

.2   the approximate time of closure for hinged fire doors shall be no more than 40 s and no less than 10 s from the beginning of their movement with the ship in upright position. The approximate uniform rate of closure for sliding doors shall be of no more than 0.2 m/s and no less than 0.1 m/s with the ship in upright position;

.3   the doors, except those for emergency escape trunks, shall be capable of remote release from the continuously manned central control station, either simultaneously or in groups, and shall be capable of release also individually from a position at both sides of the door. Release switches shall have an on-off function to prevent automatic resetting of the system;

.4   hold-back hooks not subject to central control station release are prohibited;

.5   a door closed remotely from the central control station shall be capable of being re-opened from both sides of the door by local control. After such local opening, the door shall automatically close again;

.6   indication shall be provided at the fire door indicator panel in the continuously manned central control station whether each door is closed;

.7   the release mechanism shall be so designed that the door will automatically close in the event of disruption of the control system or central power supply;

.8   local power accumulators for power-operated doors shall be provided in the immediate vicinity of the doors to enable the doors to be operated at least ten times (fully opened and closed) after disruption of the control system or central power supply using the local controls;

.9   disruption of the control system or central power supply at one door shall not impair the safe functioning of the other doors;

.10   remote-released sliding or power-operated doors shall be equipped with an alarm that sounds at least 5 s but no more than 10 s, after the door is released from the central control station and before the door begins to move and continues sounding until the door is completely closed;

.11   a door designed to re-open upon contacting an object in its path shall re-open not more than 1 m from the point of contact;

.12   double-leaf doors equipped with a latch necessary for their fire integrity shall have a latch that is automatically activated by the operation of the doors when released by the system;

.13   doors giving direct access to special category spaces which are power-operated and automatically closed need not be equipped with the alarms and remote-release mechanisms required in paragraphs 4.1.1.4.3 and 4.1.1.4.10;

.14   the components of the local control system shall be accessible for maintenance and adjusting;

.15   power-operated doors shall be provided with a control system of an approved type which shall be able to operate in case of fire and be in accordance with the Fire Test Procedures Code. This system shall satisfy the following requirements:

.15.1   the control system shall be able to operate the door at the temperature of at least 200°C for at least 60 min, served by the power supply;

.15.2   the power supply for all other doors not subject to fire shall not be impaired; and

.15.3   at temperatures exceeding 200°C the control system shall be automatically isolated from the power supply and shall be capable of keeping the door closed up to at least 945°C.

4.1.1.5 In ships carrying not more than 36 passengers, where a space is protected by an automatic sprinkler fire detection and fire alarm system complying with the provisions of the Fire Safety Systems Code or fitted with a continuous "B" class ceiling, openings in decks not forming steps in main vertical zones nor bounding horizontal zones shall be closed reasonably tight and such decks shall meet the "A" class integrity requirements in so far as is reasonable and practicable in the opinion of the Administration.

4.1.1.6 The requirements for "A" class integrity of the outer boundaries of a ship shall not apply to glass partitions, windows and sidescuttles, provided that there is no

REGULATION
9

requirement for such boundaries to have "A" class integrity in paragraph 4.1.3.3. The requirements for "A" class integrity of the outer boundaries of the ship shall not apply to exterior doors, except for those in superstructures and deckhouses facing life-saving appliances, embarkation and external assembly station areas, external stairs and open decks used for escape routes. Stairway enclosure doors need not meet this requirement.

4.1.1.7 Except for watertight doors, weathertight doors (semi-watertight doors), doors leading to the open deck and doors which need to be reasonably gastight, all "A" class doors located in stairways, public spaces and main vertical zone bulkheads in escape routes shall be equipped with a self-closing hose port. The material, construction and fire resistance of the hose port shall be equivalent to the door into which it is fitted, and shall be a 150 mm square clear opening with the door closed and shall be inset into the lower edge of the door, opposite the door hinges or, in the case of sliding doors, nearest the opening.

4.1.1.8 Where it is necessary that a ventilation duct passes through a main vertical zone division, a fail-safe automatic closing fire damper shall be fitted adjacent to the division. The damper shall also be capable of being manually closed from each side of the division. The operating position shall be readily accessible and be marked in red light-reflecting colour. The duct between the division and the damper shall be of steel or other equivalent material and, if necessary, insulated to comply with the requirements of paragraph 3.1. The damper shall be fitted on at least one side of the division with a visible indicator showing whether the damper is in the open position.

4.1.2   Openings in "B" class divisions

4.1.2.1 Doors and door frames in "B" class divisions and means of securing them shall provide a method of closure which shall have resistance to fire equivalent to that of the divisions, this being determined in accordance with the Fire Test Procedures Code except that ventilation openings may be permitted in the lower portion of such doors. Where such opening is in or under a door, the total net area of any such opening or openings shall not exceed 0.05 m². Alternatively, a non-combustible air balance duct routed between the cabin and the corridor, and located below the sanitary unit, is permitted where the cross-sectional area of the duct does not exceed 0.05 m². All ventilation openings shall be fitted with a grill made of non-combustible material. Doors shall be non-combustible.

4.1.2.2 Cabin doors in "B" class divisions shall be of a self-closing type. Hold-back hooks are not permitted.

4.1.2.3 The requirements for "B" class integrity of the outer boundaries of a ship shall not apply to glass partitions, windows and sidescuttles. Similarly, the requirements for "B" class integrity shall not apply to exterior doors in superstructures and deckhouses. For ships carrying not more than 36 passengers, the Administration may permit the use of combustible materials in doors separating cabins from the individual interior sanitary spaces such as showers.

4.1.2.4 In ships carrying not more than 36 passengers, where an automatic sprinkler system complying with the provisions of the Fire Safety Systems Code is fitted:

.1 openings in decks not forming steps in main vertical zones nor bounding horizontal zones shall be closed reasonably tight and such decks shall meet the "B" class integrity requirements in so far as is reasonable and practicable in the opinion of the Administration; and

.2 openings in corridor bulkheads of "B" class materials shall be protected in accordance with the provisions of paragraph 2.2.2.

4.1.3 Windows and sidescuttles

4.1.3.1 Windows and sidescuttles in bulkheads within accommodation and service spaces and control stations other than those to which the provisions of paragraphs 4.1.1.6 and 4.1.2.3 apply shall be so constructed as to preserve the integrity requirements of the type of bulkheads in which they are fitted, this being determined in accordance with the Fire Test Procedures Code.

4.1.3.2 Notwithstanding the requirements of tables 9.1 to 9.4, windows and sidescuttles in bulkheads separating accommodation and service spaces and control stations from weather shall be constructed with frames of steel or other suitable material. The glass shall be retained by a metal glazing bead or angle.

4.1.3.3 Windows facing life-saving appliances, embarkation and assembly stations, external stairs and open decks used for escape routes, and windows situated below liferaft and escape slide embarkation areas shall have fire integrity as required in table 9.1. Where automatic dedicated sprinkler heads are provided for windows, "A–0" windows may be accepted as equivalent. To be considered under this paragraph, the sprinkler heads shall either be:

.1 dedicated heads located above the windows, and installed in addition to the conventional ceiling sprinklers; or

.2 conventional ceiling sprinkler heads arranged such that the window is protected by an average application rate of at least 5 l/min per square metre and the additional window area is included in the calculation of the area of coverage.

Windows located in the ship's side below the lifeboat embarkation area shall have fire integrity at least equal to "A–0" class.

4.2 Doors in fire-resisting divisions in cargo ships

4.2.1 The fire resistance of doors shall be equivalent to that of the division in which they are fitted, this being determined in accordance with the Fire Test Procedures Code. Doors and door frames in "A" class divisions shall be constructed of steel. Doors in "B" class divisions shall be non-combustible. Doors fitted in boundary bulkheads of machinery spaces of category A shall be reasonably gastight and self-closing. In ships constructed according to method IC, the Administration may permit the use of combustible materials in doors separating cabins from individual interior sanitary accommodation such as showers.

4.2.2 Doors required to be self-closing shall not be fitted with hold-back hooks. However, hold-back arrangements fitted with remote release devices of the fail-safe type may be utilized.

4.2.3 In corridor bulkheads, ventilation openings may be permitted in and under the doors of cabins and public spaces. Ventilation openings are also permitted in "B" class doors leading to lavatories, offices, pantries, lockers and store-rooms. Except as permitted below, the openings shall be provided only in the lower half of a door. Where such an opening is in or under a door, the total net area of any such opening or openings shall not exceed 0.05 m2. Alternatively, a non-combustible air balance duct routed between the cabin and the corridor, and located below the sanitary unit, is permitted where the cross-sectional area of the duct does not exceed 0.05 m^2. Ventilation openings, except those under the door, shall be fitted with a grill made of non-combustible material.

4.2.4 Watertight doors need not be insulated.

Guidance 9

G53 Openings in 'A' Class divisions

G53.1 Hatches

G53.1.1 A hatch in a deck separating special category spaces and/or Ro-Ro cargo spaces, which are in the same horizontal zone, is not required to have any fire standard.

G53.1.2 However a hatch in a deck separating such spaces which are in different horizontal zones should be constructed and insulated to the required 'A' Class standard.

G53.1.3 See detail denoted – superscription 'h' – in paragraph 2.3.3.2 regarding hatches fitted in decks separating Ro-Ro spaces.

G53.2 Watertight doors

G53.2.1 Watertight doors which are sliding doors fitted below the bulkhead deck need not be fire tested, and may be fitted with hard rubber or neoprene seals provided no part of the seals are exposed when the door is closed. The doors should be designed to remain substantially watertight if such seals were to become heat damaged.

G53.3 External doors – relaxation from requirements

G53.3.1 Doors in the outer boundaries of superstructures and deckhouses are permitted to not have 'A' Class integrity by paragraph 4.1.1.6 may be of any material subject to compliance with loadline requirements.

G53.3.2 'A' Class door assemblies designed for interior use may not be suitable for use in positions exposed to the weather because of their light construction and susceptibility to corrosion.

G53.4 Doors and shutters in 'A' Class divisions

G53.4.1 For cargo ships and tankers the requirement for doors to be self-closing, only applies to the doors when the ship is in the upright position even though the Regulations do not specifically state this.

G54 'A' Class doors and shutters

G54.1 Doors and shutters

G54.1.1 Every door or shutter assembly which is used to close openings in 'A' Class bulkheads, should be of an approved type and its construction and method of installation should be in accordance with the conditions specified by the manufacturer or approval certificate.

G54.1.2 When a door or shutter is used to close an opening in an 'A' Class bulkhead constructed of aluminium alloy, it should be fitted in a stiffened steel panel attached to the aluminium alloy bulkhead by 12mm diameter steel bolts spaced 300mm apart. The steel plate should extend 450mm beyond the sides and top of the frame of the door or shutter. The steel plate and bolts should be suitably isolated from the aluminium alloy to the satisfaction of the surveyor.

G54.1.3 In no case should a primary deck covering or a surface floor covering be fitted under an 'A' Class door or shutter. The sill plate, sill channel or coaming, whichever is applicable, should be welded to the deck plating and such coverings stopped on each side of it.

G54.1.4 Grilles or louvres should not be fitted in 'A' Class doors or shutters.

G54.2 Doors only

G54.2.1 A door should have the same or higher 'A' Class standard as the bulkhead in which it is fitted.

G54.2.2 A window may be fitted in the upper half of an 'A' Class door provided that:

.1   it is positioned no closer than 150mm to any edge of the door leaf;

.2   the window is of toughened safety glass and the window frame and glazing bar are of steel; and

.3   the door incorporating the window has been successfully fire tested.

G54.3 Shutters only

G54.3.1 In no case should a rolling shutter be fitted in an 'A' Class bulkhead other than a bulkhead of A–O standard. A rolling shutter should be capable of automatic closure after initial release and subsequently if the shutter is raised to approximately three quarters of the height of the clear opening.

G54.4 Instructions to open

G54.4.1 To avoid any doubts in an emergency, all sliding 'A' Class doors and drop-rolling 'A' Class shutters should be provided with the following notices to indicate how they are to be opened:

.1   Sliding doors

G54.4.2 The notice illustrated below left should be painted on each side of the door leaf:

G54.4.3 The notice should be painted in letters 100mm in height and positioned close to the door handle. The letters and arrow should be painted white on a green background.

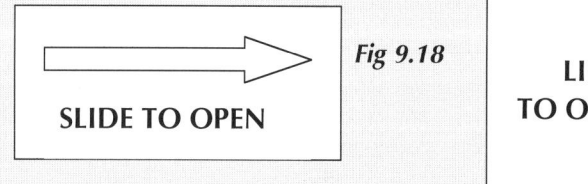
Fig 9.18

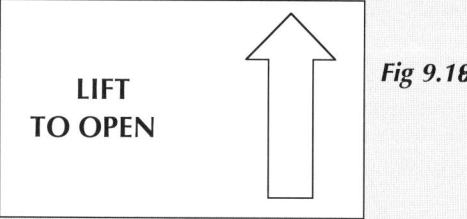
Fig 9.18

.1   Drop-rolling shutters

G54.4.4 The notice illustrated above right should be painted on each side of the shutter curtain:

G54.4.5 The notice should be painted in white letters 100mm in height on a green background and positioned close to the lifting handle.

G54.5 'A' Class doors – gaskets

G54.5.1 Approved 'A' Class door assemblies are not designed to accommodate gaskets of any material in the bosom of the door frames or housing channels in order to make them gas tight, doors have been seriously damaged when this has been done in the past. Consequently under no circumstances should this be done. Each approved 'A' Class door assembly is considered to comply with the Regulations without the necessity to fit gaskets.

G54.5.2 If it is necessary for any other purpose to fit gaskets to an 'A' Class door assembly they may be fitted to the door frame and bear on the surface of the door leaf as shown for a hinged door in figure 9.20. The gaskets should be of flame retardant neoprene or similar. It may be necessary at the bottom of the door to attach the gasket to the bottom edge of the door leaf and bear on the sill or coaming rather than the other way round because it would be vulnerable to damage in the latter situation. However it should be noted that the MCA is not prepared to take any responsibility with regard to the effectiveness of such gaskets where there is a pressure differential across the door.

G54.6 'A' Class doors – identification plates

G54.6.1 Each door or shutter should be fitted with a thin metal identification plate which indicates clearly the manufacturers name, the 'A' Class standard of the door or shutter and the number of the approved drawing to which it has been manufactured or the manufacturers type designation or reference number (e.g. Smith + Co.; A30 grade; Ref Nos 123/A).

G54.6.2 The identification plate should be screwed or pop riveted to the vertical edge of the door (hinged side).

G54.6.3 In the case of a shutter the identification plate is to be screwed or pop riveted to the vertical flange of the bottom bar of the shutter or to the underside of its boxing.

G54.7 Doors assemblies with coamings

G54.7.1 The height of the door coaming may be increased or reduced from that shown on the approved drawing provided the construction of the door frame and its connection to the modified coaming is precisely the same as shown on the approved drawing.

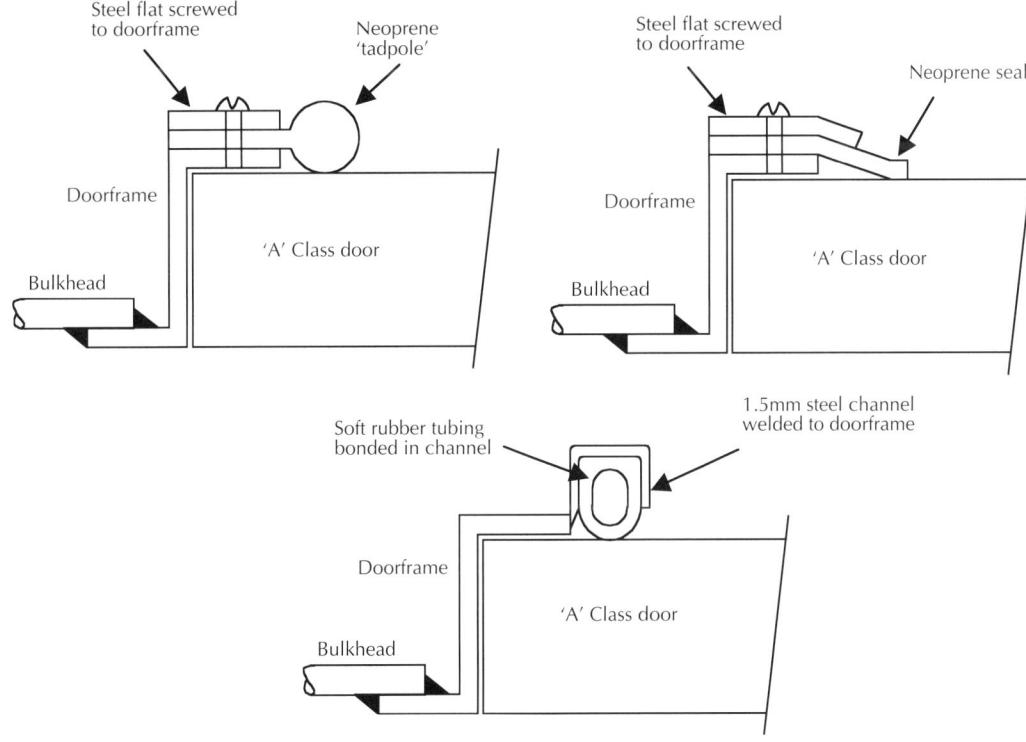

Figure 9.20 Acceptable seals for 'A' Class doors

G54.8 Doors in spaces of high humidity

G54.8.1 'A' Class doors which are fitted in the boundary bulkheads of boiler rooms, refrigerated machinery spaces and similar spaces having atmospheres of high humidity, may be constructed of stainless steel instead of mild steel without the necessity to retest the doors provided that all other materials and details of construction are the same as shown on the appropriate approved drawings.

G54.9 Electrical release arrangements for 'A' Class doors and shutters

G54.9.1 Arrangements may be provided for fire doors or shutters to be held in the open position, by means of energised electro-magnets which may be controlled from a central control point, but they must also be capable of release at each door. Such devices should be arranged to 'fail-safe', i.e. they should cause the door to close in the event of their failure.

G54.9.2 When the arrangements incorporate direct acting solenoids, they should be capable of exerting a pull which equates to at least half the weight of the door, plus that force required to overcome any self-closing mechanism, thus being capable of holding the door open under a possible rolling condition of up to at least 15° either way. Other retaining devices, e.g. solenoid controlled latches, should be capable of exerting a restraint equivalent to the above. When de-energised, the residual magnetism should not be so great as to impede the door from closing at inclinations of $3^1/_2$° either way.

G54.9.3 Full details of the performance, construction and enclosure of the proposed solenoids should be submitted to MCA Headquarters, together with the door manufacturer's assessment of the hold-on pull required for the type of door under consideration in the above mentioned conditions. The hold-on power of a solenoid should be established by tests, appreciating that a small reduction in air gap greatly reduces the hold-on power, and that cleanliness of the magnet faces is essential.

G54.9.4 The solenoid coils should be rated for continuous operation.

G54.10 Door control systems

G54.10.1 It will be essential for the solenoids to release the doors when de-energised, from both the remote and local positions, and the solenoids must remain de-energised so that should the door thereafter be opened, it would not be retained in the open position.

G54.10.2 Grouping of release circuits should be so arranged that doors bounding, or lying in a main fire zone should normally be grouped together, and follow the same group nomenclature as the fire alarm indicators. Proposals for grouping should be forwarded to MCA Headquarters for consideration at an early stage.

G54.10.3 Local switches, and the group release switches at the control station, should be of the 'on-off' or 'stay-put' type so that the solenoids remain de-energised when the switches are operated, until deliberately re-set after an emergency.

G54.10.4 Where a door or shutter is permitted to have a local release switch on one side only it should be easily accessible and conspicuous to anyone passing through the door opening.

G54.11 Door indicators

G54.11.1 Where remote indication of door closure is required by the Regulations, the sensing device for such purposes should activate only on the final movement of closure. Where large numbers of doors require remote indication then grouping of indicators may be accepted provided the doors in any such group are in reasonable proximity to each other.

G54.12 Double swing doors

G54.12.1 Double swing doors which often form the access to and from the kitchen in a restaurant are not acceptable as 'A' Class doors because they are not fitted with latches and their frames do not overlap the door leaves. Furthermore the door leaves of a double leaf swing door do not overlap each other.

G54.13 Revolving doors

G54.13.1 Revolving doors are not acceptable as 'A' Class doors because their leaves are capable of being 'feathered' and locked in the open position. They do not overlap the frame. Such doors should not be fitted in escape routes because they may inhibit escape particularly when in the revolving mode.

G55 Openings in 'B' Class divisions

G55.1 When a 'B' Class division is intersected by structure or penetrated for any purpose, the fire integrity and insulation standard of the division should be maintained in way of such an intersection or penetration.

G55.2 Pipes and cables penetrating 'B' Class divisions should be dealt with as indicated in guidance G9.49 and G9.50.

G55.3 Ventilation ducting which penetrates 'B' Class divisions should be dealt with as indicated in guidance G9.67.

G55.4 See guidance G9.52.2 for lighting fittings in 'B' Class ceilings and for access panels in 'B' Class ceilings or linings.

G55.5 'B' Class doors

G55.5.1 Every door assembly which is used to close openings in 'B' Class bulkheads should be of an approved type and its construction and method of installation should be in accordance with the conditions specified in the approval certificate.

G55.6 Attachment of door to bulkhead

G55.6.1 A doorframe of a 'B' Class door assembly should not be screwed or bolted to 'B' Class bulkheads constructed of board type materials because the expansion of the steel frame could cause serious cracking in boards during a fire situation which could result in an integrity failure of the bulkhead.

G55.7 Ventilation openings in doors

G55.7.1 The 0.05m^2 total net area limitation for openings in and/or under 'B' Class doors is applicable to single and double leaf doors. In the case of the double leaf door the limitation should apply to the whole door and not to each leaf individually.

G55.7.2 When a door is fitted with an escape panel the ventilation opening should be incorporated in it.

G55.7.3 In addition to a ventilation grille being capable of manual closure from each side of the door it may be closed by means of a spring activated by the melting of a fusible link or similar. In no case should the automatic means be accepted without the manual means of closure.

G55.8 Self closing doors

G55.8.1 Doors which are required to self close, should close and latch after opening wide enough to allow the passage of at least one adult, with the ship in an upright condition.

G55.9 External doors in outer boundaries

G55.9.1 Doors in the outer boundaries of superstructures and deckhouses are permitted to not have 'B' Class integrity by paragraph 4.1.2.3 and may be of any material or construction, subject to compliance with any requirements imposed by the Load Line Regulations. 'B' Class door assemblies are not considered suitable for use in positions exposed to the weather.

G55.10 Doors in 'B' Class divisions on cargo ships and tankers

G55.10.1 The foregoing guidance applies in the same manner except that a ventilation opening should not be provided in a door fitted in a 'B' Class bulkhead forming a stairway enclosure, the gap under such a door should not exceed 6mm.

G55.10.2 Additionally any door fitted in a 'B' Class bulkhead forming a stairway enclosure is required to be fitted with a closing device which will close the door in the upright position when the door is released from an open position. Any such door is permitted by paragraph 4.2.2 to be held in the open position subject to the hold-back arrangements having remote release fittings which, on disruption of the control system, will permit the closing device to close the door, and the arrangements also allowing the door to be closed manually. When energised, electro-magnets are used to hold-back such doors the arrangements should comply with guidance G9.54.9 on electrical release arrangements for 'A' Class doors and shutters except that the requirement for doors to be self-closing only applies to the doors when in the upright position. When a shipbuilder or shipowner proposes to use hold-back arrangements other than those incorporating energised electro-magnets, full system details should be submitted by the builder for consideration.

G56   Windows and sidescuttles

G56.1 In internal bulkheads

G56.1.1 Proposals to fit glazed openings in internal 'A' or 'B' Class bulkheads, together with particulars of the glass, framing arrangements and any test reports which are available, should be submitted to MCA Headquarters for consideration.

G56.1.2 Every window or sidescuttle within accommodation spaces, service spaces and control stations other than those fitted in the boundaries of the hull, superstructures and deckhouses referred to in paragraphs 4.1.1.6 and 4.1.2.3 are required to be constructed such that the integrity standards of the bulkheads in which they are fitted are not impaired. Since insulating glasses are readily available such glasses should have an insulating value equivalent to the divisions in which they are to be fitted. In addition glasses and the interior window frames in which they are fitted should satisfy the thermal radiation test stated in the International Code for Application of Fire Test Procedures – MSC 61(67) Annex 1, Part 3, Appendix 1 refers. Each window or sidescuttle which is fitted in such internal 'A' Class or 'B' Class bulkheads should be of an approved type and should be constructed and fitted in accordance with the conditions stated in the approval certificate. Note also that paragraph 5.2.6 prohibits the fitting of windows in the boundaries of machinery spaces.

G56.1.3 Every window or sidescuttle fitted within the accommodation spaces, should be constructed, with glass which breaks safely.

G56.2 In way of lifeboat, liferaft, marine escape system positions and external escape routes.

G56.2.1 The fire resisting glass recommended to be fitted in windows facing life saving appliances, external escape routes and in windows situated below such spaces should be of an approved type and be fitted in accordance with the conditions stated in the certificate of approval.

G56.3 Windows facing lifeboat and liferaft positions etc on passenger ships

G56.3.1 Windows facing lifeboat, liferaft or marine escape system embarkation, stowage, handling and lowering positions and windows within 3m of such positions and windows facing or within 3m of any deck which is used for transferring passengers or crew from a muster station to an embarkation deck, should be fitted with an approved fire resisting glass. The glass should be fitted in accordance with the conditions in the approval certificate.

5 *Protection of openings in machinery spaces boundaries*

5.1 Application

5.1.1 The provision of this paragraph shall apply to machinery spaces of category A and, where the Administration considers it desirable, to other machinery spaces.

5.2 Protection of openings in machinery space boundaries

5.2.1 The number of skylights, doors, ventilators, openings in funnels to permit exhaust ventilation and other openings to machinery spaces shall be reduced to a minimum consistent with the needs of ventilation and the proper and safe working of the ship.

5.2.2 Skylights shall be of steel and shall not contain glass panels.

5.2.3 Means of control shall be provided for closing power-operated doors or actuating release mechanisms on doors other than power-operated watertight doors. The controls shall be located outside the space concerned, where they will not be cut off in the event of fire in the space it serves.

5.2.4 In passenger ships, the means of control required in paragraph 5.2.3 shall be situated at one control position or grouped in as few positions as possible, to the satisfaction of the Administration. Such positions shall have safe access from the open deck.

5.2.5 In passenger ships, doors, other than power-operated watertight doors, shall be so arranged that positive closure is assured in case of fire in the space by power-operated closing arrangements or by the provision of self-closing doors capable of closing against an inclination of 3.5° opposing closure, and having a fail-safe hold-back arrangement, provided with a remotely operated release device. Doors for emergency escape trunks need not be fitted with a fail-safe hold-back facility and a remotely operated release device.

5.2.6 Windows shall not be fitted in machinery space boundaries. However, this does not preclude the use of glass in control rooms within the machinery spaces.

Guidance 9

G57 Machinery space boundaries – protection of openings

G57.1 Skylights

G57.1.1 Windows and sidescuttles should not be fitted in skylights serving machinery spaces of Category A or cargo pump-rooms in compliance with paragraphs 5.2.2 and 2.4.2.6 respectively. The steel skylights should be of substantial construction and capable of preventing the passage of flame and smoke as far as is reasonably practicable.

G57.2 Windows and sidescuttles

G57.2.1 Sidescuttles should be regarded as windows for the purpose of paragraph 5.2.6.

G57.2.2 The windows and sidescuttles which are permitted by paragraph 5.2.6 to be fitted in a bulkhead separating a machinery space of Category A and a machinery control room located within its boundaries, are not required to meet any 'A' Class or 'B' Class standard but their construction should be compatible with their size and should be fitted with an approved toughened safety glass.

G57.2.3 Where a machinery control room abuts a machinery space, the window may be fire resistant glass fitted with a steel closing plate or alternatively the control room boundary must be treated as if the machinery space incorporates the control room. Glass shall not be fitted in watertight divisions.

6   *Protection of cargo space boundaries*

6.1   *In passenger ships carrying more than 36 passengers, the boundary bulkheads and decks of special category and ro-ro spaces shall be insulated to "A–60" class standard. However, where a category (5), (9) or (10) space, as defined in paragraph 2.2.3, is on one side of the division, the standard may be reduced to "A–0". Where fuel oil tanks are below a special category space, the integrity of the deck between such spaces may be reduced to "A–0" standard.*

6.2   *In passenger ships carrying not more than 36 passengers, the boundary bulkheads of special category spaces shall be insulated as required for category (11) spaces in table 9.3 and the horizontal boundaries as required for category (11) spaces in table 9.4.*

6.3   *In passenger ships carrying not more than 36 passengers, the boundary bulkheads and decks of closed and open ro-ro spaces shall have a fire integrity as required for category (8) spaces in table 9.3 and the horizontal boundaries as required for category (8) spaces in table 9.4.*

6.4   *In passenger ships, indicators shall be provided on the navigation bridge which shall indicate when any fire door leading to or from the special category spaces is closed.*

6.5   *In tankers, for the protection of cargo tanks carrying crude oil and petroleum products having a flashpoint not exceeding 60°C, materials readily rendered ineffective by heat shall not be used for valves, fittings, tank opening covers, cargo vent piping, and cargo piping so as to prevent the spread of fire to the cargo.*

7   *Ventilation systems*

7.1   Duct and dampers

7.1.1 *Ventilation ducts shall be of non-combustible material. However, short ducts, not generally exceeding 2 m in length and with a free cross-sectional area* not exceeding 0.02 m^2, need not be non-combustible subject to the following conditions:*

.1   *the ducts are made of a material which has low flame spread characteristics;*

.2   *the ducts are only used at the end of the ventilation device; and*

.3   *the ducts are not situated less than 600 mm, measured along the duct, from an opening in an "A" or "B" class division, including continuous "B" class ceiling.*

---

*   The term *free cross-sectional area* means, even in the case of a pre-insulated duct, the area calculated on the basis of the inner diameter of the duct.

7.1.2 The following arrangements shall be tested in accordance with the Fire Test Procedures Code:

.1   fire dampers, including their relevant means of operation; and

.2   duct penetrations through "A" class divisions. However, the test is not required where steel sleeves are directly joined to ventilation ducts by means of riveted or screwed flanges or by welding.

7.2   Arrangement of ducts

7.2.1 The ventilation systems for machinery spaces of category A, vehicle spaces, ro-ro spaces, galleys, special category spaces and cargo spaces shall, in general, be separated from each other and from the ventilation systems serving other spaces, except that the galley ventilation systems on cargo ships of less than 4,000 gross tonnage and in passenger ships carrying not more than 36 passengers need not be completely separated, but may be served by separate ducts from a ventilation unit serving other spaces. In any case, an automatic fire damper shall be fitted in the galley ventilation duct near the ventilation unit. Ducts provided for the ventilation of machinery spaces of category A, galleys, vehicle spaces, ro-ro spaces or special category spaces shall not pass through accommodation spaces, service spaces or control stations unless they comply with the conditions specified in paragraphs 7.2.1.1.1 to 7.2.1.1.4 or 7.2.1.2.1 and 7.2.1.2.2 below:

.1.1   the ducts are constructed of steel having a thickness of at least 3 mm and 5 mm for ducts the widths or diameters of which are up to and including 300 mm and 760 mm and over respectively and, in the case of such ducts, the widths or diameters of which are between 300 mm and 760 mm having a thickness obtained by interpolation;

.1.2   the ducts are suitably supported and stiffened;

.1.3   the ducts are fitted with automatic fire dampers close to the boundaries penetrated; and

.1.4   the ducts are insulated to "A–60" class standard from the machinery spaces, galleys, vehicle spaces, ro-ro spaces or special category spaces to a point at least 5 m beyond each fire damper;

or

.2.1   the ducts are constructed of steel in accordance with paragraphs 7.2.1.1.1 and 7.2.1.1.2; and

.2.2   the ducts are insulated to "A–60" class standard throughout the accommodation spaces, service spaces or control stations;

except that penetrations of main zone divisions shall also comply with the requirements of paragraph 4.1.1.8.

7.2.2 Ducts provided for ventilation to accommodation spaces, service spaces or control stations shall not pass through machinery spaces of category A, galleys, vehicle spaces, ro-ro spaces or special category spaces unless they comply with the conditions specified in paragraphs 7.2.2.1.1 to 7.2.2.1.3 or 7.2.2.2.1 and 7.2.2.2.2 below:

.1.1 *the ducts where they pass through a machinery space of category A, galley, vehicle space, ro-ro space or special category space, are constructed of steel in accordance with paragraphs 7.2.1.1.1 and 7.2.1.1.2;*

.1.2 *automatic fire dampers are fitted close to the boundaries penetrated; and*

.1.3 *the integrity of the machinery space, galley, vehicle space, ro-ro space or special category space boundaries is maintained at the penetrations;*
or

.2.1 *the ducts, where they pass through a machinery space of category A, galley, vehicle space, ro-ro space or special category space, are constructed of steel in accordance with paragraphs 7.2.1.1.1 and 7.2.1.1.2; and*

.2.2 *the ducts are insulated to "A–60" standard within the machinery space, galley, vehicle space, ro-ro space or special category space;*

except that penetrations of main zone divisions shall also comply with the requirements of paragraph 4.1.1.8.

7.3 Details of duct penetrations

7.3.1 Where a thin plated duct with a free cross-sectional area equal to, or less than, 0.02 m^2 passes through "A" class bulkheads or decks, the opening shall be lined with a steel sheet sleeve having a thickness of at least 3 mm and a length of at least 200 mm, divided preferably into 100 mm on each side of the bulkhead or, in the case of the deck, wholly laid on the lower side of the decks pierced. Where ventilation ducts with a free cross-sectional area exceeding 0.02 m^2 pass through "A" class bulkheads or decks, the opening shall be lined with a steel sheet sleeve. However, where such ducts are of steel construction and pass through a deck or bulkhead, the ducts and sleeves shall comply with the following:

.1 *The sleeves shall have a thickness of at least 3 mm and a length of at least 900 mm. When passing through bulkheads, this length shall be divided preferably into 450 mm on each side of the bulkhead. These ducts, or sleeves lining such ducts, shall be provided with fire insulation. The insulation shall have at least the same fire integrity as the bulkhead or deck through which the duct passes; and*

.2 *Ducts with a free cross-sectional area exceeding 0.075 m^2 shall be fitted with fire dampers in addition to the requirements of paragraph 7.3.1.1. The fire damper shall operate automatically, but shall also be capable of being closed manually from both sides of the bulkhead or deck. The damper shall be provided with an indicator which shows whether the damper is open or closed. Fire dampers are not required, however, where ducts pass through spaces surrounded by "A" class divisions, without serving those spaces, provided those ducts have the same fire* *integrity as the divisions which they pierce. Fire dampers shall be easily accessible. Where they are placed behind ceilings or linings, these ceilings or linings shall be provided with an inspection door on which a plate reporting the identification number of the fire damper is provided. The fire damper identification number shall also be placed on any remote controls required.*

7.3.2 Ventilation ducts with a free cross-sectional area exceeding 0.02 m2 passing through "B" class bulkheads shall be lined with steel sheet sleeves of 900 mm in length, divided preferably into 450 mm on each side of the bulkheads unless the duct is of steel for this length.

7.4   Ventilation systems for passenger ships carrying more than 36 passengers

7.4.1 The ventilation system of a passenger ship carrying more than 36 passengers shall be in compliance with the following additional requirements.

7.4.2 In general, the ventilation fans shall be so disposed that the ducts reaching the various spaces remain within the main vertical zone.

7.4.3 Where ventilation systems penetrate decks, precautions shall be taken, in addition to those relating to the fire integrity of the deck required by paragraphs 3.1 and 4.1.1.5, to reduce the likelihood of smoke and hot gases passing from one 'tween-deck space to another through the system. In addition to insulation requirements contained in paragraph 7.4, vertical ducts shall, if necessary, be insulated as required by the appropriate tables 9.1 and 9.2.

7.4.4 Except in cargo spaces, ventilation ducts shall be constructed of the following materials:

.1   *ducts not less than 0.075 m^2 in free cross-sectional area and all vertical ducts serving more than a single 'tween-deck space shall be constructed of steel or other equivalent material;*

.2   *ducts less than 0.075 m^2 in free cross-sectional area other than the vertical ducts referred to in paragraph 7.4.4.1, shall be constructed of non-combustible materials. Where such ducts penetrate "A" or "B" class divisions, due regard shall be given to ensuring the fire integrity of the division; and*

.3   *short lengths of duct, not in general exceeding 0.02m^2 in free cross-sectional area nor 2 m in length, need not be non-combustible provided that all of the following conditions are met:*

.3.1   *the duct is constructed of a material which has low flame spread characteristics;*

.3.2   *the duct is used only at the terminal end of the ventilation system; and*

.3.3   *the duct is not located closer than 600mm measured along its length to a penetration of an "A" or "B" class division, including continuous "B" class ceilings.*

7.4.5 Stairway enclosures shall be ventilated and served by an independent fan and duct system which shall not serve any other spaces in the ventilation systems.

7.4.6 Exhaust ducts shall be provided with hatches for inspection and cleaning. The hatches shall be located near the fire dampers.

7.5   Exhaust ducts from galley ranges

7.5.1 Requirements for passenger ships carrying more than 36 passengers

Exhaust ducts from galley ranges shall meet the requirements of paragraphs 7.2.1.2.1 and 7.2.1.2.2 and shall be fitted with:

.1   *a grease trap readily removable for cleaning unless an alternative approved grease removal system is fitted;*

.2   *a fire damper located in the lower end of the duct which is automatically and remotely operated, and, in addition, a remotely operated fire damper located in the upper end of the duct;*

.3   *a fixed means for extinguishing a fire within the duct;*

.4   *remote-control arrangements for shutting off the exhaust fans and supply fans, for operating the fire dampers mentioned in paragraph 7.5.1.2 and for operating the fire-extinguishing system, which shall be placed in a position close to the entrance to the galley. Where a multi-branch system is installed, a remote means located with the above controls shall be provided to close all branches exhausting through the same main duct before an extinguishing medium is released into the system; and*

.5   *suitably located hatches for inspection and cleaning.*

7.5.2 Requirements for cargo ships and passenger ships carrying not more than 36 passengers.

7.5.2.1 Where they pass through accommodation spaces or spaces containing combustible materials, the exhaust ducts from galley ranges shall be constructed of "A" class divisions. Each exhaust duct shall be fitted with:

.1   *a grease trap readily removable for cleaning;*

.2   *a fire damper located in the lower end of the duct;*

.3   *arrangements, operable from within the galley, for shutting off the exhaust fans; and*

.4   *fixed means for extinguishing a fire within the duct.*

Guidance 9

G58   Fire dampers

G58.1 Manual control of dampers

> G58.1.1 Manual control of a fire damper is to be independent of and capable of overriding any automatic means of control.

> G58.1.2 Manual closing is normally by means of a handle linked directly to the damper blade spindle, but may be achieved by local operation of the fire damper by means of a fail-safe electrical switch or pneumatic release (spring loaded, etc.), on both sides of the division, with indication of fire damper status.

G58.2 Automatic closure of dampers

> G58.2.1 When a fire damper is required to be closed automatically, the means of operation shall be situated inside the coaming or spigot such that it can be activated by hot gases passing through the ventilation ducting. The MCA is prepared to accept any additional means of operating the damper automatically, subject to compliance with preceding paragraphs.

> G58.2.2 The means of operation shall be activated at temperatures within the range of 68°C to 79°C inclusive, except that in exhaust ducts serving spaces with high ambient temperatures such as galleys and drying rooms, the temperature at which the means of operation is activated may be increased to not more than 30°C above the maximum deckhead temperature.

> G58.2.3 When the means of operating a fire damper automatically is a spring and fusible link, the link is required to be capable of being released manually from outside the duct by withdrawing the pin over which the link is hooked except that any other effective means of release would be considered.

> G58.2.4 A pneumatic or electrical system must be such that the fire damper closes on release of the air or failure of any one of the components or power supply.

G58.3 Manual operation of dampers from both sides of a division

> G58.3.1 In order to satisfy the requirements to operate a fire damper from both sides of a bulkhead or deck as indicated in the Regulations, a damper may be fitted on each side of the division within the coaming or spigot, the dampers being operated independently of each other. Only one of the two dampers need be capable of being closed automatically when automatic operation is required by the Regulations.

> G58.3.2 Alternatively a single manual or automatic damper as appropriate may be fitted on one side of the bulkhead or deck, arranged for local manual operation, and in addition for manual operation from the blind side of such a division using a suitable linkage. The instructions of this section should be complied with at both operating positions.

G58.4 Open/closed indicator (on damper)

> G58.4.1 Each damper is required by the Regulations to be fitted with a visible indicator to show whether the damper is in the open or closed position. The method of indication should be visible from the operating position.

G59   Components clear of coaming

G59.1 The manual and automatic controls, indicator, access panels and any other component should be sufficiently clear of the coaming to enable the coaming to be properly insulated.

G60   Damper controls clear of obstructions

G60.1 Manual and automatic controls of a damper are to be clear of the division, the insulation on the division or any other obstruction when the damper is in the open and closed positions.

G61   Ducts passing through 'A' Class divisions

G61.1 Attention is also drawn to the guidance dealing with Regulations referring specifically to the fitting of fire dampers in ventilation ducts passing through 'A' Class divisions and ventilation systems in general.

G61.2 The other spaces referred to in paragraph 7.2.1 are accommodation spaces, service spaces and control stations.

G61.3 Where the ventilation ducting serving a space or group of spaces fitted with a fixed gas fire-extinguishing system passes through any space not served by the system, the ducting should be of steel and of gas tight construction.

G61.4 The ventilation system serving a space in which gas cylinders are stored should not serve any other space and should be capable of freeing the space of any gas which may leak from the cylinders. Any ducting of such a system which passes through any other space should be of steel and of gas tight construction.

G62   Systems within main zones

G62.1 Wherever practicable the ventilation system leading from each ventilation fan shall be within one main vertical or horizontal zone. The fan room should also be within the same main zone otherwise an excessive number of fail-safe automatic closing fire dampers may be required where ducts penetrate the main zone division.

G63   Smoke control

G63.1 Where the arrangement of ducts and fire dampers in a ventilation system is such that smoke and hot gases may pass from one 'tween-deck to another through the system, a damper should be fitted in the duct on the upper side of the deck separating the 'tween-decks. The dampers may be simple manually controlled steel dampers fitted in a readily accessible position, and need not be of a fire tested type. Alternatively when the ducts are of steel their closure may be achieved by the shutting of punkah louvres or grilles fitted to the openings in the branch trunking within a 'tween-deck.

G63.2 Where individual ducts serve a single 'tween-deck the smoke damper may be at the fan unit or other location providing suitable isolation.

G64   Vertical ducts

G64.1 Paragraph 7.4.3 requires vertical ducts to be insulated as required by the tables in paragraph 2.2.3. Compliance with this Regulation may be achieved in the case of vertical ducts which are fitted with fire dampers, by insulating each damper coaming to the 'A' Class standard of the deck through which the duct passes.

G64.2 Vertical ducts having a cross sectional area not exceeding 0.075m² which pass through 'A' Class decks other than those which are main zone divisions, are not required to be fitted with fire dampers. Such vertical ducts should be insulated to the same 'A' Class standard as the decks through which they pass by continuing the insulation fitted to the deck plating along the ducts for a distance of not less than 450mm from the deck plating.

G64.3 Openings for recirculation of air or balancing a ventilation system may be provided between corridors in separate 'tween-decks provided that they are trunked into the corridors with no openings into the ceiling or lining voids. In addition they should comply with the constructional requirements and the requirements for the provision of fire and smoke dampers of paragraph 7. They should normally be fitted with sliding or hinged steel shutters at their ends.

G64.4 The recommended thickness of the steel coamings incorporating fire dampers for closing openings in ventilation ducts is indicated in the following table:

Table 9.1

Width or diameter of duct	Minimum thickness of coaming or sleeve
Up to and including 300mm	3mm
760mm and over	5mm

G64.5 When any duct not exceeding $0.075m^2$ in cross sectional area, passes through an insulated 'A' Class division the duct or steel sleeve should be insulated for a distance of not less than 380 mm from the division with 'A' Class mineral wool insulation having a thickness equivalent to that fitted over the plating of the division.

G64.6 When any duct exceeding $0.075m^2$ in cross sectional area, passes through an insulated 'A' Class division the steel coaming incorporating the fire dampers should be insulated with an 'A' Class mineral wool insulation having a thickness equivalent to that fitted over the plating of the division as indicated in figures 9.21 and 9.22. The insulation is to be attached by means of welded steel pins, wire netting and spring steel washers.

Note: Illustrations of insulation fitted to coamings are on following pages.

G65 Ducts in service trunks

G65.1 Where ventilation ducts are grouped in a service trunk only the service trunk need be insulated at the deck penetration; provided the trunk is closed and has A Class integrity at all points.

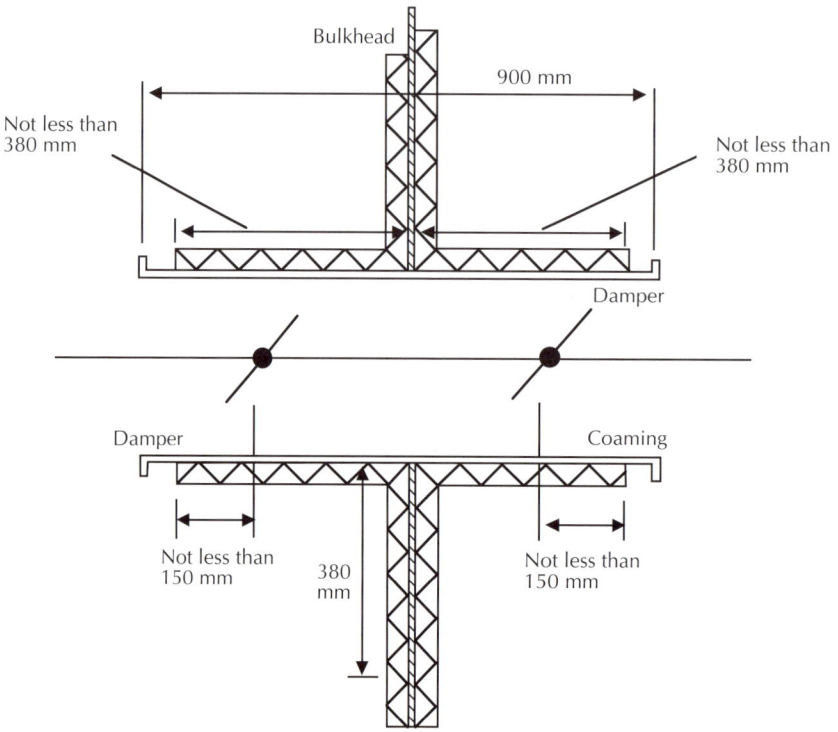

(a) Insulation fitted on coaming incorporating double dampers

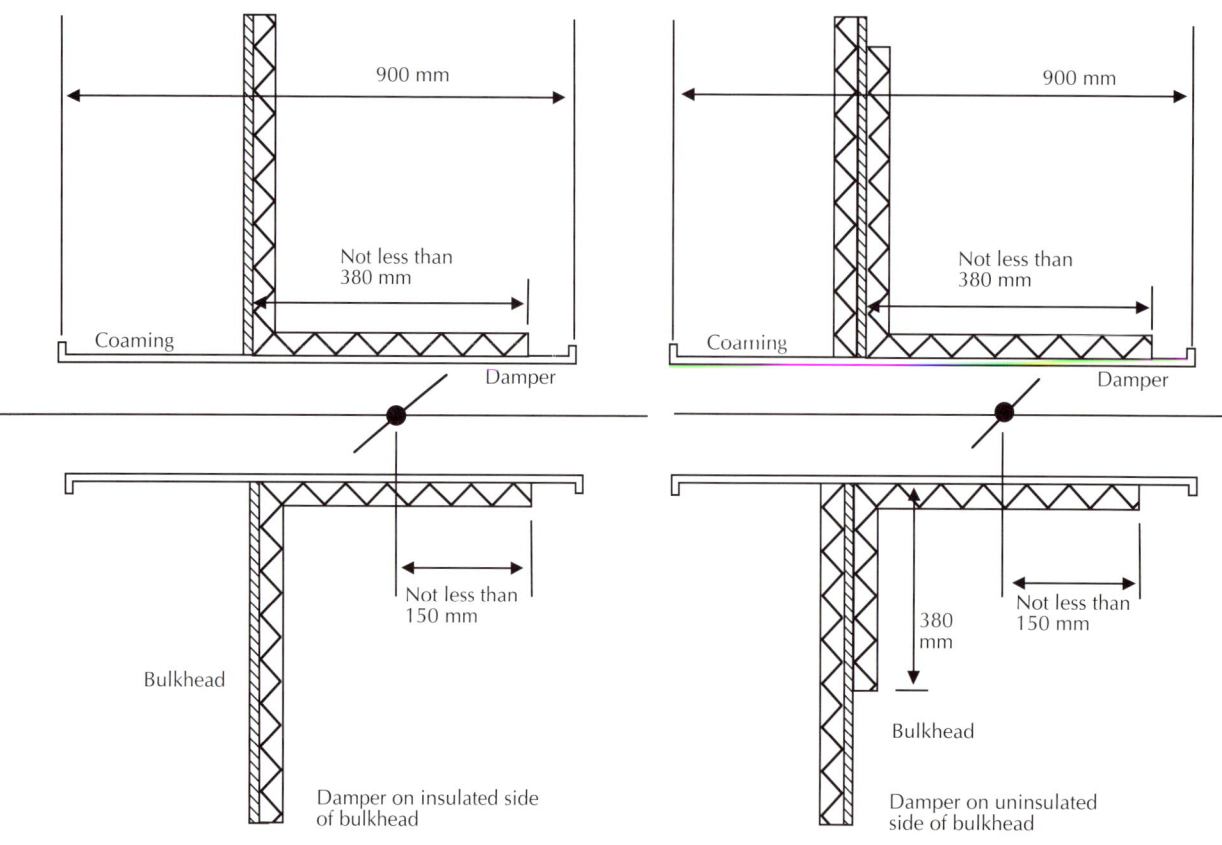

(b) Insulation fitted on coaming incorporating single dampers.

Figure 9.21

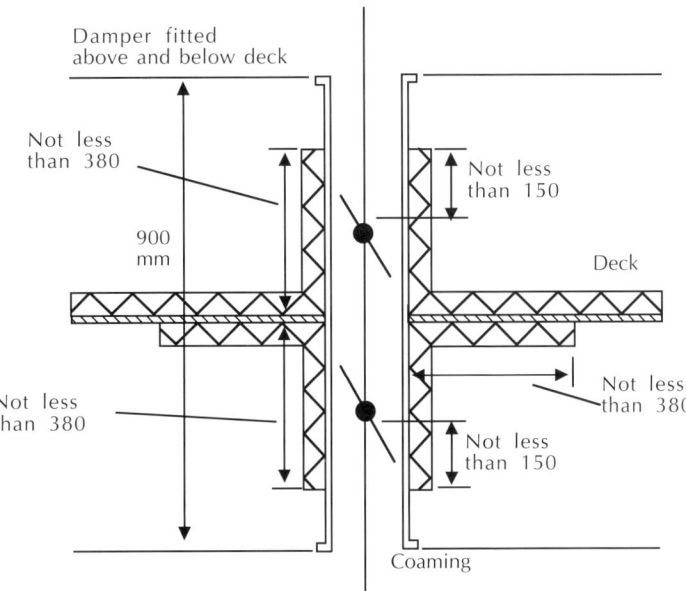

(a) Insulation fitted on coaming incorporating double dampers.

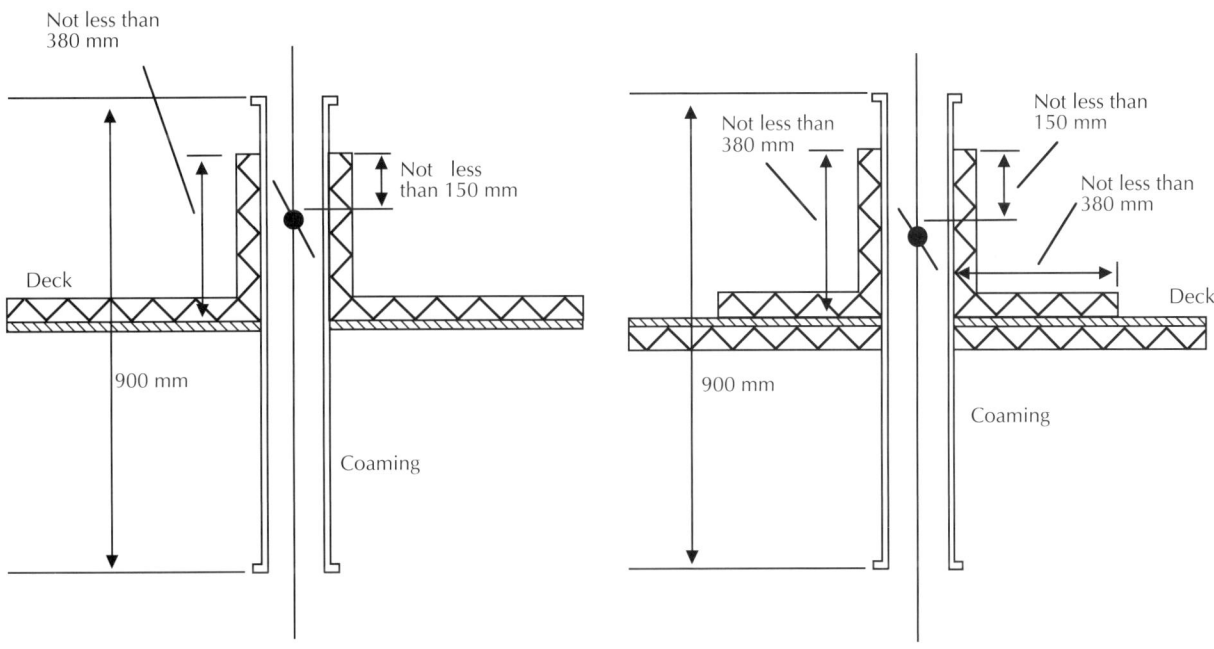

(i) Deck insulated on upper side

(ii) Deck insulated on under side

(b) Insulation fitted on coaming incorporating single dampers

Figure 9.22

G66   Fire resisting ducts

G66.1 Fire dampers are not required to be fitted in a duct which passes through a space surrounded by 'A' Class divisions and has no openings into the space, subject to following main paragraph and provided that the duct:

.1   has the same thickness as a duct as indicated in paragraph 7.2.1.1.1;

.2   is adequately supported and stiffened; and

.3   is insulated to the same 'A' Class standard as the divisions through which it passes or to the higher standard when the divisions have differing 'A' Class standards. This is illustrated by figure 9.23 below.

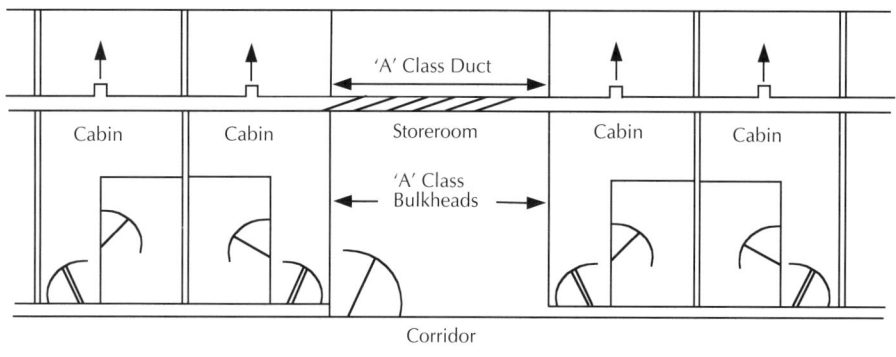

Figure 9.23

G66.2 The dispensing of fire dampers in this manner shall not apply when a duct passes through a main zone division, because paragraph 4.1.1.8 still applies.

G66.3 Notwithstanding the preceding main paragraph when a duct serves spaces bounded by 'A' Class divisions and which are situated on each side of another space into which the duct has no openings, fire dampers are still required to be fitted at each end of the 'A' Class ducting in order to maintain the integrity of the two outer spaces from each other. This is illustrated by figure 9.24.

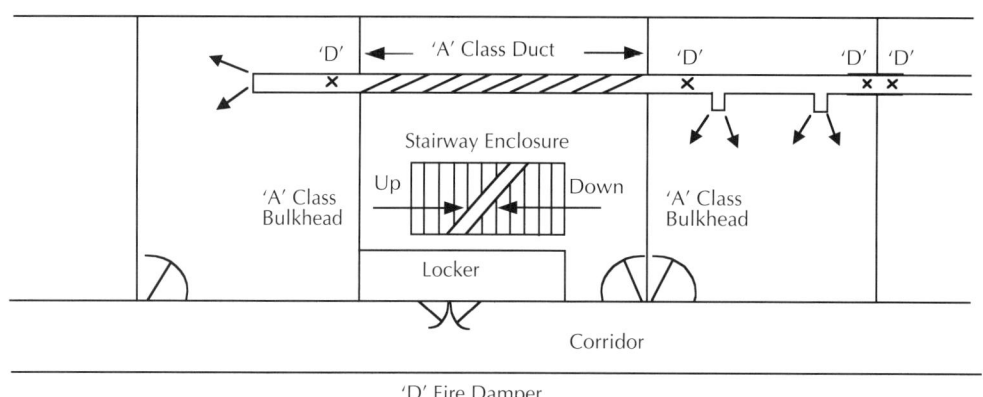

'D' Fire Damper

Figure 9.24

G67   Ducts passing through 'B' Class divisions (paragraph 7.3.2)

G67.1 Ventilation ducts passing through 'B' Class bulkheads, ceilings or linings should be treated as indicated in the following table;

Table 9.2

Cross sectional Area of duct	Type of duct	Treatment
Not exceeding 0.02m²	Steel ducts other than single skinned spiroducts.	To be collared to the division. The collars may be of steel or of the same material and thickness as the division.
	Single skinned spiroducts. Aluminium alloy ducts.	To be passed through a steel sleeve having a length and thickness of not less than 600 mm and 1.0 mm respectively collared to the division. The collars may be of steel or of the same material and thickness as the division. The gap between the sleeve and the duct should be effectively packed with a non-combustible material and the ends sealed with a suitable flexible sealant.
Exceeding 0.02 m² but not exceeding 0.075 m²	Steel ducts other than single skinned spiroducts.	To be collared to the division with steel collars.
	Single skinned spiroducts. Aluminium alloy ducts.	To be passed through a steel sleeve having a length and thickness of not less than 900 mm and 1.0 mm respectively collared to the division. The collars are to be of steel. The gap between the sleeve and the duct should be effectively packed with a non-combustible material and the ends sealed with a suitable flexible sealant.
Exceeding 0.075 m²	Steel ducts other than spiroducts.	To be collared to the division with steel collars.
	Double and single skinned spiroducts. Aluminium alloy ducts.	To be passed through a sleeve having a length and thickness of 900 mm and 1.5 mm respectively collared to the division. The collars are to be of steel. The gap between the sleeve and the duct should be effectively packed with a non-combustible material and the ends sealed with a suitable flexible sealant.

G68   Ducts from machinery of Category A, galleys etc. (Paragraph 7.2.1)

G68.1 It should be noted that double and single skinned spiroducts are precluded from use in the situations referred to because they are not constructed of steel of the required thickness.

G68.2 The automatic closing fire damper required by paragraph 7.2.1.1.3 should be fitted on the opposite side of the boundary penetrated to that of the spaces which it serves. The manual controls of the dampers should be readily accessible and the operating position clearly marked.

G68.3 Care should be taken to ensure that the A–60 standard of the portion of ducting which is required by paragraph 7.2.1.1.4 to be insulated, is not impaired where the ducting passes through a deck or adjoins another structure. It should be borne in mind that the intention of the requirement is to protect the accommodation spaces etc. from a fire in the machinery space of Category A, galley etc.

G68.4 When the measures specified in paragraph 7.2.1.2.2 or 7.2.2.2.2 are adopted and the boundary of the machinery space of Category A, galley, Ro-Ro space or special category space which is being penetrated by the duct is a main zone division, in addition to the duct being insulated for its full length to A–60 standard, paragraph 4.1.1.8 must also be complied with.

G68.5 Similar care with insulation should be taken when the alternative method of protecting accommodation spaces etc. indicated in paragraph 7.2.1.2.1 and 7.2.1.2.2, is adopted.

G69   Ducts from accommodation spaces etc. (Paragraph 7.2.2)

G69.1 See guidance G9.68, which applies in a similar manner.

G70   Galley ventilation

G70.1 The automatic closing fire damper referred to in paragraph 7.5.2.1.2 should be positioned immediately above the grease trap and the fixed means of extinguishing a fire referred to in paragraph 7.5.2.1.4 should be capable of extinguishing a fire situated anywhere above it from the exhaust duct. The fire damper should be provided with control operable from an accessible position clear of the equipment which the exhaust duct serves.

G70.2 In all cases when an exhaust duct is fitted with branches serving different items of galley equipment, the requirements of paragraph 7.5.2.1.4 should apply to each branch. In such cases remote control of the fire dampers in the exhaust trunk branches may be necessary; even in those ships which are not required to comply with paragraph 7.5.2.1.2. Where compliance with these standards is not necessary because a galley exhaust duct does not pass through accommodation spaces or spaces containing combustibles e.g. when the duct goes directly to the open air from the galley, then regulations 5.2.1.1 and 5.2.1.2 should be complied with in respect of stopping the fan and providing a means of closure at the duct outlet. It would be sensible in such a case to fit a grease trap in the duct.

G71   Ducts passing through 'A' Class divisions (on cargo ships and tankers)

G71.1 See guidance G9.61 which also applies in a similar manner to cargo ships and tankers.

G72   Fire resisting ducts (on cargo ships and tankers)

G72.1 See guidance G9.66 which also applies in a similar manner to cargo ships and tankers.

G73   Openings for recirculating or exhausting air or balancing systems

G73.1 Paragraph 4.2.3, for cargo ships, paragraph 4.1.2.1, for passenger ships, permits openings in the lower part of 'B' Class doors through which air from cabins or similar spaces and from cabins and public spaces respectively may be taken via the corridors and ducting to the air conditioning machinery room for recirculation or to the atmosphere. 'B' Class bulkheads should not be penetrated by openings other than those in the lower part of the doors or within ducting irrespective of the openings being fitted with shutters or dampers. Open-ended steel coamings should not be regarded as ducting.

G73.2 Air from spaces surrounded by 'A' Class divisions should not be exhausted directly into corridors for recirculating or for return to the atmosphere through openings or open-ended coamings irrespective of the openings or coamings being fitted with shutters or dampers. Such spaces should be fitted with exhaust ducting to the fan room or to the atmosphere. Similarly high risk spaces such as galleys should not be provided with recirculating, balancing or exhaust openings or open-ended coamings into adjacent accommodation spaces.

G73.3 Openings for recirculation of air or balancing a ventilation system may be provided between corridors in separate 'tween-decks provided that they are trunked into the corridors with no openings into the ceiling or lining voids. Also, they should comply with constructional requirements (including the provision of fire and smoke dampers) of paragraph 7. They should normally be fitted with sliding or hinged steel shutters at their ends.

Fire fighting

1   Purpose

The purpose of this regulation is to suppress and swiftly extinguish a fire in the space of origin. For this purpose, the following functional requirements shall be met:

> *.1   fixed fire-extinguishing systems shall be installed, having due regard to the fire growth potential of the protected spaces; and*

> *.2   fire-extinguishing appliances shall be readily available.*

2   Water supply systems

Ships shall be provided with fire pumps, fire mains, hydrants and hoses complying with the applicable requirements of this regulation.

2.1   Fire mains and hydrants

2.1.1 General

Materials readily rendered ineffective by heat shall not be used for fire mains and hydrants unless adequately protected. The pipes and hydrants shall be so placed that the fire hoses may be easily coupled to them. The arrangement of pipes and hydrants shall be such as to avoid the possibility of freezing. Suitable drainage provisions shall be provided for fire main piping. Isolation valves shall be installed for all open deck fire main branches used for purposes other than fire fighting. In ships where deck cargo may be carried, the positions of the hydrants shall be such that they are always readily accessible and the pipes shall be arranged as far as practicable to avoid risk of damage by such cargo.

2.1.2 Ready availability of water supply

The arrangements for the ready availability of water supply shall be:

> *.1   in passenger ships:*

>> *.1.1   of 1,000 gross tonnage and upwards such that at least one effective jet of water is immediately available from any hydrant in an interior location and so as to ensure the continuation of the output of water by the automatic starting of one required fire pump;*

>> *.1.2   of less than 1,000 gross tonnage by automatic start of at least one fire pump or by remote starting from the navigation bridge of at least one fire pump. If the pump starts automatically or if the bottom valve cannot be opened from where the pump is remotely started, the bottom valve shall always be kept open; and*

>> *.1.3   if fitted with periodically unattended machinery spaces in accordance with regulation II–1/54, the Administration shall determine provisions for fixed water fire-extinguishing arrangement for such spaces equivalent to those required for normally attended machinery spaces;*

.2   in cargo ships:

.2.1   to the satisfaction of the Administration; and

.2.2   with a periodically unattended machinery space or when only one person is required on watch, there shall be immediate water delivery from the fire main system at a suitable pressure, either by remote starting of one of the main fire pumps with remote starting from the navigation bridge and fire control station, if any, or permanent pressurization of the fire main system by one of the main fire pumps, except that the Administration may waive this requirement for cargo ships of less than 1,600 gross tonnage if the fire pump starting arrangement in the machinery space is in an easily accessible position.

2.1.3 Diameter of fire mains

The diameter of the fire main and water service pipes shall be sufficient for the effective distribution of the maximum required discharge from two fire pumps operating simultaneously, except that in the case of cargo ships the diameter need only be sufficient for the discharge of 140 m³/h.

2.1.4   Isolating valves and relief valves

2.1.4.1 Isolating valves to separate the section of the fire main within the machinery space containing the main fire pump or pumps from the rest of the fire main shall be fitted in an easily accessible and tenable position outside the machinery spaces. The fire main shall be so arranged that when the isolating valves are shut all the hydrants on the ship, except those in the machinery space referred to above, can be supplied with water by another fire pump or an emergency fire pump. The emergency fire pump, its seawater inlet, and suction and delivery pipes and isolating valves shall be located outside the machinery space. If this arrangement cannot be made, the sea-chest may be fitted in the machinery space if the valve is remotely controlled from a position in the same compartment as the emergency fire pump and the suction pipe is as short as practicable. Short lengths of suction or discharge piping may penetrate the machinery space, provided they are enclosed in a substantial steel casing or are insulated to "A–60" class standards. The pipes shall have substantial wall thickness, but in no case less than 11 mm, and shall be welded except for the flanged connection to the sea inlet valve.

2.1.4.2 A valve shall be fitted to serve each fire hydrant so that any fire hose may be removed while the fire pumps are in operation.

2.1.4.3 Relief valves shall be provided in conjunction with fire pumps if the pumps are capable of developing a pressure exceeding the design pressure of the water service pipes, hydrants and hoses. These valves shall be so placed and adjusted as to prevent excessive pressure in any part of the fire main system.

2.1.4.4 In tankers, isolation valves shall be fitted in the fire main at the poop front in a protected position and on the tank deck at intervals of not more than 40 m to preserve the integrity of the fire main system in case of fire or explosion.

2.1.5 Number and position of hydrants

2.1.5.1 The number and position of hydrants shall be such that at least two jets of water not emanating from the same hydrant, one of which shall be from a single length of hose, may reach any part of the ship normally accessible to the passengers or crew while the ship is being navigated and any part of any cargo space when empty, any ro-ro space or any vehicle space in which latter case the two jets shall reach any part of the space, each from a single length of hose. Furthermore, such hydrants shall be positioned near the accesses to the protected spaces.

2.1.5.2 In addition to the requirements in paragraph 2.1.5.1, passenger ships shall comply with the following:

.1 *in the accommodation, service and machinery spaces, the number and position of hydrants shall be such that the requirements of paragraph 2.1.5.1 may be complied with when all watertight doors and all doors in main vertical zone bulkheads are closed; and*

.2 *where access is provided to a machinery space of category A at a low level from an adjacent shaft tunnel, two hydrants shall be provided external to, but near the entrance to, that machinery space. Where such access is provided from other spaces, in one of those spaces two hydrants shall be provided near the entrance to the machinery space of category A. Such provision need not be made where the tunnel or adjacent spaces are not part of the escape route.*

2.1.6 Pressure at hydrants

With the two pumps simultaneously delivering water through the nozzles specified in paragraph 2.3.3, with the quantity of water as specified in paragraph 2.1.3, through any adjacent hydrants, the following minimum pressures shall be maintained at all hydrants:

.1 *for passenger ships:*
4,000 gross tonnage and upwards 0.40 N/mm^2
less than 4,000 gross tonnage 0.30 N/mm^2

.2 *for cargo ships:*
6,000 gross tonnage and upwards 0.27 N/mm^2
less than 6,000 gross tonnage 0.25 N/mm^2
and

.3 *the maximum pressure at any hydrant shall not exceed that at which the effective control of a fire hose can be demonstrated.*

2.1.7 International shore connection

2.1.7.1 Ships of 500 gross tonnage and upwards shall be provided with at least one international shore connection complying with the Fire Safety Systems Code.

2.1.7.2 Facilities shall be available enabling such a connection to be used on either side of the ship.

2.2   Fire pumps

2.2.1 Pumps accepted as fire pumps

Sanitary, ballast, bilge or general service pumps may be accepted as fire pumps, provided that they are not normally used for pumping oil and that if they are subject to occasional duty for the transfer or pumping of oil fuel, suitable change-over arrangements are fitted.

2.2.2 Number of fire pumps

Ships shall be provided with independently driven fire pumps as follows:

.1   in passenger ships of:

4,000 gross tonnage and upwards	*at least three*
less than 4,000 gross tonnage	*at least two*

.2   in cargo ships of:

1,000 gross tonnage and upwards	*at least two*
less than 1,000 gross tonnage	*at least two power-driven pumps, one of which shall be independently driven.*

2.2.3 Arrangement of fire pumps and fire mains

2.2.3.1 Fire pumps

The arrangement of sea connections, fire pumps and their sources of power shall be as to ensure that:

.1   in passenger ships of l,000 gross tonnage and upwards, in the event of a fire in any one compartment, all the fire pumps will not be put out of action; and

.2   in passenger ships of less than 1,000 gross tonnage and in cargo ships, if a fire in any one compartment could put all the pumps out of action, there shall be an alternative means consisting of an emergency fire pump complying with the provisions of the Fire Safety Systems Code with its source of power and sea connection located outside the space where the main fire pumps or their sources of power are located.

2.2.3.2 Requirements for the space containing the emergency fire pump

2.2.3.2.1 Location of the space

The space containing the fire pump shall not be contiguous to the boundaries of machinery spaces of category A or those spaces containing main fire pumps. Where this is not practicable, the common bulkhead between the two spaces shall be insulated to a standard of structural fire protection equivalent to that required for a control station.

2.2.3.2.2 Access to the emergency fire pump

No direct access shall be permitted between the machinery space and the space containing the emergency fire pump and its source of power. When this is impracticable, the Administration may accept an arrangement where the access is by means of an airlock with the door of the machinery space being of "A–60" class standard and the other door being at least steel, both reasonably gastight, self-closing and without any hold-back arrangements. Alternatively, the access may be through a watertight door capable of being operated from a space remote from the machinery space and the space containing the emergency fire pump and unlikely to be cut off in the event of fire in those spaces. In such cases, a second means of access to the space containing the emergency fire pump and its source of power shall be provided.

2.2.3.2.3 Ventilation of the emergency fire pump space

Ventilation arrangements to the space containing the independent source of power for the emergency fire pump shall be such as to preclude, as far as practicable, the possibility of smoke from a machinery space fire entering or being drawn into that space.

2.2.3.3   Additional pumps for cargo ships

In addition, in cargo ships where other pumps, such as general service, bilge and ballast, etc., are fitted in a machinery space, arrangements shall be made to ensure that at least one of these pumps, having the capacity and pressure required by paragraphs 2.1.6.2 and 2.2.4.2, is capable of providing water to the fire main.

2.2.4   Capacity of fire pumps

2.2.4.1   Total capacity of required fire pumps

The required fire pumps shall be capable of delivering for fire-fighting purposes a quantity of water, at the pressure specified in paragraph 2.1.6, as follows:

.1   pumps in passenger ships: the quantity of water is not less than two thirds of the quantity required to be dealt with by the bilge pumps when employed for bilge pumping; and

.2   pumps in cargo ships, other than any emergency pump: the quantity of water is not less than four thirds of the quantity required under regulation II–1/21 to be dealt with by each of the independent bilge pumps in a passenger ship of the same dimension when employed in bilge pumping, provided that in no cargo ship need the total required capacity of the fire pumps exceed 180 m³/h.

2.2.4.2   Capacity of each fire pump

Each of the required fire pumps (other than any emergency pump required in paragraph 2.2.3.1.2 for cargo ships) shall have a capacity not less than 80% of the total required capacity divided by the minimum number of required fire pumps but in any case not less than 25 m³/h, and each such pump shall in any event be capable of delivering at least the two required jets of water. These fire pumps shall be capable of supplying the fire main system under the required conditions. Where more pumps than the minimum of required pumps are installed, such additional pumps shall have a capacity of at least 25 m³/h and shall be capable of delivering at least the two jets of water required in paragraph 2.1.5.1.

2.3   Fire hoses and nozzles

2.3.1   General specifications

2.3.1.1 Fire hoses shall be of non-perishable material approved by the Administration and shall be sufficient in length to project a jet of water to any of the spaces in which they may be required to be used. Each hose shall be provided with a nozzle and the necessary couplings. Hoses specified in this chapter as "fire hoses" shall, together with any necessary fittings and tools, be kept ready for use in conspicuous positions near the water service hydrants or connections. Additionally, in interior locations in passenger ships carrying more than 36 passengers, fire hoses shall be connected to the hydrants at all times. Fire hoses shall have a length of at least 10 m, but not more than:

.1   15 m in machinery spaces;

.2   20 m in other spaces and open decks; and

.3   25 m for open decks on ships with a maximum breadth in excess of 30 m.

2.3.1.2 Unless one hose and nozzle is provided for each hydrant in the ship, there shall be complete interchangeability of hose couplings and nozzles.

2.3.2   Number and diameter of fire hoses

2.3.2.1 Ships shall be provided with fire hoses, the number and diameter of which shall be to the satisfaction of the Administration.

2.3.2.2 In passenger ships, there shall be at least one fire hose for each of the hydrants required by paragraph 2.1.5 and these hoses shall be used only for the purposes of extinguishing fires or testing the fire-extinguishing apparatus at fire drills and surveys.

2.3.2.3 In cargo ships:

.1   of 1,000 gross tonnage and upwards, the number of fire hoses to be provided shall be one for each 30 m length of the ship and one spare, but in no case less than five in all. This number does not include any hoses required in any engine-room or boiler room. The Administration may increase the number of hoses required so as to ensure that hoses in sufficient number are available and accessible at all times, having regard to the type of ship and the nature of trade in which the ship is employed. Ships carrying dangerous goods in accordance with regulation 19 shall be provided with three hoses and nozzles, in addition to those required above; and

.2   of less than 1,000 gross tonnage, the number of fire hoses to be provided shall be calculated in accordance with the provisions of paragraph 2.3.2.3.1. However, the number of hoses shall in no case be less than three.

2.3.3   Size and types of nozzles

2.3.3.1 For the purposes of this chapter, standard nozzle sizes shall be 12 mm, 16 mm and 19 mm or as near thereto as possible. Larger diameter nozzles may be permitted at the discretion of the Administration.

2.3.3.2 For accommodation and service spaces, a nozzle size greater than 12 mm need not be used.

2.3.3.3 For machinery spaces and exterior locations, the nozzle size shall be such as to obtain the maximum discharge possible from two jets at the pressure mentioned in paragraph 2.1.6 from the smallest pump, provided that a nozzle size greater than 19 mm need not be used.

2.3.3.4 Nozzles shall be of an approved dual-purpose type (i.e. spray/jet type) incorporating a shutoff.

Guidance 10

G1   Independently driven power operated emergency fire pumps

G1.1 When the emergency pump is the only means of providing water for the operation of, or use in connection with, a required fixed fire extinguishing installation for the machinery space, regard should be paid particularly to the ready accessibility of the pump controls in all weather conditions so that the system can be brought quickly into use.

G1.2 In tankers, there should, in general, be a cofferdam or void space between the space containing the emergency fire pump and any adjacent cargo oil tank, unless the pump is driven from a prime mover situated in a non-hazardous area outside the space. The means for driving the pump, e.g. pneumatic or hydraulic transmission, should be safe and suitable for use within the space containing the emergency fire pump, the pump suction and discharge valves should be capable of being operated from outside the space and the prime mover should be in a non-hazardous area. Notwithstanding the above, it is considered undesirable for the emergency fire pump so driven to be placed in a hazardous area of a tanker having common boundaries with the machinery space containing the main fire pumps or their source of power. Where it is impracticable for the pump to be sited elsewhere, however, proposals to locate it within the main cargo pump room would be considered on their merits.

G1.3 Where the emergency fire pump is used for the production of foam for a machinery space fixed foam system, or for recharging a pre-mixed foam installation, the pump capacity should be sufficient for this purpose in addition to the jets of water required by the Regulations.

G1.4 Starting arrangements for emergency fire pumps must be outside and independent of the space containing the main fire pumps. If manual starting is impracticable the other means of starting should include those by compressed air, electricity or other sources of stored energy, hydraulic power or starting cartridges.

G1.5 For the purposes of the Regulations and this guidance the fire main should be deemed to start at the fire pump discharge valve and hence includes all parts of the fire main and branches both within and outside the machinery space.

G1.6 For the purposes of the Regulations the fire main should be deemed to start at the fire pump discharge valve and hence includes all parts of the fire main and branches both within and outside the machinery space.

G1.7 In every ship of Class I, II, or II(A) any emergency fire pump shall be situated in a position aft of the ship's collision bulkhead.

G2   Hydrants

G2.1 Where the Regulations require a fire hydrant to be fitted in the tunnel the arrangements should ensure that the hydrant can be supplied by the emergency fire pump when the machinery space fire main is isolated. When not required by Regulations, because of the advantages in attacking a machinery space fire from a low level, the provision of a light steel door at the tunnel entrance for fire fighting purposes is strongly recommended. It should have an aperture, with hinged cover, through which a hose nozzle may be directed.

G2.2 Hydrant valves fitted in fire mains should be designed to open with an anti-clockwise rotation of the hand wheel.

G2.3 It is recommended that if blank caps are fitted on the outlets of hydrant valves, they should be so designed, e.g. by the incorporation of radial vent holes, manually or automatically operated release valves, plastic plugs etc. as to permit the safe release of any accumulated air or vapour pressure prior to the removal of the blank cap.

G2.4 In every Class VII ship of 500 tons or over fitted with oil-fire boilers or internal combustion type propelling machinery, there shall be provided in each space containing such boilers or machinery at least two fire hydrants, one on the port side and one on the starboard side. In addition where there is access to the machinery space of any such ship by way of a shaft tunnel, a fire hydrant shall be provided in the tunnel at the end adjacent to that space. A fire hose and nozzle shall be provided at every such fire hydrant.

G2.5 The water pipes shall not be made of cast iron and if made of iron or steel shall be galvanised or alternatively the pipe wall thickness shall be increased by a corrosion allowance.

G2.6 Every fire hose provided in compliance with these Regulations together with the tools and fittings necessary for its use, shall be kept in a conspicuous position near the hydrants or connections with which it is intended to be used. In interior locations in passenger ships, fire hoses shall be connected to the hydrants at all times. Hose diameters shall be not less than 64mm if unlined or 45mm if lined except that smaller diameter hoses may be permitted in small ships.

G3 Testing

G3.1 Where the working pressure in the fire main at the pump discharge exceeds 7 bar, the individual lengths of pipe, fittings and valves comprising the fire main should be tested to twice the maximum working pressure to which the system can be subjected in service. Subject to the surveyor having witnessed such tests, or that such tests have been satisfactorily completed, then the fire main after installation need only be subjected to the maximum pressure attainable by the fire pumps under normal service conditions.

G4 Expansion glands and couplings

G4.1 Where glands or couplings are used in fire mains, they should be of an approved type and the surveyor should be satisfied with the arrangements provided to maintain their integrity under the action of the internal pressure. Acceptance of such fittings will be conditional on their suitability taking into account loadline and sub-division requirements.

G4.2 No permanent connections to the fire main except for the purposes of fire fighting or washing down (e.g. hawse pipes and deck washing arrangements) are permissible under the Regulations. Exceptionally, where the use of water from the fire main is required to operate intermittently an isolated bilge water ejector or services of similar importance, the Regulations will not be deemed to be contravened providing the water connection is temporary, i.e. by hose and the fire hydrants used are easily accessible and in a place where they can easily be seen. In such cases a suitable warning notice should be positioned adjacent to the hydrant stressing that the hose should be disconnected when not in use. The position of the hydrant serving these ejectors should be indicated on the Fire Control Plan.

G5 Tank cleaning

G5.1 The fire main may be used for supplying a tank cleaning system in tankers providing all the following conditions are satisfied:

.1 the vessel is equipped with a separate and complete deck foam system, the foam main of which can be used as a water main having hose connections identical to the hose connections fitted on the fire main;

.2   the main fire pumps are capable of supplying that part of the fire main serving the machinery and accommodation spaces and the deck foam system when tank cleaning is in progress using the tank deck fire main;

.3   adequate means are provided against excessive pressure in the fire main if the tank washing pump is used on fire duty.

G6   Materials

G6.1   Materials readily rendered ineffective by heat must not be used for fire mains, hydrants, valves or cocks. Where doubt exists about the suitability of a particular fitting full details should be submitted to MCA Headquarters.

G7   Availability of water supply

G7.1   To obtain the maximum benefits from such a pressurised system it is desirable for permanently connected hose reel units using smaller diameter non-collapsible hoses to be provided in accommodation spaces; this will allow one person to attack any small fire without delay. Such hose reels, if provided, should be in addition to the hydrants and hoses required by the Regulations, as the latter would still be required when fighting a larger fire. However the MCA would be prepared to consider the use of hose reels, for statutory purposes, having a throughput of about half that of a 12mm nozzle at the appropriate pressure, with an acceptable throw, on the basis that two such reels together with one hose and nozzle of regulation size provide the equivalent throughput of two jets of water required by the Regulations to be available at any part of the accommodation spaces. In such an arrangement, the hose reels must be served by the ship's fire main and be at all times under a water pressure at least as great as that required by the Regulations. Hose reels that use the ships fresh water supply shall not be considered as being part of the statutory requirements.

G8   Isolating arrangements

G8.1   The arrangements should permit the supply of water from the emergency fire pump to the machinery space hydrants; e.g. the isolating valve may be a screw lift valve.

G8.2   Isolating valves should also be fitted in the fire main on the tank deck at the poop front in a protected position to protect the integrity of the fire main system in case of fire or explosion. Fire mains should be routed clear of tanker pump rooms. When this is impracticable full details of the arrangements should be submitted by the builder for consideration.

G9   Bore of stand pipes and hydrant valves

G9.1   In the interest of standardisation, and having regard to the loss of performance over a period of time due to internal corrosion, the internal bore of hydrant stand pipes of galvanised steel, and of hydrant valves of ferrous material should not in general be less than 64mm but a lesser diameter may be acceptable in small ships providing all requirements are complied with. Subject to the same proviso, stand pipes and hydrant valves of copper alloy may be accepted with bores not less than 50mm.

G10   Fire hoses, nozzles and spray nozzles

G10.1   Hoses should be efficiently connected to their end couplings. Fire hoses of 64mm diameter unlined canvas are considered as standard, but lined fire hoses of smaller diameter may be accepted provided tests have shown that the pressure drop across an 18m length approximates to that across an 18m length of unlined 64mm canvas at corresponding pressures. Certain lined hoses of 45mm bore have been shown to have a throughput comparable to that of a 64mm bore unlined canvas hose and as the smaller bore hose is more easily handled its use is recommended, particularly for machinery spaces and other interior locations. Fire hoses of a diameter not less than 32mm may be accepted in small passenger launches and other small craft.

G11   Nozzles

G11.1 The approximate discharges in m3/hour (which for practical purposes may be considered equivalent to tonnes/hour) through well designed plain nozzles of 12mm, 16mm and 19mm for pressure drops of 2.1, 2.5, 2.7 and 3.1 bars are given in the following table.

G12   Pressure Discharge for Various Nozzle Diameters m^3/hour

kPa	12mm	16mm	19mm
210	9	14	20.5
250	10	15	22.5
270	10.5	16	23.5
310	11	17	25

Note: nozzle sizes may be rounded up or down to the nearest standard dimension.

G12.1 Dual purpose nozzles should be capable of a performance in the plain jet setting without undue spread, and have a throw of at least 12m. The spray setting should produce a reasonably fine spray which can be arranged to form a curtain behind which it would be possible to approach a fire. An acceptable diameter of the cone of spray would be 5m at a distance of 2m from the end of the nozzle.

G12.2 Nozzles provided for use with deck fire hoses in tankers and ships carrying cargoes having a similar fire hazard should not be of aluminium alloy. Such dual purpose nozzles should be of robust construction, easy to operate and made of materials suitable for the intended duty.

G13   Fixed fire extinguishing installations

G13.1 For the periodic inspection, testing and maintenance of transportable gas containers (excluding dissolved acetylene containers) reference should be made to BS 5430: Part 2: 1990.

G13.2 The following extract from the "Report of the Home Office Gas Cylinders and Containers Committee" should also be taken into account: Testing of containers used for fire fighting, in some cases such as containers filled with carbon dioxide, the containers may remain charged for long periods and are unlikely to deteriorate seriously if filled with dry gas and kept under suitable conditions. It is not considered advisable that these containers should remain charged for indefinite periods without examination and test. It is however considered unreasonable that they should be discharged every five years in order to be submitted to the examination and test which we have recommended. We accordingly recommend that for these containers the first examination and test, after initial manufacturing test, should not be mandatory for new containers until a period of ten years (twenty years in cases where an external examination of the containers is carried out by a competent person at intervals not greater than one year) has elapsed from the time of installation. This relaxation would not apply to any container which had been discharged, showed a loss of pressure or weight or was excessively corroded externally. If, after the first periodic examination and test, containers are found to be in a satisfactory condition then the inspecting authority should certify that they may continue in service for a further period of ten years before being again submitted to examination and test, subject to the exceptions mentioned above. Subsequently the containers should be examined and tested at intervals of five years.

3   Portable fire extinguishers

3.1   Type and design

Portable fire extinguishers shall comply with the requirements of the Fire Safety Systems Code.

3.2   Arrangement of fire extinguishers

3.2.1 Accommodation spaces, service spaces and control stations shall be provided with portable fire extinguishers of appropriate types and in sufficient number to the satisfaction of the Administration. Ships of 1,000 gross tonnage and upwards shall carry at least five portable fire extinguishers.

3.2.2 One of the portable fire extinguishers intended for use in any space shall be stowed near the entrance to that space.

3.2.3 Carbon dioxide fire extinguishers shall not be placed in accommodation spaces. In control stations and other spaces containing electrical or electronic equipment or appliances necessary for the safety of the ship, fire extinguishers should be provided whose extinguishing media are neither electrically conductive nor harmful to the equipment and appliances.

3.2.4 Fire extinguishers shall be situated ready for use at easily visible places, which can be reached quickly and easily at any time in the event of a fire, and in such a way that their serviceability is not impaired by the weather, vibration or other external factors. Portable fire extinguishers shall be provided with devices which indicate whether they have been used.

3.3   Spare charges

3.3.1 Spare charges shall be provided for 100% of the first ten extinguishers and 50% of the remaining fire extinguishers capable of being recharged on board. Not more than sixty total spare charges are required. Instructions for recharging shall be carried on board.

3.3.2 For fire extinguishers which cannot be recharged on board, additional portable fire extinguishers of the same quantity, type, capacity and number as determined in paragraph 3.3.1 above shall be provided in lieu of spare charges.

Guidance 10

G14   In every passenger ship at least one portable fire extinguisher should be provided for use in each control station.

G15   In every passenger ship there should be provided on each deck below the bulkhead deck a sufficient number of portable fire extinguishers so that at least two are readily available for use in every accommodation space, service space and control station between main vertical zones. In enclosed accommodation spaces, service spaces and control stations above the bulkhead deck at least one such extinguisher should be provided for use on each side of the ship in such spaces. The number of such extinguishers in such spaces should not be less than five in a ship of 1,000 tons or over. In addition at least one portable fire extinguisher and a fire blanket should be provided in every galley; provided that where the deck area of any galley exceeds 45m², at least two such extinguishers and two such blankets should be provided.

G16   One of the portable fire extinguishers intended for use in any space should be available near the entrance to that space.

G17   Fire extinguishers

G17.1 The extinguishers should be examined annually by a competent person. During these examinations plastic collars etc. which may conceal the condition of the steel underneath should be removed.

G17.2 Each extinguisher should be provided with a sign indicating it has been examined.

G17.3 Containers of permanently pressurised and non-permanently pressurised fire extinguishers should be hydraulically pressure tested every 10 years.

G17.4 In the corridors of the accommodation area the fire extinguishers should be located as follows:

.1 Passenger ships:

Within each deck and main vertical zone the extinguishers should be so located that no point in the space is more than 15m walking distance from an extinguisher;

.2 Cargo ships:

one extinguisher on each deck.

G18 General

G18.1 The general requirements for fire extinguishers are contained in the relevant Regulations and in BS EN3 Series: 1996, in respect of portable extinguishers. In view of the ability of aluminium to produce incentive smears on steel, aluminium fire extinguishers should not be provided for use on tankers and ships carrying similar flammable cargoes, or which carry vehicles with petrol in their tanks.

G19 Charges

G19.1 Ships' personnel responsible for them should be informed that the charges of portable and non-portable fire extinguishers should, in general, be checked for condition annually. The charges of extinguishers other than those referred to below should be renewed if on checking there is any indication of deterioration and in any case at intervals not exceeding four years.

G19.2 Carbon dioxide extinguishers and gas expellent cartridges of other extinguishers should be recharged or renewed if the loss of gas by weight exceeds 10% of the original charge as stamped on the bottle or cartridge, and the reason for the loss investigated. Spare charges should have the maker's instructions for charging the extinguishers clearly shown and, where the chemicals are liable to deteriorate, the containers should be marked with the date of packing and the date before which renewal is necessary. These spare charges should be supplied either by the makers of the extinguishers or by a firm having an agreement with the makers guaranteeing to supply charges to the original specification.

G19.3 Dry powder extinguishers may suffer from compaction when subject to vibration. At least one should be discharged annually and the retention of contents checked. Where the retention is found to be in excess of 15% of the initial charge, further extinguishers should be discharged.

G19.4 The portable extinguishers provided for machinery spaces must be of a type which discharges a medium suitable for extinguishing oil fires. Portable extinguishers required in the firing spaces and at the oil fuel installations of motor ships having auxiliary oil-fired boilers need not, in general, be additional to similar extinguishers already provided in the combined spaces to meet other Regulations. Where a heating boiler of less than 73.2 kW is installed, one or more of the portable extinguishers already provided in the space should be so positioned as to be readily available for use at the boiler. Where such a heating boiler is located outside the machinery space paragraph G19.5 below applies.

G19.5 Particular attention should be given to positioning portable fire extinguishers in periodically unattended machinery spaces. Generally, a number of extinguishers should be sited at, or adjacent to, the entrance to such spaces having regard to the possible need to attack a fire from outside the space as well as from inside.

G19.6 In galleys which are fitted with oil-fired, gas-fired or electric cooking appliances, and in spaces in which oil-fired or gas-fired domestic boilers are fitted, a sufficient number of portable extinguishers should be provided. The types discharging foam, CO_2 or dry powder will be found most suitable for dealing with oil fires and CO_2 or dry powder for fires at electrical cooking appliances and electrical switchboards

G19.7 Extinguishers of less than 5 kg capacity, provided in addition to regulation requirements, for use in special positions in service spaces e.g. radio room, switchboards, etc. may be accepted provided they comply with the relevant British Standard specifications.

G19.8 The number of such extinguishers in accommodation, cargo and service spaces should not be less than five in passenger ships of 1,000 tons or over. In addition at least one portable fire extinguisher and a fire blanket should be provided in every galley.

G19.9 Every cargo ship of 500 tons or over should be provided with a sufficient number of portable fire extinguishers to ensure that at least one such extinguisher will be readily available for use in any part of the accommodation spaces, service spaces and control stations. The number of such extinguishers should not be less than five in a ship of 1,000 tons or over and not less than three in a ship of 500 tons or over but under 1,000 tons.

G19.10 Non-portable foam, carbon dioxide and dry powder fire extinguishers provided in compliance with these Regulations shall be of approved types and designs and shall meet the requirements of Schedules 2, 3 and 4 in Merchant Shipping Notice MSN 1665 respectively.

G19.11 Portable fire extinguishers provided in compliance with these Regulations shall be approved to the Marine Equipment Directive and be wheelmarked.

G19.12 The number of spare charges for vessels operating on short sea routes may be reduced where arrangements have been made for the ready availability of spare extinguishers or charges. Equivalence may be granted only while the vessel is in service on the designated route, an arrangement is made with an identified reputable supplier and the arrangements for supply of spares can be verified.

G19.13 Dry powder extinguishers should not exceed one half of the total number of extinguishers in either the accommodation spaces or machinery spaces. Flag-in vessels which have only dry powder should, when extinguishers need replacement, replace with foam extinguishers in accordance with this guidance.

4   Fixed fire-extinguishing systems

4.1   Types of fixed fire-extinguishing systems

4.1.1 A fixed fire-extinguishing system required by paragraph 5 below may be any of the following systems:

.1   a fixed gas fire-extinguishing system complying with the provisions of the Fire Safety Systems Code;

.2   a fixed high-expansion foam fire-extinguishing system complying with the provisions of the Fire Safety Systems Code; and

.3   *a fixed pressure water-spraying fire-extinguishing system complying with the provisions of the Fire Safety Systems Code.*

4.1.2 Where a fixed fire-extinguishing system not required by this chapter is installed, it shall meet the requirements of the relevant regulations of this chapter and the Fire Safety Systems Code.

4.1.3 Fire-extinguishing systems using Halon 1211, 1301, and 2402 and perfluorocarbons shall be prohibited.

4.1.4 In general, the Administration shall not permit the use of steam as a fire-extinguishing medium in fixed fire-extinguishing systems. Where the use of steam is permitted by the Administration, it shall be used only in restricted areas as an addition to the required fire-extinguishing system and shall comply with the requirements of the Fire Safety System Code.

4.2   Closing appliances for fixed gas fire-extinguishing systems

Where a fixed gas fire-extinguishing system is used, openings which may admit air to, or allow gas to escape from, a protected space shall be capable of being closed from outside the protected space.

4.3   Storage rooms of fire-extinguishing medium

When the fire-extinguishing medium is stored outside a protected space, it shall be stored in a room which is located behind the forward collision bulkhead, and is used for no other purposes. Any entrance to such a storage room shall preferably be from the open deck and shall be independent of the protected space. If the storage space is located below deck, it shall be located no more than one deck below the open deck and shall be directly accessible by a stairway or ladder from the open deck. Spaces which are located below deck or spaces where access from the open deck is not provided shall be fitted with a mechanical ventilation system designed to take exhaust air from the bottom of the space and shall be sized to provide at least 6 air changes per hour. Access doors shall open outwards, and bulkheads and decks, including doors and other means of closing any opening therein, which form the boundaries between such rooms and adjacent enclosed spaces shall be gastight. For the purpose of the application of tables 9.1 to 9.8, such storage rooms shall be treated as fire control stations.

4.4   Water pumps for other fire-extinguishing systems

Pumps, other than those serving the fire main, required for the provision of water for fire-extinguishing systems required by this chapter, their sources of power and their controls shall be installed outside the space or spaces protected by such systems and shall be so arranged that a fire in the space or spaces protected will not put any such system out of action.

Guidance 10

G20   Smothering gas installations

G20.1 Any gas used as a fire smothering medium in cargo spaces and in boiler and machinery spaces must not either by itself or under expected conditions of use, give off toxic or anaesthetic vapours such as to endanger persons. Gases carried in liquid form should, after discharge into the space for which they are provided, readily evaporate into the gaseous form.

G21   Carbon Dioxide systems

G21.1   Gas cylinders should be constructed in accordance with the BS 5396: 1976 which requires inter alia the tare weight and the water capacity to be stamped on it. The weight of CO_2 permitted in each cylinder should not exceed two-thirds of a kilogram for every litre of water capacity of the cylinder at 15°C. Each cylinder head discharge valve assembly must be fitted with a bursting disc guaranteed to rupture at a pressure of between 177 and 193 bar. The arrangements should permit the free escape of gas from a cylinder when the bursting disc is ruptured but non-return valves should be provided in the discharge system to allow any cylinder or flexible discharge pipe to be disconnected without affecting the use of other cylinders in the system and to prevent any discharge to the CO_2 cylinder storage room when the system is put into operation to smother a fire. Cylinder head discharge valves, if arranged for remote release should be capable of being opened manually in the event of malfunction of the remote release system.

G22   Carbon Dioxide storage rooms

G22.1   The Carbon Dioxide storage rooms should provide access from the open deck in an emergency for personnel wearing breathing apparatus, be well illuminated, dry and well ventilated and there should be no risk to personnel from leakage or from bursting disc rupture. The storage rooms should not be accessible directly from boiler, machinery, accommodation or cargo spaces. The space should be reserved solely for the purpose of the CO_2 fire extinguishing system. The ambient temperature should not exceed 60°C and where adjacent spaces are likely to be at higher temperatures, special precautions such as insulation of boundaries or power assisted ventilation should be provided to prevent the overheating. Suitable means should be provided for the cylinders to be weighed as necessary. Attention is drawn to the inability of liquid level detectors to operate satisfactorily when the ambient temperature is near or above the critical temperature which for CO_2 is 30.5°C. The space should permit inspection, testing, maintenance and operation of the system to be carried out easily and safely.

G22.2   As the discharge must be maintained from the liquid content of the cylinder a suitable internal pipe must be fitted for this purpose. Cylinders fitted with such internal pipes should be marked such that they can be easily distinguished from CO_2 cylinders not fitted with an internal pipe and used for refrigeration purposes. It should be noted that small CO_2 cylinders used for providing the control gas for gas operated discharge systems are not provided with internal pipes.

G23   Distribution and release arrangements and test requirements

G23.1   The distribution valves should be of quick opening type to avoid wire drawing and consequent freezing. All power and automatically operated valves should be capable of being manually controlled from a local position in case of malfunction. Where gas pressure from pilot cylinders is used as a means of releasing the remaining cylinders at least two such cylinders should be used simultaneously for such operation. Effective safeguards should be provided against the gas being accidentally released when a CO_2 system is being serviced on board and to guard against the inadvertent, and as far as practicable, the malicious use of the controls after the system has been installed or serviced. To achieve this the discharge of CO_2 from the storage cylinders should be isolated from the machinery space by means of a sector valve and so arranged that the control cabinet door cannot be closed unless the sector valve is in the fully closed position. In installations where the sector valves are gas operated equivalent means of safeguarding the system against inadvertent discharge should be provided on the actuation position. The release arrangements should give an indication if the system has been operated. Automatic time delays should not be incorporated in any of the release arrangements for the system.

G23.2   Distribution piping systems should be of a permanent character and arranged so that CO_2 is effectively distributed throughout the protected spaces through suitably designed nozzles. The arrangements should be such that part of the charge is distributed below the floor plates and over the tank top.

G23.3 The Regulations require that 85% of the required concentrations for machinery spaces and cargo pump rooms is achieved in such spaces within two minutes. However the arrangements should additionally provide for a discharge of at least 50% of the required amount of gas in the first minute of operation. Nozzle sizes determined in accordance with BS 5306: Part 4: 2001 are acceptable provided full details are submitted to enable the designs to be checked against the formulae in the British Standard. Otherwise surveyors may accept distribution systems where the nominal bore of the main supply pipes and associated valves to machinery and cargo pumprooms is not less than the commonly accepted values shown against gas throughput in the table below.

Maximum quantity of required CO_2 in Kg	Nominal bore (mm)
45	12
100	20
125	25
270	32
450	40
1,100	50
1,600	65
2,000	80
3,200	90
4,700	100
7,000	125

G23.4 Distribution pipes should normally be not less than 20mm nominal bore but short lengths of dual terminal pipes may be 12mm nominal bore. The distribution manifolds and the pipes or flexible hoses between the cylinders and the distribution manifolds should be guaranteed by the makers or suppliers to have been satisfactorily tested to a pressure of at least 190 bar. Any fittings in this section of pipework should be of steel or acceptable non-ferrous material and be capable of withstanding the same test pressure. The makers or suppliers should guarantee that not less than 10% of the pipes from the distribution manifolds to the spaces to be protected have been satisfactorily tested to a hydraulic pressure of at least 122 bar. Any fittings in the open ended pipework downstream of the distribution valves should be capable of withstanding the same test pressure and be suitable for their intended duty.

G23.5 Carbon dioxide pipes to cargo holds should not pass through machinery spaces where this can possibly be avoided. When CO_2 pipes have to pass through machinery spaces no objection need be raised subject to the following:

.1 the suppliers should confirm that all CO_2 pipes used within the machinery space have been tested to 122 bar; and

.2 the surveyor should satisfy himself, e.g. by testing a sample joint to 122 bar or by other means, that the jointing arrangements are sufficient for the intended service.

G23.6 The joints of CO_2 gas pipes should be made by suitable barrel couplings, cone connections, flanges or welding. The pipes should not be weakened by exposed screw threads, and running couplings are not acceptable. If jointing material is used it should be as thin as practicable. After installation, all pipes should be tested, either by a discharge of the smothering gas into the pipes or with compressed air to a pressure of about 7 bar with the discharge opening closed to ensure no leaking will occur. There should be no permanent connections between the CO_2 system and any compressed air system. After the pressure tests have been completed, it should be ensured that all plugs and blank flanges have been removed from the distribution system and that all pipes are clear and correctly connected according to the marking on the distribution valve chest.

G24   Operation and instructions

G24.1 Instructions for operating the installation must be displayed near the remote operating controls, distribution control valves and also near the gas cylinders. Such instructions should state that when the remote release controls are used, the cylinder storage room should be checked to confirm that the medium has been discharged. When the installation is used to protect the pump room or cargo tanks of a tanker and similar spaces, a notice should be displayed indicating that the system should not be used for inerting purposes unless the compartment is gas free since the injection of CO_2 may generate a static charge capable of igniting flammable atmospheres.

G24.2 When the means for putting the system into operation are located within a compartment which may be locked, e.g. the CO_2 cylinder room, one key to such a compartment should be provided adjacent to the entrance in a suitably marked glass-fronted box. Normally, mechanical ventilation of the protected space should be capable of being shut down manually. Where this is achieved automatically on release of CO_2, over ride facilities that can be rapidly operated without entry into the protected space should be provided to enable spaces to be ventilated after the injection of CO_2. Suitable notices should be posted by the ventilation system controls to indicate that provisions for automatic ventilation shut down have been fitted and where these are located. Notices should be posted on the entrances to every space protected by CO_2 indicating that the space is so protected and that personnel should evacuate the space immediately on hearing the CO_2 alarm.

G25   Alarms

G25.1 The means provided for giving audible alarm referred to in the Regulations should be distinct from all other alarms. When such means are electric, the power should be obtained from the emergency source batteries or through the emergency switchboard. Supplies for air operated devices should be taken from the main air receivers through a safeguarded supply system. When fitted in pump rooms, such alarms if electric should be intrinsically safe and if of the air operated type should be connected to a safeguarded moisture free supply. The arrangements should be such that the alarm is given automatically before the release of CO_2. Interlocks or time delays to delay operation of the release mechanisms are not acceptable.

G26   Exhaust ducts from galley ranges

G26.1 When CO_2 is to be used as the fixed means of extinguishing fires in galley ducts, the following criteria are recommended:

    .1   the system should comply with the appropriate recommendations set out in NFPA 12: 2000 (Standards on CO_2 Extinguishing Systems);

    .2   the recommended flooding factor should be 2 kg/m3 of duct volume, representing a concentration of 65%; and

    .3   the duct must be designed to withstand the calculated pressure which will occur within the duct after discharge of the gas, with the dampers closed.

G27   Bulk CO_2 systems

G27.1 In systems in which refrigerated liquid CO_2 stored in bulk is utilised the design of the storage vessel and details of the relief devices, fittings, instrumentation and control equipment, together with details and specifications of the distribution pipework arrangements should have been approved by or on behalf of the MCA and for which a certificate of approval has been issued.

G27.2   The total charge must not be less than regulation capacity and may be contained in more than one tank. Because the availability of bulk CO_2 on a world-wide basis may be uncertain and that the inability to make good any leakage may cause the ship to be considered unseaworthy, the MCA recommends that about 5% additional capacity be provided.

G27.3   The number of CO_2 leakage paths should be kept to a minimum and be monitored with audible and visual alarms where necessary.

G27.4   Refrigerating units should be duplicated and arranged for automatic standby duties.

G27.5   An automatic alarm should be fitted to operate at not more than 2% loss of contents.

G27.6   Duplicate means of ascertaining contents measurements should be fitted or supplied.

G27.7   Alarm systems should be powered from two sources, one of which should be the emergency source of electrical power.

G27.8   One complete refrigerating unit should be powered by the emergency source of power; cooling water to condensers may be obtained from the emergency fire pump through temporary connections from the fire main.

G27.9   Relief valve arrangements should be in duplicate on a changeover valve assembly to permit replacements in service, means being provided to ensure that at least one relief valve is in communication with the tank. The discharge should be led to a safe place outside the room in which the tank is situated. Alternative proposals will be considered on their merits.

G28   Distribution and test requirement

G28.1   Distribution and test requirements should generally follow the instructions for high pressure systems except that the piping sizes given for guidance in G10.23.3 are too small for the discharge rates required by regulation in the case of bulk systems due to the lower initial pressure in the storage containers. Full details of the distribution pipe which should comply with the requirements of BS 5306: Part 4: 2001 or equivalent should be submitted to MCA Headquarters for consideration.

G29   Foam installations

G29.1   As the present tendency in machinery space arrangements is to site items of machinery on flats, especially in vessels having aft engine room installations, the arrangements for distributing foam in connection with oil-fired boilers, oil fuel units, etc. should be considered in relation to the possibility of fire spreading from one place to another or of oil spraying from a burst pipe being ignited. Means should be provided for foam to be effectively directed by fixed sprayers on to the main fire hazards. Sufficient foam should be provided to cover to a depth of 150mm all areas over which oil is liable to spread.

G29.2   The provision of coamings in way of boilers, diesel generators etc. whilst preventing the spread of fire in some instances, cannot always be guaranteed to do so, e.g. oil spraying from leaking flanges, and the flats on which such items are situated should therefore be protected by the foam installation and their areas included with the tank top area in the assessment of the required quantity of foam. The emergency fire pump capacity should be suitably increased if it is necessary to maintain water supply from that source. Distribution pipes should in general be of steel, galvanised inside and outside, and provision for flushing with fresh water should be incorporated.

5   *Fire-extinguishing arrangements in machinery spaces*

5.1   Machinery spaces containing oil-fired boilers or oil fuel units

5.1.1 Fixed fire-extinguishing systems

Machinery spaces of category A containing oil-fired boilers or oil fuel units shall be provided with any one of the fixed fire-extinguishing systems in paragraph 4.1. In each case, if the engine-room and boiler room are not entirely separate, or if fuel oil can drain from the boiler room into the engine-room, the combined engine and boiler rooms shall be considered as one compartment.

5.1.2   Additional fire-extinguishing arrangements

5.1.2.1 There shall be in each boiler room or at an entrance outside of the boiler room at least one portable foam applicator unit complying with the provisions of the Fire Safety Systems Code.

5.1.2.2 There shall be at least two portable foam extinguishers or equivalent in each firing space in each boiler room and in each space in which a part of the oil fuel installation is situated. There shall be not less than one approved foam-type extinguisher of at least 135 l capacity or equivalent in each boiler room. These extinguishers shall be provided with hoses on reels suitable for reaching any part of the boiler room. In the case of domestic boilers of less than 175 kW an approved foam-type extinguisher of at least 135 l capacity is not required.

5.1.2.3 In each firing space there shall be a receptacle containing at least 0.1 m3 sand, sawdust impregnated with soda, or other approved dry material, along with a suitable shovel for spreading the material. An approved portable extinguisher may be substituted as an alternative.

5.2   Machinery spaces containing internal combustion machinery

5.2.1   Fixed fire-extinguishing systems

Machinery spaces of category A containing internal combustion machinery shall be provided with one of the fixed fire-extinguishing systems in paragraph 4.1.

5.2.2   Additional fire-extinguishing arrangements

5.2.2.1 There shall be at least one portable foam applicator unit complying with the provisions of the Fire Safety Systems Code.

5.2.2.2 There shall be in each such space approved foam-type fire extinguishers, each of at least 45 l capacity or equivalent, sufficient in number to enable foam or its equivalent to be directed on to any part of the fuel and lubricating oil pressure systems, gearing and other fire hazards. In addition, there shall be provided a sufficient number of portable foam extinguishers or equivalent which shall be so located that no point in the space is more than 10 m walking distance from an extinguisher and that there are at least two such extinguishers in each such space. For smaller spaces of cargo ships the Administration may consider relaxing this requirement.

5.3   Machinery spaces containing steam turbines or enclosed steam engines

5.3.1   Fixed fire-extinguishing systems

In spaces containing steam turbines or enclosed steam engines used for main propulsion or other purposes having in the aggregate a total output of not less than 375 kW, one of the fire-extinguishing systems specified in paragraph 4.1 shall be provided if such spaces are periodically unattended.

5.3.2   Additional fire-extinguishing arrangements

5.3.2.1 There shall be approved foam fire extinguishers, each of at least 45 l capacity or equivalent, sufficient in number to enable foam or its equivalent to be directed on to any part of the pressure lubrication system, on to any part of the casings enclosing pressure-lubricated parts of the turbines, engines or associated gearing, and any other fire hazards. However, such extinguishers shall not be required if protection, at least equivalent to that required by this subparagraph, is provided in such spaces by a fixed fire-extinguishing system fitted in compliance with paragraph 4.1.

5.3.2.2 There shall be a sufficient number of portable foam extinguishers or equivalent which shall be so located that no point in the space is more than 10 m walking distance from an extinguisher and that there are at least two such extinguishers in each such space, except that such extinguishers shall not be required in addition to any provided in compliance with paragraph 5.1.2.2.

5.4   Other machinery spaces

Where, in the opinion of the Administration, a fire hazard exists in any machinery space for which no specific provisions for fire-extinguishing appliances are prescribed in paragraphs 5.1, 5.2 and 5.3, there shall be provided in, or adjacent to, that space such a number of approved portable fire extinguishers or other means of fire extinction as the Administration may deem sufficient.

5.5   Additional requirements for passenger ships

In passenger ships carrying more than 36 passengers, each machinery space of category A shall be provided with at least two suitable water fog applicators.*

5.6   Fixed local application fire-fighting systems

5.6.1   Paragraph 5.6 shall apply to passenger ships of 500 gross tonnage and above and cargo ships of 2,000 gross tonnage and above.

5.6.2   Machinery spaces of category A above 500 m³ in volume shall, in addition to the fixed fire-extinguishing system required in paragraph 5.1.1, be protected by an approved type of fixed water-based or equivalent local application fire-fighting

---

* A water fog applicator might consist of a metal L-shaped pipe, the long limb being about 2 m in length, capable of being fitted to a fire hose, and the short limb being about 250 mm in length, fitted with a fixed water fog nozzle or capable of being fitted with a water spray nozzle.

system, based on the guidelines developed by the Organization.‡ In the case of periodically unattended machinery spaces, the fire-extinguishing system shall have both automatic and manual release capabilities. In the case of continuously manned machinery spaces, the fire-extinguishing system is only required to have a manual release capability.

5.6.3 Fixed local application fire-extinguishing systems are to protect areas such as the following without the necessity of engine shutdown, personnel evacuation, or sealing of the spaces:

.1 the fire hazard portions of internal combustion machinery used for the ship's main propulsion and power generation;

.2 boiler fronts;

.3 the fire hazard portions of incinerators; and

.4 purifiers for heated fuel oil.

5.6.4 Activation of any local application system shall give a visual and distinct audible alarm in the protected space and at continuously manned stations. The alarm shall indicate the specific system activated. The system alarm requirements described within this paragraph are in addition to, and not a substitute for, the detection and fire alarm system required elsewhere in this chapter.

Guidance 10

G30   Non-portable extinguishers in machinery spaces

G30.1 The length of hose on non-portable extinguishers should not in general exceed that provided by the makers except where the lengthening of the hose will not reduce the projection of the froth below the distance specified in the Regulations, i.e. 14m for extinguishers of 135 l and over, and 10 m for extinguishers of under 135 l. Non-portable dry powder extinguishers are not acceptable as the equivalents of non-portable carbon dioxide or foam extinguishers. No objection need be raised to their acceptance as additional equipment. When used in conjunction with foam equipment the powder used should be of a foam compatible type.

G30.2 It is recommended that non-portable extinguishers be secured by a band type bracket fitted in halves round the body of the extinguisher with a non-corrodible hinge and securing pin. Whatever method is chosen to secure the extinguisher, it should be capable of ready release without the use of tools.

G30.3 Because of the deterioration to which the ingredients of foam making liquids are liable at temperatures of 38°C or over, portable foam fire extinguishers should be kept in as cool a place as possible. Additionally, they should not be stowed in a position where the ambient temperature is liable to fall below 0°C. Dry powder and CO_2 extinguishers are generally considered suitable for use at temperatures down to –30°C, but the latter type should not be exposed to corrosive conditions or to a temperature exceeding 60°C. The extinguishing media provided adjacent to any given fire risk should be suitable for the type of fire risk involved.

‡ Refer to the Guidelines for the approval of fixed water-based local application fire-fighting systems for use in category A machinery spaces (MSC/Circ.913).

6   *Fire-extinguishing arrangements in control stations, accommodation and service spaces*

6.1   Sprinkler systems in passenger ships

6.1.1 Passenger ships carrying more than 36 passengers shall be equipped with an automatic sprinkler, fire detection and fire alarm system of an approved type complying with the requirements of the Fire Safety Systems Code in all control stations, accommodation and service spaces, including corridors and stairways. Alternatively, control stations, where water may cause damage to essential equipment, may be fitted with an approved fixed fire-extinguishing system of another type. Spaces having little or no fire risk such as voids, public toilets, carbon dioxide rooms and similar spaces need not be fitted with an automatic sprinkler system.

6.1.2 In passenger ships carrying not more than 36 passengers, when a fixed smoke detection and fire alarm system complying with the provisions of the Fire Safety Systems Code is provided only in corridors, stairways and escape routes within accommodation spaces, an automatic sprinkler system shall be installed in accordance with regulation 7.5.3.2.

6.2   Sprinkler systems for cargo ships

In cargo ships in which method IIC specified in regulation 9.2.3.1.1.2 is adopted, an automatic sprinkler, fire detection and fire alarm system shall be fitted in accordance with the requirements in regulation 7.5.5.2.

6.3   Spaces containing flammable liquid

6.3.1 Paint lockers shall be protected by:

.1   *a carbon dioxide system, designed to give a minimum volume of free gas equal to 40% of the gross volume of the protected space;*

.2   *a dry powder system, designed for at least 0.5 kg powder/m³;*

.3   *a water spraying or sprinkler system, designed for 5 l/m² min. Water spraying systems may be connected to the fire main of the ship; or*

.4   *a system providing equivalent protection, as determined by the Administration.*

In all cases, the system shall be operable from outside the protected space.

6.3.2 Flammable liquid lockers shall be protected by an appropriate fire-extinguishing arrangement approved by the Administration.

6.3.3 For lockers of a deck area of less than 4 m², which do not give access to accommodation spaces, a portable carbon dioxide fire extinguisher sized to provide a minimum volume of free gas equal to 40% of the gross volume of the space may be accepted in lieu of a fixed system. A discharge port shall be arranged in the locker to allow the discharge of the extinguisher without having to enter into the protected space. The required portable fire extinguisher shall be stowed adjacent to the port. Alternatively, a port or hose connection may be provided to facilitate the use of fire main water.

6.4   Deep-fat cooking equipment

Deep-fat cooking equipment shall be fitted with the following:

.1   *an automatic or manual fire-extinguishing system tested to an international standard acceptable to the Organization;**

.2   *a primary and backup thermostat with an alarm to alert the operator in the event of failure of either thermostat;*

.3   *arrangements for automatically shutting off the electrical power upon activation of the fire-extinguishing system;*

.4   *an alarm for indicating operation of the fire-extinguishing system in the galley where the equipment is installed; and*

.5   *controls for manual operation of the fire-extinguishing system which are clearly labelled for ready use by the crew.*

Guidance 10

G31   Automatic sprinkler systems

G31.1 Paragraph 2.3.3.2 of Chapter 8 of the FSS Code – the nominal area is defined as being the gross, horizontal projection of the area to be covered.

G31.2 Instructions for carrying out of periodic tests should be exhibited prominently at the control station.

G32   Deep fat fryer standards

G32.1 Deep fat fryers are included in the Marine Equipment Directive and on UK ships should be so approved and wheel marked.

7   Fire-extinguishing arrangements in cargo spaces

7.1   Fixed gas fire-extinguishing systems for general cargo

7.1.1 Except as provided for in paragraph 7.2, the cargo spaces of passenger ships of 1,000 gross tonnage and upwards shall be protected by a fixed carbon dioxide or inert gas fire-extinguishing system complying with the provisions of the Fire Safety Systems Code or by a fixed high-expansion foam fire-extinguishing system which gives equivalent protection.

7.1.2 Where it is shown to the satisfaction of the Administration that a passenger ship is engaged on voyages of such short duration that it would be unreasonable to apply the requirements of paragraph 7.1.1 and also in ships of less than 1,000 gross tonnage, the arrangements in cargo spaces shall be to the satisfaction of the Administration, provided that the ship is fitted with steel hatch covers and effective means of closing all ventilators and other openings leading to the cargo spaces.

---

* Refer to the recommendations by the International Organization for Standardization, in particular publication ISO 15371:2000, Fire-extinguishing systems for protection of galley deep-fat cooking equipment.

7.1.3 Except for ro-ro and vehicle spaces, cargo spaces on cargo ships of 2,000 gross tonnage and upwards shall be protected by a fixed carbon dioxide or inert gas fire-extinguishing system complying with the provisions of the Fire Safety Systems Code, or by a fire-extinguishing system which gives equivalent protection.

7.1.4 The Administration may exempt from the requirements of paragraphs 7.1.3 and 7.2, cargo spaces of any cargo ship if constructed, and solely intended for, the carriage of ore, coal, grain, unseasoned timber, non-combustible cargoes or cargoes which, in the opinion of the Administration, constitute a low fire risk.* Such exemptions may be granted only if the ship is fitted with steel hatch covers and effective means of closing all ventilators and other openings leading to the cargo spaces. When such exemptions are granted, the Administration shall issue an Exemption Certificate, irrespective of the date of construction of the ship concerned, in accordance with regulation I/12(a)(vi), and shall ensure that the list of cargoes the ship is permitted to carry is attached to the Exemption Certificate.

7.2   Fixed gas fire-extinguishing systems for dangerous goods

A ship engaged in the carriage of dangerous goods in any cargo spaces shall be provided with a fixed carbon dioxide or inert gas fire-extinguishing system complying with the provisions of the Fire Safety Systems Code or with a fire-extinguishing system which, in the opinion of the Administration, gives equivalent protection for the cargoes carried.

Guidance 10

G33   Fire extinguishing arrangements in cargo spaces

G33.1 For vessels described in paragraph 7.1.3 and carrying Cargoes listed in table 2 of MSC Circular 671 and for which a fixed gas system is ineffective, the cargo space shall be provided with an approved fire extinguishing system which can be shown to give equivalent fire protection.

8   Cargo tank protection

8.1   Fixed deck foam fire-extinguishing systems

8.1.1 For tankers of 20,000 tonnes deadweight and upwards, a fixed deck foam fire-extinguishing system shall be provided complying with the provisions of the Fire Safety Systems Code, except that, in lieu of the above, the Administration, after having given consideration to the ship's arrangement and equipment, may accept other fixed installations if they afford protection equivalent to the above, in accordance with regulation I/5. The requirements for alternative fixed installations shall comply with the requirements in paragraph 8.1.2.

8.1.2 In accordance with paragraph 8.1.1, where the Administration accepts an equivalent fixed installation in lieu of the fixed deck foam fire-extinguishing system, the installation shall:

---

* Refer to the Code of Safe Practice for Solid Bulk Cargoes, emergency schedule B14, entry for coal, and to the List of solid bulk cargoes which are non-combustible or constitute a low fire risk or for which a fixed gas fire-extinguishing system is ineffective (MSC/Circ.671).

.1   be capable of extinguishing spill fires and also preclude ignition of spilled oil not yet ignited; and

.2   be capable of combating fires in ruptured tanks.

8.1.3 Tankers of less than 20,000 tonnes deadweight shall be provided with a deck foam fire-extinguishing system complying with the requirements of the Fire Safety Systems Code.

Guidance 10

G34   Deck foam systems

G34.1 Foam mains should be routed clear of tanker pump rooms. When this is impracticable details of alternative arrangements should be submitted for consideration.

G34.2 In any chemical tanker the type of foam concentrate should be appropriate for the chemicals listed on the Certificate of Fitness i.e. either a regular foam or an alcohol resistant foam. In cases where a foam concentrate of each type is required an all-purpose foam should be used.

9   Protection of cargo pump-rooms in tankers

9.1   Fixed fire-extinguishing systems

Each cargo pump-room shall be provided with one of the following fixed fire-extinguishing systems operated from a readily accessible position outside the pump-room. Cargo pump-rooms shall be provided with a system suitable for machinery spaces of category A.

9.1.1 A carbon dioxide fire-extinguishing system complying with the provisions the Fire Safety Systems Code and with the following:

.1   the alarms giving audible warning of the release of fire-extinguishing medium shall be safe for use in a flammable cargo vapour/air mixture; and

.2   a notice shall be exhibited at the controls stating that, due to the electrostatic ignition hazard, the system is to be used only for fire extinguishing and not for inerting purposes.

9.1.2 A high-expansion foam fire-extinguishing system complying with the provisions of the Fire Safety Systems Code, provided that the foam concentrate supply is suitable for extinguishing fires involving the cargoes carried.

9.1.3 A fixed pressure water-spraying fire-extinguishing system complying with the provisions of the Fire Safety Systems Code.

9.2   Quantity of fire-extinguishing medium

Where the fire-extinguishing medium used in the cargo pump-room system is also used in systems serving other spaces, the quantity of medium provided or its delivery rate need not be more than the maximum required for the largest compartment.

10   *Fire-fighter's outfits*

10.1   Types of fire-fighter's outfits

Fire-fighter's outfits shall comply with the Fire Safety Systems Code.

10.2   Number of fire-fighter's outfits

10.2.1   Ships shall carry at least two fire-fighter's outfits.

10.2.2   In addition, in passenger ships there shall be provided:

.1   *for every 80 m, or part thereof, of the aggregate of the lengths of all passenger spaces and service spaces on the deck which carries such spaces or, if there is more than one such deck, on the deck which has the largest aggregate of such lengths, two fire-fighter's outfits and, in addition, two sets of personal equipment, each set comprising the items stipulated in the Fire Safety Systems Code. In passenger ships carrying more than 36 passengers, two additional fire-fighter's outfits shall be provided for each main vertical zone. However, for stairway enclosures which constitute individual main vertical zones and for the main vertical zones in the fore or aft end of a ship which do not contain spaces of categories (6), (7), (8) or (12) defined in regulation 9.2.2.3, no additional fire-fighter's outfits are required; and*

.2   *on ships carrying more than 36 passengers, for each pair of breathing apparatus, one water fog applicator which shall be stored adjacent to such apparatus.*

10.2.3   In addition, in tankers, two fire-fighter's outfits shall be provided.

10.2.4   The Administration may require additional sets of personal equipment and breathing apparatus, having due regard to the size and type of the ship.

10.2.5   Two spare charges shall be provided for each required breathing apparatus. Passenger ships carrying not more than 36 passengers and cargo ships that are equipped with suitably located means for fully recharging the air cylinders free from contamination need carry only one spare charge for each required apparatus. In passenger ships carrying more than 36 passengers, at least two spare charges for each breathing apparatus shall be provided.

10.3   Storage of fire-fighter's outfits

10.3.1   The fire-fighter's outfits or sets of personal equipment shall be kept ready for use in an easily accessible location that is permanently and clearly marked and, where more than one fire-fighter's outfit or more than one set of personal equipment is carried, they shall be stored in widely separated positions.

10.3.2   In passenger ships, at least two fire-fighter's outfits and, in addition, one set of personal equipment shall be available at any one position. At least two fire-fighter's outfits shall be stored in each main vertical zone.

Guidance 10

G35   The adjustable safety belt or harness together with the snap hook should be to BS EN 354, 355, 358, 361 and 365 requirements. To ensure that the safety belt or harness is compatible with the breathing apparatus, each type of safety belt or harness supplied by the manufacturers should be submitted for the drop test at the same time as the apparatus is submitted for approval.

G36   The point of attachment of the life and signalling line to the safety belt or harness should be such as to be easily removable by the wearer. Where it is necessary to use a pennant for this purpose the attachment of pennant to the safety harness should be such that it cannot readily be detached. Snap hooks should be of materials so far as possible resistant to incendive sparking on impact.

G37   The firemen's outfits required by the Regulations should be stowed in readily accessible positions which are not likely to be easily cut off by fire.

G38   Air compressors

G38.1 Where special compressors intended solely for the charging of compressed air cylinders are carried on board, surveyors should ensure that they are of adequate capacity and that the air intakes are sited so as to preclude the ingress of water or noxious fumes, even under adverse weather conditions. Also the vessel's standing orders should contain the manufacturer's detailed instructions for operating and servicing the compressor and ancillary equipment, e.g. filters, dryers, etc. At least one member of the crew should be competent in the use of the equipment.

G39   Marking

G39.1 Where in any ship breathing apparatus cylinders are carried having different working pressures, in addition to the normal marking on the cylinder the working pressure should be prominently marked in paint on the cylinder.

G40   Training

G40.1 In addition to the fully charged spare cylinders required by the Regulations it is recommended that where no means for recharging such cylinders is provided additional cylinder capacity be provided for training purposes. Cylinders intended for such purposes should be prominently marked to indicate their intended use, e.g. by the use of waterproof adhesive labels or tape.

G41   Safety lamps

G41.1 They may be either the hand lamp or cap-lamp type. The batteries must be re-chargeable and the hand lamps must be fitted with means for easy attachment of the lamp to the user at about waist level.

G41.2 Safety lamps for use with firemen's outfits they should be Class I. These lamps are intended for use in any ship, including those carrying cargoes which are, or may give rise to, flammable gases and vapours. All lamps accepted in this Class are suitable for use in petroleum tankers but may not be suitable for all flammable cargoes; special attention should be paid to ensure that certification is suitable for use with the cargoes of bulk chemical carriers and liquefied gas carriers.

Structural integrity

1   Purpose

The purpose of this regulation is to maintain structural integrity of the ship, preventing partial or whole collapse of the ship structures due to strength deterioration by heat. For this purpose, materials used in the ships' structure shall ensure that the structural integrity is not degraded due to fire.

2   Material of hull, superstructures, structural bulkheads, decks and deckhouses

The hull, superstructures, structural bulkheads, decks and deckhouses shall be constructed of steel or other equivalent material. For the purpose of applying the definition of steel or other equivalent material as given in regulation 3.43, the "applicable fire exposure" shall be according to the integrity and insulation standards given in tables 9.1 to 9.4. For example, where divisions such as decks or sides and ends of deckhouses are permitted to have "B–0" fire integrity, the "applicable fire exposure" shall be half an hour.

Guidance 11

G1   Hinged or portable decks

G1.1   Moveable decks with their connecting ramps should be constructed of steel or equivalent material. Proposals to construct such decks with aluminium should be referred initially to MCA Headquarters.

G2   False decks

G2.1   False decks should be constructed of steel or equivalent material except that small areas used for dancing in dining rooms may be constructed of wood which should be included in the total volume of combustibles referred to in regulation 5.3.2.3. A false deck is any deck which is fitted above the level of a structural deck for any purpose and is sometimes referred to as a false or raised floor.

G3   'A' Class division

G3.1   Subject to any additional requirements for watertight or load-bearing structure, the minimum scantlings required for steel and aluminium alloy 'A' Class divisions should be derived from the following tables and should be insulated as indicated in the guidance G11.8.2 to paragraph 3.

G4   Scantlings of steel 'A' Class divisions

G4.1   Where swedges are used to stiffen 'A' Class bulkheads the spacing should not exceed 760mm.

Table showing the geometrical properties required when using steel stiffeners or beams spaced 760mm apart and without end connections.

Span of Stiffener or Beam	Plating Thickness	Geometrical Properties in conjunction with plating 610mm x thickness	
Metres	*mm*	*Moment of Inertia (I)* *cm4*	*Section Modulus (I/Y)* *cm3*
2.4	4.0	87.5	12.0
2.7	4.5	130.0	17.0
3.0	5.0	175.0	22.0
3.3	5.5	237.5	27.0
3.6	6.0	305.0	32.0

(Note: The spacing of stiffeners or beams should not normally exceed 760mm. However, where stiffeners or beams are spaced other than 760mm apart their moment of inertia and section modulus should be increased or decreased in direct proportion to the distance apart.)

G5 Scantlings of aluminium alloy 'A' Class divisions

G5.1 Where 'A' Class divisions are constructed of aluminium alloy the aluminium structure should have the equivalent strength and stiffness to that of steel having the same length of unsupported span – see table.

Table giving the ratios to be used to obtain equivalent strength values when using aluminium alloys

Required Plating thickness of aluminium alloy	=	1.4 x thickness of steel plating
Required Inertia (I) of aluminium alloy stiffeners or beams	=	2.8 x inertia (I) of steel stiffeners or beams
Required Modulus (I/Y) of aluminium alloy stiffeners or beams	=	2.35 x Modulus (I/Y) of steel stiffeners or beams

G6 Scantlings of steel or aluminium alloy 'B' Class divisions

G6.1 Subject to any additional requirements for load-bearing structure, the minimum scantlings required for steel or aluminium alloy 'B' Class divisions should be the same as those for steel and aluminium alloy 'A' Class divisions as derived from the preceding tables.

G6.2 Aluminium alloy 'B' Class divisions of B–15 and B–0 should be insulated respectively to the same standards as aluminium alloy 'A' Class divisions of A–15 and A–0 standards unless an approval certificate has been issued for the appropriate 'B' Class standard.

> *3 Structure of aluminium alloy*
>
> *Unless otherwise specified in paragraph 2, in cases where any part of the structure is of aluminium alloy, the following shall apply:*
>
> > *.1 the insulation of aluminium alloy components of "A" or "B" class divisions, except structure which, in the opinion of the Administration, is non-load-bearing, shall be such that the temperature of the structural core does not rise more than 200°C above the ambient temperature at any time during the applicable fire exposure to the standard fire test; and*
> >
> > *.2 special attention shall be given to the insulation of aluminium alloy components of columns, stanchions and other structural members required to support lifeboat and liferaft stowage, launching and embarkation areas, and "A" and "B" class divisions to ensure:*
> >
> > > *.2.1 that for such members supporting lifeboat and liferaft areas and "A" class divisions, the temperature rise limitation specified in paragraph 3.1 shall apply at the end of one hour; and*
> > >
> > > *.2.2 that for such members required to support "B" class divisions, the temperature rise limitation specified in paragraph 3.1 shall apply at the end of half an hour.*

Guidance 11

G7 Structure supporting lifeboats and liferafts

G7.1 Notwithstanding preceding paragraphs and guidance G9.20, on separation of machinery spaces from other spaces, any aluminium alloy structure which supports the lifeboat, liferaft and marine escape system embarkation, stowage, handling and lowering positions is required to be insulated such that the temperature rise limitation of the structural core shall apply for 60 minutes duration. Such structure should be insulated in the same manner as an aluminium alloy 'A' Class division of A–0 standard.

G8   Aluminium structure for passenger ships

G8.1   Insulating the structure

G8.1.1   Tables 9.1, 9.2, 9.3 and 9.4 of regulation 9 require all bulkheads and decks to be 'A' Class or 'B' Class divisions except for those decks referred to in guidance G9.27 and a limited number of bulkheads in the tables which are permitted to be 'C' Class divisions. Consequently all aluminium alloy bulkheads and decks including the ships side and boundaries of superstructures and deckhouses, except for the decks referred to above and 'C' Class bulkheads, are required by paragraph 3 to be insulated such that the temperature of their structural core does not rise more than 200°C above the ambient temperature when subjected to a standard fire test of 60 and 30 minutes duration in the case of 'A' Class and 'B' Class divisions respectively.

G8.2   Insulating aluminium alloy 'A' Class divisions

G8.2.1   Aluminium alloy has a low melting point and its strength properties are severely diminished at elevated temperatures. 'A' Class divisions constructed of alloy have therefore to be protected against the effect of heat by the fitting of approved fire insulation to all surfaces which may be exposed to a fire. Paragraph 3.1 requires that the insulation of 'A' Class divisions shall be such that the temperature of the aluminium alloy core does not rise more than 200°C above ambient temperature at any time during the standard fire test of 60 minutes duration. This requirement applies to aluminium alloy 'A' Class divisions A–60, A–30, A–15 or A–0 standard. Such divisions should be insulated on both sides, except for decks which should be insulated at least on their underside. Where such divisions form the outer boundaries of the ship's hull, superstructures or deckhouses, only their inside surfaces need to be insulated. Flanges and webs of deep girders should be insulated as part of the structural core, even when they exceed the dimensions of the stiffeners included in the standard structural core of IMO Resolution A 754(18) on which the insulation was tested.

G8.3   Steel or aluminium alloy 'B' Class divisions

G8.3.1   Paragraph 3 requires that the insulation of aluminium alloy 'B' Class divisions shall be such that the temperature of the aluminium alloy core does not rise more than 200°C above the ambient temperature at any time during a standard fire test of 30 minutes duration. This requirement applies to 'B' Class divisions of any standard i.e. B–15 or B–0.

G8.3.2   Steel 'B' Class divisions of B–15 standard should be insulated to the same standard as steel 'A' Class divisions of A–15 standards and aluminium alloy 'B' Class divisions of B–15 and B–0 should be insulated respectively to the same standards as aluminium alloy 'A' Class divisions of A–15 and A–0 unless an approval certificate has been issued for the appropriate 'B' Class standard.

G8.4   Approved insulations

G8.4.1   Approved materials should be used to insulate the aluminium alloy 'A' Class and 'B' Class divisions in accordance with the conditions indicated in the appropriate approval certificates. In the absence of any approvals covering the use of materials as the insulating media for aluminium alloy 'A' Class or 'B' Class divisions of a particular standard then a material which has been approved for a higher standard for aluminium alloy 'A' Class or 'B' Class divisions should be used.

G8.4.2   Any 'C' Class bulkheads constructed of aluminium alloy which are structural bulkheads supporting 'A' Class or 'B' Class decks are also required by paragraph 3 to be insulated such that the temperature of their structural core does not rise more than 200°C above the ambient temperature when subjected to a standard fire test for the same periods as required for the divisions which they are supporting.

G8.4.3 However where 'C' Class bulkheads constructed of aluminium alloy support a deck, parts of which are 'A' Class and 'B' Class divisions, then the bulkheads should be insulated in the same manner as an aluminium alloy 'A' Class bulkhead of A–0 standard.

G8.5   Structure supporting lifeboats and liferafts (paragraph 3.2)

G8.5.1 Paragraph 3.2 should also be applied to structure supporting marine escape system embarkation and stowage areas.

G8.6   Bulkheads and decks not required to be 'A' Class or 'B' Class divisions

G8.6.1 Any 'C' Class bulkheads, or any bulkheads and decks to which the asterisk of tables 9.3 or 9.4 apply and are not thereby required to be of 'A' Class standard which are constructed of aluminium alloy and are structural bulkheads or decks supporting 'A' Class or 'B' Class divisions are required to be insulated such that the temperature of their structural core does not rise more than 200°C above the ambient temperature when subjected to a standard fire test for the same periods of time as required for the divisions which they are supporting.

G8.6.2 Any structural bulkheads and decks referred to in the preceding paragraph, which are constructed of aluminium alloy and do not support any 'A' Class or 'B' Class divisions, are still required (9.2.2.4) to be of an 'equivalent material' which, as defined, implies that they should be insulated in order to provide structural and integrity properties equivalent to steel at the end of an appropriate fire test for such bulkheads and decks as they do for 'A' Class and 'B' Class divisions. Nor do the Regulations indicate that the core temperature limitations of 200°C should apply to such bulkheads and decks. Consequently those bulkheads and decks need only be protected respectively by a non-combustible lining or ceiling, or, in the absence of a non-combustible lining or ceiling, by a 25mm thickness of an approved 'A' Class mineral wool insulation.

G9   Aluminium structure for cargo ships and tankers

G9.1   Cargo ships

G9.1.1 Insulating the structure

G9.1.1.1 Tables 9.5 and 9.6 in regulation 9.2.3.3 require all bulkheads and decks to be 'A' Class or 'B' Class divisions except for those bulkheads which are permitted to be 'C' Class divisions and those bulkheads and decks which have an asterisk notation and are consequently permitted to be of aluminium alloy with no 'A' Class standard.

G9.1.1.2 Therefore all aluminium alloy bulkheads and decks except for 'C' Class bulkheads and bulkheads and decks with no 'A' Class standard are to be insulated such that the temperature of their structural core does not rise more than 200°C above the ambient temperature when subjected to a standard fire test of 60 minutes and 30 minutes duration in the case of 'A' Class division and 'B' Class division respectively. See paragraph 3 of this regulation. Guidance G8.2 to G8.6 apply similarly to cargo ships.

G9.2   Tankers

G9.2.1 Insulating the structure

G9.2.1.1 Tables 9.7 and 9.8 in regulation 9.2.4.2 require all bulkheads and decks to be 'A' Class or 'B' Class divisions except for those bulkheads which are permitted to be 'C' Class divisions and those bulkheads and decks which have an asterisk notation and are consequently permitted to be of aluminium alloy with no 'A' Class standard.

G9.2.1.2 Additionally however, all aluminium alloy bulkheads and decks except for 'C' Class bulkheads and bulkheads and decks with no 'A' Class standard are to be insulated such that the temperature of their structural core does not rise more than 200°C above the ambient temperature when subjected to a standard fire test of 60 minutes and 30 minutes duration in the case of 'A' Class divisions and 'B' Class division respectively. See paragraph 3 of this regulation. Guidance G11.8.2 to G11.8.6 apply similarly to tankers.

4   Machinery spaces of category A

4.1   Crowns and casings

Crowns and casings of machinery spaces of category A shall be of steel construction and shall be insulated as required by tables 9.5 and 9.7, as appropriate.

4.2   Floor plating

The floor plating of normal passageways in machinery spaces of category A shall be made of steel.

5   Materials of overboard fittings

Materials readily rendered ineffective by heat shall not be used for overboard scuppers, sanitary discharges, and other outlets which are close to the waterline and where the failure of the material in the event of fire would give rise to danger of flooding.

6   Protection of cargo tank structure against pressure or vacuum in tankers

6.1   General

The venting arrangements shall be so designed and operated as to ensure that neither pressure nor vacuum in cargo tanks shall exceed design parameters and be such as to provide for:

> .1   the flow of the small volumes of vapour, air or inert gas mixtures caused by thermal variations in a cargo tank in all cases through pressure/vacuum valves; and
>
> .2   the passage of large volumes of vapour, air or inert gas mixtures during cargo loading and ballasting, or during discharging.

6.2   Openings for small flow by thermal variations

Openings for pressure release required by paragraph 6.1.1 shall:

> .1   have as great a height as is practicable above the cargo tank deck to obtain maximum dispersal of flammable vapours, but in no case less than 2 m above the cargo tank deck; and
>
> .2   be arranged at the furthest distance practicable, but not less than 5 m, from the nearest air intakes and openings to enclosed spaces containing a source of ignition and from deck machinery and equipment which may constitute an ignition hazard. Anchor windlass and chain locker openings constitute an ignition hazard.

6.3 Safety measures in cargo tanks

6.3.1 Preventive measures against liquid rising in the venting system

Provisions shall be made to guard against liquid rising in the venting system to a height which would exceed the design head of cargo tanks. This shall be accomplished by high-level alarms or overflow control systems or other equivalent means, together with independent gauging devices and cargo tank filling procedures. For the purposes of this regulation, spill valves are not considered equivalent to an overflow system.

6.3.2 Secondary means for pressure/vacuum relief

A secondary means of allowing full flow relief of vapour, air or inert gas mixtures to prevent over-pressure or under-pressure in the event of failure of the arrangements in paragraph 6.1.2. Alternatively, pressure sensors may be fitted in each tank protected by the arrangement required in paragraph 6.1.2, with a monitoring system in the ship's cargo control room or the position from which cargo operations are normally carried out. Such monitoring equipment shall also provide an alarm facility which is activated by detection of over-pressure or under-pressure conditions within a tank.

6.3.3 Bypasses in vent mains

Pressure/vacuum valves required by paragraph 6.1.1 may be provided with a bypass arrangement when they are located in a vent main or masthead riser. Where such an arrangement is provided there shall be suitable indicators to show whether the bypass is open or closed.

6.3.4 Pressure/vacuum-breaking devices

One or more pressure/vacuum-breaking devices shall be provided to prevent the cargo tanks from being subject to:

.1 *a positive pressure, in excess of the test pressure of the cargo tank, if the cargo were to be loaded at the maximum rated capacity and all other outlets are left shut; and*

.2 *a negative pressure in excess of 700 mm water gauge if the cargo were to be discharged at the maximum rated capacity of the cargo pumps and the inert gas blowers were to fail.*

Such devices shall be installed on the inert gas main unless they are installed in the venting system required by regulation 4.5.3.1 or on individual cargo tanks. The location and design of the devices shall be in accordance with regulation 4.5.3 and paragraph 6.

6.4 Size of vent outlets

Vent outlets for cargo loading, discharging and ballasting required by paragraph 6.1.2 shall be designed on the basis of the maximum designed loading rate multiplied by a factor of at least 1.25 to take account of gas evolution, in order to prevent the pressure in any cargo tank from exceeding the design pressure. The master shall be provided with information regarding the maximum permissible loading rate for each cargo tank and, in the case of combined venting systems, for each group of cargo tanks.

Part D – Escape

Notification of Crew and Passengers

1   Purpose

The purpose of this regulation is to notify crew and passengers of a fire for safe evacuation. For this purpose, a general emergency alarm system and a public address system shall be provided.

2   General emergency alarm system

A general emergency alarm system required by regulation III/6.4.2 shall be used for notifying crew and passengers of a fire.

3   Public address systems in passenger ships

A public address system or other effective means of communication complying with the requirements of regulation III/6.5 shall be available throughout the accommodation and service spaces and control stations and open decks.

Means of Escape

1   Purpose

The purpose of this regulation is to provide means of escape so that persons onboard can safely and swiftly escape to the lifeboat and liferaft embarkation deck. For this purpose, the following functional requirements shall be met:

.1   *safe escape routes shall be provided;*

.2   *escape routes shall be maintained in a safe condition, clear of obstacles; and*

.3   *additional aids for escape shall be provided as necessary to ensure accessibility, clear marking, and adequate design for emergency situations.*

2   General requirements

2.1   Unless expressly provided otherwise in this regulation, at least two widely separated and ready means of escape shall be provided from all spaces or groups of spaces.

2.2   Lifts shall not be considered as forming one of the means of escape as required by this regulation.

Guidance 13

G1   Escape panels in doors

G1.1 It is generally considered that escape panels in 'B' Class doors are unnecessary. However they may be fitted if an owner requires them. In such cases the panels should be constructed in accordance with any details shown on the approved drawings, provided they do not exceed 410mm x 410mm in size. A ventilation opening, when fitted, should be incorporated in the escape panel. Where no details of an escape panel are given the door manufacturer should be requested to submit details of the construction to MCA Headquarters for consideration before use.

G1.2 Escape panels should only be capable of being operated from that side of the door from which a person needs to escape and should be of such a design as to preserve the integrity and insulation standard of the door and prevent any unlawful entry into a space.

G1.3 Escape panels should be marked with the words 'ESCAPE PANEL – KICK OUT' in white letters on a green background.

G2   Locks in doors

G2.1 Every 'B' Class door fitted in a cabin bulkhead should be capable, when locked, of being opened manually from the cabin side other than by means of the key or key card.

G2.2 Any 'B' Class door, other than a cabin door, which is fitted to an opening forming part of an escape route should not be capable of being locked shut, except that when such a door is required to be locked shut by the owner for security reasons keys should be provided on each side of the door in glass fronted boxes fitted close to the door.

G2.3 Alternatively a door which is unlocked in the escape direction may be 'access controlled' subject to suitable safeguards. Digital locks for which the access code is known to appropriate crew members, may be accepted on such doors. (See also specific guidance G13.11 on "doors in crew accommodation").

G3   General requirements – applicable to all ships

G3.1   The general requirements apply to the escape arrangements of all ships – passenger ships, cargo ships and tankers – except where specifically indicated otherwise.

G4   Stairways and ladderways

G4.1   The width is to be measured on the tread within the sides or between the handrails, whichever is the least.

G4.2   Stairways should not extend in a single flight more than one 'tweendeck or a vertical distance of 3.5m whichever is the least. Stairways in adjacent 'tweendecks within the same enclosure should, wherever possible, be offset if sloping in the same direction or slope in different directions.

G4.3   In either case, the stairways should be separated by a landing having its shorter dimension not less than the width of the wider stairway. However when it is only possible to arrange such stairways to slope in the same direction without being offset, they should be separated by a landing having a length not less than 2m.

G4.4   Curved stairways should be such that they do not present a hazard to passengers and crew. It should be borne in mind that such stairways may be used in an emergency situation by both elderly and very young passengers (see also guidance G13.15.2 at the end of paragraph 3).

G4.5   Nosings on treads should be kept to minimum dimensions in order to reduce the risk of passengers and crew tripping over them and should be of the same sectional shape on all treads of a stairway.

G4.6   Stairways and ladderways should be fitted on each side with an efficient handrail, which in the case of stairways should be continued unbroken from the slope of the stairway round each landing to the entrance to the stairway enclosure or connected to the handrails in the corridor whenever the Regulations permit a stairway to be open to the corridor.

G4.7   Stairways and ladderways should, as far as possible, be pitched fore and aft, not athwartships, and should normally be inclined at not less than 45° to the vertical.

G4.8   In general the rise of each step should be kept constant to facilitate easy movement up (or down) the stairway, especially in an emergency situation.

G5   Corridors and doorways

G5.1   Corridors and doorways providing access to and from stairways or open decks should be of sufficient width to prevent congestion and, in the case of those serving stairways, should not be less than the width of the stairways.

G5.2   Handrails should be fitted in corridors at an approximate height of 1000mm above the deck.

G5.3   The width of a corridor should be measured between handrails or the handrail and the opposite bulkhead whichever is applicable.

G6   Escalators

G6.1   Escalators may be treated as stationary stairways for the purpose of this Regulation. (In such cases the surveyor should ensure that adequate deck area is provided in the enclosure at each end of the escalator in order to avoid any congestion. In addition the doors in the enclosure bulkheads should be wide enough to permit passengers to disperse quickly. Due regard should be paid to the design and positioning of the controls so as to reduce the risk of their unauthorised use. The emergency stop controls should however be in positions readily accessible from the escalator).

G7   Hatches

G7.1   Where hatches are provided as the second means of escape for crew from accommodation spaces, the hatches should be of such dimensions as will allow a person to escape wearing a lifejacket.

G7.2   Any hatch provided for escape from crew accommodation or working spaces should not be capable of being locked and should be operable from below and above. It is preferable for such a hatch to be provided with a counter-balance weight for ease of opening. Access to the hatch should be by means of a fixed steel ladder.

G7.3   The surveyor should ensure that escape hatches are so sited that they cannot be overstowed with deck cargo or stores or, in the case of spaces below a special category space or Ro-Ro cargo space, that vehicles cannot be parked over them or prevent them from being opened fully. In some cases it may be necessary to site the hatches on raised kerbs or be protected by substantial stanchions and rails. In no case should painted lines be accepted as the means of protecting such hatches.

G7.4   When the hatches are fitted in 'A' Class or 'B' Class decks, their construction should be such that the integrity and insulation standards of the decks are not impaired.

G8   Escape panels

G8.1   In certain instances, 'escape panels' may be used with advantage to provide an alternative means of escape. However, in no case should an escape route incorporate more than one escape panel.

G8.2   An 'escape panel' should be fitted so that it can be kicked-out with the minimum of effort and should be clearly marked to indicate its purpose. Where an escape panel is utilised to provide an escape to another compartment, the surveyor should ensure that the door to that compartment opens onto a corridor and is capable of being opened from inside at all times.

G8.3   Escape panels should not be fitted in any escape route providing access for passengers to the muster stations or lifeboat, liferaft and marine escape system embarkation positions.

G8.4   Escape panels should not be fitted in 'A' Class bulkheads or doors and when they are fitted in 'B' Class bulkheads or doors their construction should be such that the integrity and insulation standards of the bulkheads and doors are not impaired.

G9   Sleeping rooms in crew accommodation

G9.1   It is necessary to provide an emergency means of escape from sleeping rooms where access to such a sleeping room is by way of a dayroom, there being no direct access by means of a door to the sleeping room from a corridor. Ideally the crew accommodation should be designed so that a sleeping room is so positioned that an emergency escape therefrom is not required. However, where there is a need to provide an emergency escape from a sleeping room, this should be achieved by fitting a clearly marked escape panel to an adjacent room or corridor as indicated in the previous paragraphs on "escape panels" or, where this is not possible, by an escape window or sidescuttle as indicated in guidance G13.14 to paragraph 3.

G9.2   Where a dayroom is fitted with a smoke detector as part of an approved 'fixed fire detection and fire alarm system' a second means of escape will not be required.

G10   Crew messrooms, recreation rooms etc.

G10.1 When messrooms, recreation rooms, cinemas, television rooms and similar communal spaces are provided to accommodate more than 15 crew members at any one time, such spaces in general should have two doors to the adjacent corridor. In cases where this is not possible, in addition to the provision of a door to the corridor, a door to the open deck should be provided, or if this is also not possible, an escape window or sidescuttle may be accepted as indicated in guidance G13.14 to paragraph 3.

G11   Doors in crew accommodation

G11.1 In general, all doors which are not type approved should be of the hinged type. Where it is not practicable to provide a hinged door, a sliding door may be accepted provided that in the case of a 'C' Class door it can be readily removed from its rails from each side of the door or an escape panel is fitted in the sliding door.

G11.2 Doors in an escape route should not normally be locked closed. However, doors which give access to 'sensitive areas' may be locked for security purposes, provided the surveyor is satisfied that the escape routes will remain viable.

3   *Means of escape from control stations, accommodation spaces and service spaces*

3.1   General requirements

3.1.1 Stairways and ladders shall be so arranged as to provide ready means of escape to the lifeboat and liferaft embarkation deck from passenger and crew accommodation spaces and from spaces in which the crew is normally employed, other than machinery spaces.

3.1.2 Unless expressly provided otherwise in this regulation, a corridor, lobby, or part of a corridor from which there is only one route of escape shall be prohibited. Dead-end corridors used in service areas which are necessary for the practical utility of the ship, such as fuel oil stations and athwartship supply corridors, shall be permitted, provided such dead-end corridors are separated from crew accommodation areas and are inaccessible from passenger accommodation areas. Also, a part of a corridor that has a depth not exceeding its width is considered a recess or local extension and is permitted.

3.1.3 All stairways in accommodation and service spaces and control stations shall be of steel frame construction except where the Administration sanctions the use of other equivalent material.

3.1.4 If a radiotelegraph station has no direct access to the open deck, two means of escape from, or access to, the station shall be provided, one of which may be a porthole or window of sufficient size or other means to the satisfaction of the Administration.

3.1.5 Doors in escape routes shall, in general, open in way of the direction of escape, except that:

.1   individual cabin doors may open into the cabins in order to avoid injury to persons in the corridor when the door is opened; and

.2   doors in vertical emergency escape trunks may open out of the trunk in order to permit the trunk to be used both for escape and for access.

3.2   Means of escape in passenger ships

3.2.1 Escape from spaces below the bulkhead deck

3.2.1.1 Below the bulkhead deck, two means of escape, at least one of which shall be independent of watertight doors, shall be provided from each watertight compartment or similarly restricted space or group of spaces. Exceptionally, the Administration may dispense with one of the means of escape for crew spaces that are entered only occasionally, if the required escape route is independent of watertight doors.

3.2.1.2 Where the Administration has granted dispensation under the provisions of paragraph 3.2.1.1, this sole means of escape shall provide safe escape. However, stairways shall not be less than 800 mm in clear width with handrails on both sides.

3.2.2 Escape from spaces above the bulkhead deck

Above the bulkhead deck there shall be at least two means of escape from each main vertical zone or similarly restricted space or group of spaces, at least one of which shall give access to a stairway forming a vertical escape.

3.2.3 Direct access to stairway enclosures

Stairway enclosures in accommodation and service spaces shall have direct access from the corridors and be of a sufficient area to prevent congestion, having in view the number of persons likely to use them in an emergency. Within the perimeter of such stairway enclosures, only public toilets, lockers of non-combustible material providing storage for non-hazardous safety equipment and open information counters are permitted. Only public spaces, corridors, lifts, public toilets, special category spaces and open ro-ro spaces to which any passengers carried can have access, other escape stairways required by paragraph 3.2.4.1 and external areas are permitted to have direct access to these stairway enclosures. Small corridors or "lobbies" used to separate an enclosed stairway from galleys or main laundries may have direct access to the stairway provided they have a minimum deck area of 4.5 m², a width of no less than 900 mm and contain a fire hose station.

3.2.4 Details of means of escape

3.2.4.1 At least one of the means of escape required by paragraphs 3.2.1.1 and 3.2.2 shall consist of a readily accessible enclosed stairway, which shall provide continuous fire shelter from the level of its origin to the appropriate lifeboat and liferaft embarkation decks, or to the uppermost weather deck if the embarkation deck does not extend to the main vertical zone being considered. In the latter case, direct access to the embarkation deck by way of external open stairways and passageways shall be provided and shall have emergency lighting in accordance with regulation III/11.5 and slip-free surfaces underfoot. Boundaries facing external open stairways and passageways forming part of an escape route and boundaries in such a position that their failure during a fire would impede escape to the embarkation deck shall have fire integrity, including insulation values, in accordance with tables 9.1 to 9.4, as appropriate.

3.2.4.2 Protection of access from the stairway enclosures to the lifeboat and liferaft embarkation areas shall be provided either directly or through protected internal routes which have fire integrity and insulation values for stairway enclosures as determined by tables 9.1 to 9.4, as appropriate.

3.2.4.3 Stairways serving only a space and a balcony in that space shall not be considered as forming one of the required means of escape.

3.2.4.4 Each level within an atrium shall have two means of escape, one of which shall give direct access to an enclosed vertical means of escape meeting the requirements of paragraph 3.2.4.1.

13

3.2.4.5 The widths, number and continuity of escapes shall be in accordance with the requirements in the Fire Safety Systems Code.

3.2.5 Marking of escape routes

3.2.5.1 In addition to the emergency lighting required by regulations II–1/42 and III/11.5, the means of escape, including stairways and exits, shall be marked by lighting or photoluminescent strip indicators placed not more than 300 mm above the deck at all points of the escape route, including angles and intersections. The marking must enable passengers to identify the routes of escape and readily identify the escape exits. If electric illumination is used, it shall be supplied by the emergency source of power and it shall be so arranged that the failure of any single light or cut in a lighting strip will not result in the marking being ineffective. Additionally, escape route signs and fire equipment location markings shall be of photoluminescent material or marked by lighting. The Administration shall ensure that such lighting or photoluminescent equipment has been evaluated, tested and applied in accordance with the Fire Safety Systems Code.

3.2.5.2 In passenger ships carrying more than 36 passengers, the requirements of the paragraph 3.2.5.1 shall also apply to the crew accommodation areas.

3.2.6 Normally locked doors that form part of an escape route

3.2.6.1 Cabin and stateroom doors shall not require keys to unlock them from inside the room. Neither shall there be any doors along any designated escape route which require keys to unlock them when moving in the direction of escape.

3.2.6.2 Escape doors from public spaces that are normally latched shall be fitted with a means of quick release. Such means shall consist of a door-latching mechanism incorporating a device that releases the latch upon the application of a force in the direction of escape flow. Quick release mechanisms shall be designed and installed to the satisfaction of the Administration and, in particular:

.1   *consist of bars or panels, the actuating portion of which extends across at least one half of the width of the door leaf, at least 760 mm and not more than 1,120 mm above the deck;*

.2   *cause the latch to release when a force not exceeding 67 N is applied; and*

.3   *not be equipped with any locking device, set screw or other arrangement that prevents the release of the latch when pressure is applied to the releasing device.*

3.3   Means of escape in cargo ships

3.3.1 General

At all levels of accommodation there shall be provided at least two widely separated means of escape from each restricted space or group of spaces.

3.3.2 Escape from spaces below the lowest open deck

Below the lowest open deck the main means of escape shall be a stairway and the second escape may be a trunk or a stairway.

3.3.3 Escape from spaces above the lowest open deck

Above the lowest open deck the means of escape shall be stairways or doors to an open deck or a combination thereof.

3.3.4 Dead-end corridors

No dead-end corridors having a length of more than 7 m shall be accepted.

3.3.5 Width and continuity of escape routes

The width, number and continuity of escape routes shall be in accordance with the requirements in the Fire Safety Systems Code.

3.3.6 Dispensation from two means of escape

Exceptionally, the Administration may dispense with one of the means of escape, for crew spaces that are entered only occasionally, if the required escape route is independent of watertight doors.

3.4 Emergency escape breathing devices*

3.4.1 Emergency escape breathing devices shall comply with the Fire Safety Systems Code. Spare emergency escape breathing devices shall be kept onboard.

3.4.2 All ships shall carry at least two emergency escape breathing devices within accommodation spaces.

3.4.3 In all passenger ships, at least two emergency escape breathing devices shall be carried in each main vertical zone.

3.4.4 In all passenger ships carrying more than 36 passengers, two emergency escape breathing devices, in addition to those required in paragraph 3.4.3 above, shall be carried in each main vertical zone.

3.4.5 However, paragraphs 3.4.3 and 3.4.4 do not apply to stairway enclosures which constitute individual main vertical zones and to the main vertical zones in the fore or aft end of a ship which do not contain spaces of categories (6), (7), (8) or (12) as defined in regulation 9.2.2.3.

Guidance 13

G12   Construction and insulation

G12.1 The stiles, treads, risers and, if fitted, backing plates of stairways should be constructed of steel except that they may be constructed of aluminium alloy, suitably insulated, when the structure is of aluminium alloy. Stairway enclosures constructed of steel which are required by the tables in regulation 9 to be insulated, may be insulated on either side but when the enclosures are insulated on the inside, measures should be taken to prevent heat transmission through the divisions in way of decks, landings etc.

* Refer to the Guidelines for the performance, location, use and care of emergency escape breathing devices (MSC/Circ.849).

G13   Public rooms used for concerts etc.

G13.1   When a public room in a passenger ship (any class) is to be used for concerts, cinema shows etc., and lighting is to be subdued, the illuminated signs marking the exits should be in white lettering approx. 180 mm high on a green background. Each door which does not afford a safe escape from the space should be provided with an illuminated sign indicating 'NO EXIT' in white lettering approx. 180 mm high on a red background.

G14   Escape windows and sidescuttles

G14.1   Where the second means of escape from a space such as a radio office is provided by an opening window or sidescuttle, the window should be of the fully opening type of suitable dimensions and the sidescuttle should be not less than 450mm in diameter. When such a window or sidescuttle is locked by cone nuts to prevent unauthorised opening e.g. in lieu of mosquito protection in crew spaces on air conditioned ships, a special key should be provided in a glass-fronted box adjacent to the window or sidescuttle.

G15   Requirements applicable to passenger ships

The following applies specifically to passenger ships and are additional to the general requirements for all ships.

G15.1   Widths of stairways and ladderways

G15.1.1 The minimum aggregate width of stairways and ladderways, by which passengers and crew are specifically routed to the assembly stations and/or lifeboat, liferaft and marine escape system embarkation positions, is to be determined as indicated in Chapter 13 of the Fire Safety Systems Code.

G15.2   The carriage of elderly and disabled passengers

G15.2.1 Surveyors should ensure that shipowners and shipbuilders are conversant with the contents of MGN 31(M) and the IMO publication MSC/Circ 735 of June 1996 entitled; 'Recommendation on the Design and Operation of Passenger Ships to Respond to Elderly and Disabled Persons needs'.

G15.3   Continuous fire shelters

G15.3.1 Where a stairway providing continuous fire shelter has no direct access to the lifeboat, liferaft and marine escape system embarkation decks, the corridors between the stairway and the decks should be assumed to be part of the stairway enclosure with its division having the appropriate 'A' Class standards accordingly. See also paragraph on corridor and doorways in the guidance to regulation 9.2.

G15.4   Machinery space escapes

G15.4.1 The shelter should extend from the floor plate level at which there is direct access into a space, other than a special category space, or Ro-Ro cargo space, which provides a safe escape route to the embarkation deck.

G15.4.2 The protected enclosure, referred to in paragraphs 4.1.1.1 and 4.2.1.1, should be of sufficient cross sectional dimensions (but not less than the 800 mm x 800 mm) to provide unrestricted access within its height and should not be used for pipes, cables, ducts etc. except for electric cables serving light fittings within the shelter.

G15.4.3 The cross sectional dimensions of the protected enclosure should be increased in way of each opening in order to provide a landing within the shelter and permit the door to open without affecting a person who may be climbing the ladder.

G15.4.4 An opening into the protected enclosure should be provided at floor plate level and at each flat or grating level within the height of the protected enclosure except that such an opening need not be provided at any flat or grating level at which there is a door in a boundary of the machinery space which provides a safe escape route to the embarkation deck.

G15.4.5 Each opening in the protected enclosure should be fitted with a self-closing 'A' Class door of the same 'A' Class standard as the part of the shelter in which it is fitted. Each door should open into the protected enclosure.

G15.4.6 A control room situated within a machinery space should be provided with a means of escape which does not entail entering the machinery space. This may be achieved by one of the following:

.1 direct access into the protected enclosure referred to in paragraphs 4.1.1.1 and 4.2.1.1; or

.2 direct access into an adjacent space which provides a safe escape route to the embarkation deck.

G15.4.7 When a machinery space is recessed into or under an adjacent space and neither of the two means of escape referred to in paragraph 4.1.1 or 4.2.1 is situated in the recess, an additional means of escape may be required to be provided from the recess. This will depend on the dimensions of the recess, the distance to the nearest escape in the main part of the machinery space and its accessibility and the location of items of machinery which may present a fire hazard.

G15.5 Spaces in which gas cylinders are stored

G15.5.1 A space in which gas cylinders are stored should be located preferably on an open deck or, where this is not practicable, in a 'tweendeck immediately below an open deck. Any entrance to such a space should be from the open deck and be independent of the protected space or any other space. Every access door should open outwards.

G15.5.2 Where such a space is located below an open deck, the access into the space should be by a companion and sloping stairway. Access in such a case should not be by means of a hatch and vertical ladder which are not considered suitable for rapid evacuation in the event of an accidental discharge of gas into the space. See guidance to regulation 9.7 for the ventilation of such spaces.

G15.6 Low location lighting

G15.6.1 Proposals for compliance with the requirements for 'low location lighting' in escape routes should be presented on a plan drawn to a scale of not less than 1:100. This should show the layout and type (photo luminescent or electrically powered) of low location lighting and also the position of any symbols incorporated in the system. Reference should be made to guidelines on evaluation, testing and application of low location lighting on passenger ships adopted by the Organization by resolution A.752(18). This recommends luminance testing of low location lighting systems once in five years: such periodic testing is particularly relevant to unpowered systems.

G15.7 Marking and illuminating exits and escape routes

G15.7.1 Requirements relating to the marking and illuminating of exits and escape routes are given in paragraph 3.2.5. When considering those requirements the contents of the Merchant Shipping (Emergency Information for Passengers) Regulations 1990, should be observed.

G16 Requirements applicable to cargo ships and tankers

The following applies to cargo ships and tankers and are additional to the general requirements for all ships.

G16.1 Accommodation below the weather deck

G16.1.1 The two means of escape from each group of accommodation spaces situated between main bulkheads below the weather deck should be stairways as widely separated as possible. One stairway should provide direct access to the embarkation deck or higher deck and the other stairway should lead to the deck over or a higher deck which provides access to the embarkation deck by means of internal stairways and/or doors in the boundaries of the deckhouses and external ladders. However, if this is not practicable, the stairway which leads to the deck over or higher deck may be replaced by a trunked vertical ladder which provides the same degree of access. (See also the Instructions to Surveyors on the application of the Merchant Shipping(Crew Accommodation) Regulations 1997, – paragraph 2.7 refers).

G16.1.2 In certain circumstances, depending on the layout of the spaces under consideration and the position of the stairway, it may be necessary to provide two trunked vertical ladders, one port and one starboard, in order to provide adequate means of escape from the group of spaces.

G16.2 Accommodation above the weather deck

G16.2.1 The two means of escape from each group of accommodation spaces situated above the weather deck should be stairways as widely separated as possible. One stairway should provide direct access to the embarkation deck or higher deck and the other stairway should lead to the deck over or higher deck which provides access to the embarkation deck except that this stairway need not be fitted if there is at least one door from the corridor serving the group of spaces in each side of the deckhouse which provides access to the embarkation deck. The two doors and the stairway providing direct access to the embarkation deck should be as widely separated as possible.

G16.3 Arrangement of doors along escape routes and accessibility of embarkation decks

G16.3.1 The escape routes are routes for escape and also for access. Accordingly, the locking arrangements should be such that it does not obstruct these two objectives (escape and access) and that the doors in way of the escape routes can be opened from both sides.

G16.3.2 The embarkation deck should be accessible from the open decks to which the escape routes lead.

G16.4 Spaces in tower blocks

G16.4.1 When crew accommodation, service spaces and control stations are arranged in a tower block with no outside decks, all tiers in the block should be connected to each other by means of external sloping ladderways with at least one access door in each tier and by an internal enclosed stairway.

G16.5 Spaces in which gas cylinders are stored (on cargo ships)

G16.5.1 Table 9.5 in regulation 9, which relates to the location of spaces containing the gas fire extinguishing medium for cargo spaces on cargo ships, should also be noted. See also guidance to regulation 9.7 on Independent Ventilation Systems in respect of spaces in which gas cylinders are stored.

G17   Emergency escape breathing devices

G17.1 The minimum carriage of spares is one in cargo ships and in passenger ships two spare sets. In addition when more than 40 sets are carried one additional spare set is to be carried for each further 20 units (or part there of) with a total maximum number of 4 spare sets needed to be carried on board.

G17.2 The numbers needed for machinery spaces is undefined and is a departure from the normal prescriptive requirement. Because of the different manning arrangements and machinery space layouts, IMO concluded that it would be not be possible to determine satisfactory carriage requirements. The object of the regulation is to allow personnel to evacuate a dangerous space to a place of safety. It is the owner/operator, through a risk assessment process, and in consultation with the ships crew, who is to determine the number and location of the EEBD's. If a surveyor attending a ship is not satisfied with the arrangements, he/she should ask for the assessment to be repeated in light of deficiencies identified.

4   *Means of escape from machinery spaces*

4.1   Means of escape on passenger ships

Means of escape from each machinery space in passenger ships shall comply with the following provisions.

4.1.1 Escape from spaces below the bulkhead deck

Where the space is below the bulkhead deck, the two means of escape shall consist of either:

.1   *two sets of steel ladders, as widely separated as possible, leading to doors in the upper part of the space, similarly separated and from which access is provided to the appropriate lifeboat and liferaft embarkation decks. One of these ladders shall be located within a protected enclosure that satisfies regulation 9.2.2.3, category (2), or regulation 9.2.2.4, category (4), as appropriate, from the lower part of the space it serves to a safe position outside the space. Self-closing fire doors of the same fire integrity standards shall be fitted in the enclosure. The ladder shall be fixed in such a way that heat is not transferred into the enclosure through non-insulated fixing points. The protected enclosure shall have minimum internal dimensions of at least 800 mm x 800 mm, and shall have emergency lighting provisions; or*

.2   *one steel ladder leading to a door in the upper part of the space from which access is provided to the embarkation deck and additionally, in the lower part of the space and in a position well separated from the ladder referred to, a steel door capable of being operated from each side and which provides access to a safe escape route from the lower part of the space to the embarkation deck.*

4.1.2 Escape from spaces above the bulkhead deck

Where the space is above the bulkhead deck, the two means of escape shall be as widely separated as possible and the doors leading from such means of escape shall be in a position from which access is provided to the appropriate lifeboat and liferaft embarkation decks. Where such means of escape require the use of ladders, these shall be of steel.

4.1.3 Dispensation from two means of escape

In a ship of less than 1,000 gross tonnage, the Administration may dispense with one of the means of escape, due regard being paid to the width and disposition of the upper part of the space. In a ship of 1,000 gross tonnage and above, the Administration may dispense with one means of escape from any such space, including a normally unattended auxiliary machinery space, so long as either a door or a steel ladder provides a safe escape route to the embarkation deck, due regard being paid to the nature and location of the space and whether persons are normally employed in that space. In the steering gear space, a second means of escape shall be provided when the emergency steering position is located in that space unless there is direct access to the open deck.

4.1.4 Escape from machinery control rooms

Two means of escape shall be provided from a machinery control room located within a machinery space, at least one of which will provide continuous fire shelter to a safe position outside the machinery space.

4.2   Means of escape on cargo ships

Means of escape from each machinery space in cargo ships shall comply with the following provisions.

4.2.1 Escape from machinery spaces of category A

Except as provided in paragraph 4.2.2, two means of escape shall be provided from each machinery space of category A. In particular, one of the following provisions shall be complied with:

.1   *two sets of steel ladders, as widely separated as possible, leading to doors in the upper part of the space, similarly separated and from which access is provided to the open deck. One of these ladders shall be located within a protected enclosure that satisfies regulation 9.2.3.3, category (4), from the lower part of the space it serves to a safe position outside the space. Self-closing fire doors of the same fire integrity standards shall be fitted in the enclosure. The ladder shall be fixed in such a way that heat is not transferred into the enclosure through non-insulated fixing points. The enclosure shall have minimum internal dimensions of at least 800 mm x 800 mm, and shall have emergency lighting provisions; or*

.2   *one steel ladder leading to a door in the upper part of the space from which access is provided to the open deck and, additionally, in the lower part of the space and in a position well separated from the ladder referred to, a steel door capable of being operated from each side and which provides access to a safe escape route from the lower part of the space to the open deck.*

4.2.2 Dispensation from two means of escape

In a ship of less than 1,000 gross tonnage, the Administration may dispense with one of the means of escape required under paragraph 4.2.1, due regard being paid to the dimension and disposition of the upper part of the space. In addition, the means of escape from machinery spaces of category A need not comply with the requirement for an enclosed fire shelter listed in paragraph 4.2.1.1. In the steering gear space, a second means of escape shall be provided when the emergency steering position is located in that space unless there is direct access to the open deck.

4.2.3 Escape from machinery spaces other than those of category A

From machinery spaces other than those of category A, two escape routes shall be provided except that a single escape route may be accepted for spaces that are entered only occasionally, and for spaces where the maximum travel distance to the door is 5 m or less.

4.3   Emergency escape breathing devices

4.3.1 On all ships, within the machinery spaces, emergency escape breathing devices shall be situated ready for use at easily visible places, which can be reached quickly and easily at any time in the event of fire. The location of emergency escape breathing devices shall take into account the layout of the machinery space and the number of persons normally working in the spaces.*

* Refer to the Guidelines for the performance, location, use and care of emergency escape breathing devices (MSC/Circ.849).

4.3.2 The number and location of these devices shall be indicated in the fire control plan required in regulation 15.2.4.

4.3.3 Emergency escape breathing devices shall comply with the Fire Safety Systems Code.

Guidance 13

G18 Flexible ladders (not acceptable)

G18.1 Flexible ladders, i.e. ladders having strings of flexible steel wire rope (or chains) are not acceptable as forming part of any escape route.

G19 Crew spaces

G19.1 In a space or group of spaces allocated solely to crew, the means of escape referred to in paragraphs 4.1.1 and 4.1.2 may consist of one stairway providing continuous fire shelter to the lifeboat, liferaft and marine escape system embarkation decks or, where necessary, to a higher deck and another stairway or vertical ladder giving access to the deck above through an escape hatch with access from that deck to the embarkation decks. In certain circumstances, depending upon the layout of the spaces under consideration and the positions of the stairway, it may be necessary to provide two escape hatches, one port and one starboard, in order to ensure that a fire in a particular location would not render escape impossible from some spaces.

5 Means of escape on passenger ships from special category and open ro-ro spaces to which any passengers carried can have access

5.1 In special category and open ro-ro spaces to which any passengers carried can have access, the number and locations of the means of escape both below and above the bulkhead deck shall be to the satisfaction of the Administration and, in general, the safety of access to the embarkation deck shall be at least equivalent to that provided for under paragraphs 3.2.1.1, 3.2.2, 3.2.4.1 and 3.2.4.2. Such spaces shall be provided with designated walkways to the means of escape with a breadth of at least 600 mm. The parking arrangements for the vehicles shall maintain the walkways clear at all times.

5.2 One of the escape routes from the machinery spaces where the crew is normally employed shall avoid direct access to any special category space.

Guidance 13

G20 Special category spaces

G20.1 The stairways forming the means of escape from each special category space should be suitably spaced in order to provide adequate coverage to the whole of the space. In general, at least one stairway should be provided at each end of the space and one stairway at approximately mid-length, each of which provides continuous fire shelter to the lifeboat, liferaft and marine escape system embarkation positions or, where necessary, to a higher deck. However, in ships fitted with two or more casings, this spacing of stairways providing continuous fire shelter should apply to each casing. Suitable signs to indicate the route to the escape stairways should be provided.

6 Means of escape from ro-ro spaces

At least two means of escape shall be provided in ro-ro spaces where the crew are normally employed. The escape routes shall provide a safe escape to the lifeboat and liferaft embarkation decks and shall be located at the fore and aft ends of the space.

Guidance 13

G21   Ro-Ro spaces

G21.1 Ro-Ro spaces should be fitted with at least one stairway providing continuous fire shelter to the lifeboat, liferaft and marine escape system embarkation decks or, where necessary, to a higher deck and a stairway or ladder giving access to the deck above through an escape hatch with access from that deck to the embarkation decks. The two means of escape should be situated at opposite ends of the Ro-Ro space or as near thereto as practicable. Additional means of escape may be necessary in a space which extends longitudinally over a considerable portion of the ships length. Suitable signs to indicate the route to the escape stairways should be provided.

G22   Number and location of escape routes in Ro-Ro spaces

G22.1 The escape (and access) routes in Ro-Ro spaces should be so arranged that there are adequate escape routes during both the loading and unloading process.

7   *Additional requirements for ro-ro passenger ships*

7.1   *General*

> *7.1.1 Escape routes shall be provided from every normally occupied space on the ship to an assembly station. These escape routes shall be arranged so as to provide the most direct route possible to the assembly station,* and shall be marked with symbols based on the guidelines developed by the Organization.†*
>
> *7.1.2 The escape route from cabins to stairway enclosures shall be as direct as possible, with a minimum number of changes in direction. It shall not be necessary to cross from one side of the ship to the other to reach an escape route. It shall not be necessary to climb more than two decks up or down in order to reach an assembly station or open deck from any passenger space.*
>
> *7.1.3 External routes shall be provided from open decks, as referred to in paragraph 7.1.2, to the survival craft embarkation stations.*
>
> *7.1.4 Where enclosed spaces adjoin an open deck, openings from the enclosed space to the open deck shall, where practicable, be capable of being used as an emergency exit.*
>
> *7.1.5 Escape routes shall not be obstructed by furniture and other obstructions. With the exception of tables and chairs which may be cleared to provide open space, cabinets and other heavy furnishings in public spaces and along escape routes shall be secured in place to prevent shifting if the ship rolls or lists. Floor coverings shall also be secured in place. When the ship is under way, escape routes shall be kept clear of obstructions such as cleaning carts, bedding, luggage and boxes of goods.*

7.2   *Instruction for safe escape*

> *7.2.1 Decks shall be sequentially numbered, starting with "1" at the tank top or lowest deck. The numbers shall be prominently displayed at stair landings and lift*

---

* Refer to the Indication of the assembly stations in passenger ships (MSC/Circ.777)

† Refer to Symbols related to life-saving appliances and arrangements adopted by the Organization by resolution A.760(18).

lobbies. Decks may also be named, but the deck number shall always be displayed with the name.

7.2.2 Simple "mimic" plans showing the "you are here" position and escape routes marked by arrows shall be prominently displayed on the inside of each cabin door and in public spaces. The plan shall show the directions of escape and shall be properly oriented in relation to its position on the ship.

7.3   Strength of handrails and corridors

7.3.1 Handrails or other handholds shall be provided in corridors along the entire escape route so that a firm handhold is available at every step of the way, where possible, to the assembly stations and embarkation stations. Such handrails shall be provided on both sides of longitudinal corridors more than 1.8 m in width and transverse corridors more than 1 m in width. Particular attention shall be paid to the need to be able to cross lobbies, atriums and other large open spaces along escape routes. Handrails and other handholds shall be of such strength as to withstand a distributed horizontal load of 750 N/m applied in the direction of the centre of the corridor or space, and a distributed vertical load of 750 N/m applied in the downward direction. The two loads need not be applied simultaneously.

7.3.2 The lowest 0.5 m of bulkheads and other partitions forming vertical divisions along escape routes shall be able to sustain a load of 750 N/m to allow them to be used as walking surfaces from the side of the escape route with the ship at large angles of heel.

7.4   Evacuation analysis*

Escape routes shall be evaluated by an evacuation analysis early in the design process. The analysis shall be used to identify and eliminate, as far as practicable, congestion which may develop during an abandonment, due to normal movement of passengers and crew along escape routes, including the possibility that crew may need to move along these routes in a direction opposite to the movement of passengers. In addition, the analysis shall be used to demonstrate that escape arrangements are sufficiently flexible to provide for the possibility that certain escape routes, assembly stations, embarkation stations or survival craft may not be available as a result of a casualty.

* Refer to interim Guidelines for evacuation analysis for new and existing passenger ships (MSC/Circ.1033).

Part E – Operational requirements

Operational Readiness and Maintenance

1   Purpose

The purpose of this regulation is to maintain and monitor the effectiveness of the fire safety measures the ship is provided with. For this purpose, the following functional requirements shall be met:

> *.1   fire protection systems and fire-fighting systems and appliances shall be maintained ready for use; and*

> *.2   fire protection systems and fire-fighting systems and appliances shall be properly tested and inspected.*

2   General requirements

At all times while the ship is in service, the requirements of paragraph 1.1 shall be complied with. A ship is not in service when:

> *.1   it is in for repairs or lay-up (either at anchor or in port) or in dry-dock;*

> *.2   it is declared not in service by the owner or the owner's representative; and*

> *.3   in the case of passenger ships, there are no passengers on board.*

2.1   Operational readiness

2.1.1 The following fire protection systems shall be kept in good order so as to ensure their required performance if a fire occurs:

> *.1   structural fire protection, including fire-resisting divisions, and protection of openings and penetrations in these divisions;*

> *.2   fire detection and fire alarm systems; and*

> *.3   means of escape systems and appliances.*

2.1.2 Fire-fighting systems and appliances shall be kept in good working order and readily available for immediate use. Portable extinguishers which have been discharged shall be immediately recharged or replaced with an equivalent unit.

2.2   Maintenance, testing and inspections

2.2.1 Maintenance, testing and inspections shall be carried out based on the guidelines developed by the Organization* and in a manner having due regard to ensuring the reliability of fire-fighting systems and appliances.

2.2.2 The maintenance plan shall be kept on board the ship and shall be available for inspection whenever required by the Administration.

---

* Refer to the Guidelines on maintenance and inspection of fire protection systems and appliances (MSC/Circ.850).

2.2.3 The maintenance plan shall include at least the following fire protection systems and fire-fighting systems and appliances, where installed:

.1   fire mains, fire pumps and hydrants, including hoses, nozzles and international shore connections;

.2   fixed fire detection and fire alarm systems;

.3   fixed fire-extinguishing systems and other fire-extinguishing appliances;

.4   automatic sprinkler, fire detection and fire alarm systems;

.5   ventilation systems, including fire and smoke dampers, fans and their controls;

.6   emergency shut down of fuel supply;

.7   fire doors, including their controls;

.8   general emergency alarm systems;

.9   emergency escape breathing devices;

.10   portable fire extinguishers, including space charges; and

.11   fire-fighter's outfits.

2.2.4 The maintenance programme may be computer-based.

3   Additional requirements for passenger ships

In addition to the fire protection systems and appliances listed in paragraph 2.2.3, ships carrying more than 36 passengers shall develop a maintenance plan for low-location lighting and public address systems.

4   Additional requirements for tankers

In addition to the fire protection systems and appliances listed in paragraph 2.2.3, tankers shall have a maintenance plan for:

.1   inert gas systems;

.2   deck foam systems;

.3   fire safety arrangements in cargo pump-rooms; and

.4   flammable gas detectors.

Instructions, on-board training and drills

1   Purpose

The purpose of this regulation is to mitigate the consequences of fire by means of proper instructions for training and drills of persons on board in correct procedures under emergency conditions. For this purpose, the crew shall have the necessary knowledge and skills to handle fire emergency cases, including passenger care.

2   General requirements

2.1   Instructions, duties and organization

2.1.1   Crew members shall receive instruction on fire safety onboard the ship.

2.1.2   Crew members shall receive instructions on their assigned duties.

2.1.3   Parties responsible for fire extinguishing shall be organized. These parties shall have the capability to complete their duties at all times while the ship is in service.

2.2   On-board training and drills

2.2.1   Crew members shall be trained to be familiar with the arrangements of the ship as well as the location and operation of any fire-fighting systems and appliances that they may be called upon to use.

2.2.2   Training in the use of the emergency escape breathing devices shall be considered as part of on-board training.

2.2.3   Performance of crew members assigned fire-fighting duties shall be periodically evaluated by conducting on-board training and drills to identify areas in need of improvement, to ensure competency in fire-fighting skills is maintained, and to ensure the operational readiness of the fire-fighting organization.

2.2.4   On-board training in the use of the ship's fire-extinguishing systems and appliances shall be planned and conducted in accordance with provisions of regulation III/19.4.1.

2.2.5   Fire drills shall be conducted and recorded in accordance with the provisions of regulations III/19.3 and III/19.5.

2.3   Training manuals

2.3.1   A training manual shall be provided in each crew mess room and recreation room or in each crew cabin.

2.3.2   The training manual shall be written in the working language of the ship.

2.3.3   The training manual, which may comprise several volumes, shall contain the instructions and information required in paragraph 2.3.4 in easily understood terms and illustrated wherever possible. Any part of such information may be provided in the form of audio-visual aides in lieu of the manual.

2.3.4 The training manual shall explain the following in detail:

.1 general fire safety practice and precautions related to the dangers of smoking, electrical hazards, flammable liquids and similar common shipboard hazards;

.2 general instructions on fire-fighting activities and fire-fighting procedures, including procedures for notification of a fire and use of manually operated call points;

.3 meanings of the ship's alarms;

.4 operation and use of fire-fighting systems and appliances;

.5 operation and use of fire doors;

.6 operation and use of fire and smoke dampers; and

.7 escape systems and appliances.

2.4 Fire control plans*

2.4.1 General arrangement plans shall be permanently exhibited for the guidance of the ship's officers, showing clearly for each deck the control stations, the various fire sections enclosed by "A" class divisions, the sections enclosed by "B" class divisions together with particulars of the fire detection and fire alarm systems, the sprinkler installation, the fire-extinguishing appliances, means of access to different compartments, decks, etc., and the ventilating system, including particulars of the fan control positions, the position of dampers and identification numbers of the ventilating fans serving each section. Alternatively, at the discretion of the Administration, the aforementioned details may be set out in a booklet, a copy of which shall be supplied to each officer, and one copy shall at all times be available on board in an accessible position. Plans and booklets shall be kept up to date; any alterations thereto shall be recorded as soon as practicable. Description in such plans and booklets shall be in the language or languages required by the Administration. If the language is neither English nor French, a translation into one of those languages shall be included.

2.4.2 A duplicate set of fire control plans or a booklet containing such plans shall be permanently stored in a prominently marked weathertight enclosure outside the deckhouse for the assistance of shore-side fire-fighting personnel.†

3 Additional requirements for passenger ships

3.1 Fire drills

In addition to the requirement of paragraph 2.2.3, fire drills shall be conducted in accordance with the provisions of regulation III/30, having due regard to notification of passengers and movement of passengers to assembly stations and embarkation decks.

---

* Refer to the Graphical symbols for fire control plans, adopted by the Organization by resolution A.654(16) as amplified by MSC/Circ. 1050.
† Refer to the Guidance concerning the location of fire control plans for assistance of shoreside fire-fighting personnel (MSC/Circ.451).

3.2   Fire control plans

In ships carrying more than 36 passengers, plans and booklets required by this regulation shall provide information regarding fire protection, fire detection and fire extinction based on the guidelines issued by the Organization.*

Guidance 15

G1   Fire Drills

G1.1   A proportion of portable fire extinguishers should be discharged, if possible by those likely to use them in an emergency.

G2   Fire Control Plans

G2.1   The fire control plans should also include firemans outfits and means of escape.

* Refer to the Guidelines on the information to be provided with fire control plans and booklets required by SOLAS regulations II-2/20 and 41-2, adopted by the Organization by resolution A.756(18).

REGULATION 16 Operations

1   Purpose

The purpose of this regulation is to provide information and instructions for proper ship and cargo handling operations in relation to fire safety. For this purpose, the following functional requirements shall be met:

> *.1   fire safety operational booklets shall be provided on board; and*

> *.2   flammable vapour releases from cargo tank venting shall be controlled.*

2   Fire safety operational booklets

2.1   The required fire safety operational booklet shall contain the necessary information and instructions for the safe operation of the ship and cargo handling operations in relation to fire safety. The booklet shall include information concerning the crew's responsibilities for the general fire safety of the ship while loading and discharging cargo and while underway. Necessary fire safety precautions for handling general cargoes shall be explained. For ships carrying dangerous goods and flammable bulk cargoes, the fire safety operational booklet shall also provide reference to the pertinent fire-fighting and emergency cargo handling instructions contained in the Code of Safe Practice for Solid Bulk Cargoes, the International Bulk Chemical Code, the International Gas Carrier Code and the International Maritime Dangerous Goods Code, as appropriate.

2.2   The fire safety operational booklet shall be provided in each crew mess room and recreation room or in each crew cabin.

2.3   The fire safety operational booklet shall be written in the working language of the ship.

2.4   The fire safety operational booklet may be combined with the training manuals required in regulation 15.2.3.

3   Additional requirements for tankers

3.1   General

The fire safety operational booklet referred to in paragraph 2 shall include provisions for preventing fire spread to the cargo area due to ignition of flammable vapours and include procedures of cargo tank gas-purging and/or gas-freeing, taking into account the provisions in paragraph 3.2.

3.2   Procedures for cargo tank purging and/or gas-freeing

> *3.2.1 When the ship is provided with an inert gas system, the cargo tanks shall first be purged in accordance with the provisions of regulation 4.5.6 until the concentration of hydrocarbon vapours in the cargo tanks has been reduced to less than 2% by volume. Thereafter, gas-freeing may take place at the cargo tank deck level.*

> *3.2.2 When the ship is not provided with an inert gas system, the operation shall be such that the flammable vapour is discharged initially through:*

.1   the vent outlets as specified in regulation 4.5.3.4;

.2   outlets at least 2 m above the cargo tank deck level with a vertical efflux velocity of at least 30 m/s maintained during the gas-freeing operation; or

.3   outlets at least 2 m above the cargo tank deck level with a vertical efflux velocity of at least 20 m/s and which are protected by suitable devices to prevent the passage of flame.

3.2.3 The above outlets shall be located not less than 10 m, measured horizontally, from the nearest air intakes and openings to enclosed spaces containing a source of ignition and from deck machinery, which may include anchor windlass and chain locker openings, and equipment which may constitute an ignition hazard.

3.2.4 When the flammable vapour concentration at the outlet has been reduced to 30% of the lower flammable limit, gas-freeing may be continued at cargo tank deck level.

Guidance 16

G1   Inert gas systems

G1.1   Where inert gas is being supplied by a system required by this Regulation, and the oxygen content of the inert gas in the inert gas supply main exceeds 8% by volume, it shall be the duty of the master to ensure that:

.1   immediate action is taken to improve the gas quality;

.2   if the quality of the gas does not improve, all operations in those tanks to which the inert gas is being supplied are suspended so as to avoid air being drawn into those tanks;

.3   the deck isolation valve (not being the water-seal device) is closed; and

.4   sub-standard gas is vented to the atmosphere.

G1.2   Combination carriers shall not carry solid cargoes unless all cargo tanks are empty of crude oil and other petroleum products having a closed flash point not exceeding 60°C and other liquids having a similar fire hazard and are gas freed, or unless the arrangements provided in each case are in accordance with the relevant operational requirements contained in the Guidelines for inert gas system.

Part F – Alternative design and arrangements

1   Purpose

The purpose of this regulation is to provide a methodology for alternative design and arrangements for fire safety.

2   General

2.1   Fire safety design and arrangements may deviate from the prescriptive requirements set out in parts B, C, D, E or G, provided that the design and arrangements meet the fire safety objectives and the functional requirements.

2.2   When fire safety design or arrangements deviate from the prescriptive requirements of this chapter, engineering analysis, evaluation and approval of the alternative design and arrangements shall be carried out in accordance with this regulation.

3   Engineering analysis

The engineering analysis shall be prepared and submitted to the Administration, based on the guidelines developed by the Organization* and shall include, as a minimum, the following elements:

.1   determination of the ship type and space(s) concerned;

.2   identification of prescriptive requirement(s) with which the ship or the space(s) will not comply;

.3   identification of the fire and explosion hazards of the ship or the space(s) concerned, including:

.3.1   identification of the possible ignition sources;

.3.2   identification of the fire growth potential of each space concerned;

.3.3   identification of the smoke and toxic effluent generation potential for each space concerned;

.3.4   identification of the potential for the spread of fire, smoke or of toxic effluents from the space(s) concerned to other spaces;

.4   determination of the required fire safety performance criteria for the ships or the space(s) concerned addressed by the prescriptive requirement(s), in particular:

.4.1   performance criteria shall be based on the fire safety objectives and on the functional requirements of this chapter;

.4.2   performance criteria shall provide a degree of safety not less than that achieved by using the prescriptive requirements; and

.4.3   performance criteria shall be quantifiable and measurable;

* Refer to MSC/Circ. 1002

    .5   *detailed description of the alternative design and arrangements, including a list of the assumptions used in the design and any proposed operational restrictions or conditions; and*

    .6   *technical justification demonstrating that the alternative design and arrangements meet the required fire safety performance criteria.*

4   *Evaluation of the alternative design and arrangements*

4.1   *The engineering analysis required in paragraph 3 shall be evaluated and approved by the Administration, taking into account the guidelines developed by the Organization.**

4.2   *A copy of the documentation, as approved by the Administration, indicating that the alternative design and arrangements comply with this regulation shall be carried onboard the ship.*

5   *Exchange of information*

The Administration shall communicate to the Organization pertinent information concerning alternative design and arrangements approved by them for circulation to all Contracting Governments.

6   *Re-evaluation due to change of conditions*

If the assumptions, and operational restrictions that were stipulated in the alternative design and arrangements are changed, the engineering analysis shall be carried out under the changed condition and shall be approved by the Administration.

---

* Refer to the guidelines to be developed by the Organization.

Part G – Special requirements

Helicopter Facilities

1   Purpose

The purpose of this regulation is to provide additional measures in order to address the fire safety objectives of this chapter for ships fitted with special facilities for helicopters. For this purpose, the following functional requirements shall be met:

> *.1   helideck structure shall be adequate to protect the ship from the fire hazards associated with helicopter operations;*

> *.2   fire-fighting appliances shall be provided to adequately protect the ship from the fire hazards associated with helicopter operations;*

> *.3   refueling and hangar facilities and operations shall provide the necessary measures to protect the ship from the fire hazards associated with helicopter operations; and*

> *.4   operation manuals and training shall be provided.*

2   Application

2.1   In addition to complying with the requirements of regulations in parts B, C, D and E, as appropriate, ships equipped with helidecks shall comply with the requirements of this regulation.

2.2   Where helicopters land or conduct winching operations on an occasional or emergency basis on ships without helidecks, fire-fighting equipment fitted in accordance with the requirements in part C may be used. This equipment shall be made readily available in close proximity to the landing or winching areas during helicopter operations.

2.3   Notwithstanding the requirements of paragraph 2.2 above, ro-ro passenger ships without helidecks shall comply with regulation III/28.

3   Structure

3.1   Construction of steel or other equivalent material

In general, the construction of the helidecks shall be of steel or other equivalent materials. If the helideck forms the deckhead of a deckhouse or superstructure, it shall be insulated to "A–60" class standard.

3.2   Construction of aluminium or other low melting point metals

If the Administration permits aluminium or other low melting point metal construction that is not made equivalent to steel, the following provisions shall be satisfied:

> *.1   if the platform is cantilevered over the side of the ship, after each fire on the ship or on the platform, the platform shall undergo a structural analysis to determine its suitability for further use; and*

.2   if the platform is located above the ship's deckhouse or similar structure, the following conditions shall be satisfied:

.2.1   the deckhouse top and bulkheads under the platform shall have no openings;

.2.2   windows under the platform shall be provided with steel shutters; and

.2.3   after each fire on the platform or in close proximity, the platform shall undergo a structural analysis to determine its suitability for further use.

4   Means of escape

A helideck shall be provided with both a main and an emergency means of escape and access for fire fighting and rescue personnel. These shall be located as far apart from each other as is practicable and preferably on opposite sides of the helideck.

5   Fire-fighting appliances

5.1   In close proximity to the helideck, the following fire-fighting appliances shall be provided and stored near the means of access to that helideck:

.1   at least two dry powder extinguishers having a total capacity of not less than 45 kg;

.2   carbon dioxide extinguishers of a total capacity of not less than 18 kg or equivalent;

.3   a suitable foam application system consisting of monitors or foam-making branch pipes capable of delivering foam to all parts of the helideck in all weather conditions in which helicopters can operate. The system shall be capable of delivering a discharge rate as required in table 18.1 for at least five minutes;

Table 18.1 – Foam discharge rates

Category	Helicopter Overall Length	Discharge rate foam solution (l/min.)
H1	up to but not including 15m	250
H2	from 15m up to but not including 24m	500
H3	from 24m up to but not including 35m	800

.4   the principal agent shall be suitable for use with salt water and conform to performance standards not inferior to those acceptable to the Organization;*

.5   at least two nozzles of an approved dual-purpose type (jet/spray) and hoses sufficient to reach any part of the helideck;

.6   in addition to the requirements of regulation 10.10, two sets of fire-fighter's outfits; and

* Refer to the "International Civil Aviation Organization Airport Services Manual", part 1, Rescue and Fire Fighting, chapter 8, Extinguishing Agent Characteristics, paragraph 8.1.5, Foam Specifications table 8-1, level 'B'.

.7   at least the following equipment shall be stored in a manner that provides for immediate use and protection from the elements:

.1   adjustable wrench;

.2   blanket, fire-resistant;

.3   cutters, bolt, 60 cm;

.4   hook, grab or salving;

.5   hacksaw, heavy duty complete with 6 spare blades;

.6   ladder;

.7   lift line 5 mm diameter and 15 m in length;

.8   pliers, side-cutting;

.9   set of assorted screwdrivers; and

.10 harness knife complete with sheath.

6   Drainage facilities

Drainage facilities in way of helidecks shall be constructed of steel and shall lead directly overboard independent of any other system and shall be designed so that drainage does not fall onto any part of the ship.

7   Helicopter refuelling and hangar facilities

Where the ship has helicopter refuelling and hangar facilities, the following requirements shall be complied with:

.1   a designated area shall be provided for the storage of fuel tanks which shall be:

.1.1 as remote as is practicable from accommodation spaces, escape routes and embarkation stations; and

.1.2 isolated from areas containing a source of vapour ignition;

.2   the fuel storage area shall be provided with arrangements whereby fuel spillage may be collected and drained to a safe location;

.3   tanks and associated equipment shall be protected against physical damage and from a fire in an adjacent space or area;

.4   where portable fuel storage tanks are used, special attention shall be given to:

.4.1 design of the tank for its intended purpose;

.4.2 mounting and securing arrangements;

.4.3 electric bonding; and

.4.4 inspection procedures;

.5   storage tank fuel pumps shall be provided with means which permit shutdown from a safe remote location in the event of a fire. Where a gravity fuelling system is installed, equivalent closing arrangements shall be provided to isolate the fuel source;

.6   the fuel pumping unit shall be connected to one tank at a time. The piping between the tank and the pumping unit shall be of steel or equivalent material, as short as possible, and protected against damage;

.7   electrical fuel pumping units and associated control equipment shall be of a type suitable for the location and potential hazards;

.8   fuel pumping units shall incorporate a device which will prevent over-pressurization of the delivery or filling hose;

.9   equipment used in refuelling operations shall be electrically bonded;

.10   "NO SMOKING" signs shall be displayed at appropriate locations;

.11   hangar, refuelling and maintenance facilities shall be treated as category A machinery spaces with regard to structural fire protection, fixed fire-extinguishing and detection system requirements;

.12   enclosed hangar facilities or enclosed spaces containing refuelling installations shall be provided with mechanical ventilation, as required by regulation 20.3 for closed ro-ro spaces of cargo ships. Ventilation fans shall be of non-sparking type; and

.13   electric equipment and wiring in enclosed hangar or enclosed spaces containing refuelling installations shall comply with regulations 20.3.2, 20.3.3 and 20.3.4.

8   Operations manual and fire-fighting arrangements

8.1   Each helicopter facility shall have an operations manual, including a description and a checklist of safety precautions, procedures and equipment requirements. This manual may be part of the ship's emergency response procedures.

8.2   The procedures and precautions to be followed during refuelling operations shall be in accordance with recognized safe practices and contained in the operations manual.

8.3   Fire-fighting personnel consisting of at least two persons trained for rescue and fire-fighting duties, and fire-fighting equipment shall be immediately available at all times when helicopter operations are expected.

8.4   Fire-fighting personnel shall be present during refuelling operations. However, the fire-fighting personnel shall not be involved with refuelling activities.

8.5   On-board refresher training shall be carried out and additional supplies of fire-fighting media shall be provided for training and testing of the equipment.

Carriage of Dangerous Goods*

1   Purpose

The purpose of this regulation is to provide additional safety measures in order to address the fire safety objectives of this chapter for ships carrying dangerous goods. For this purpose, the following functional requirements shall be met:

.1   fire protection systems shall be provided to protect the ship from the added fire hazards associated with carriage of dangerous goods;

.2   dangerous goods shall be adequately separated from ignition sources; and

.3   appropriate personnel protective equipment shall be provided for the hazards associated with the carriage of dangerous goods.

2   General requirements

2.1   In addition to complying with the requirements of regulations in parts B, C, D, E and regulations 18 and 20,† as appropriate, ship types and cargo spaces, referred to in paragraph 2.2, intended for the carriage of dangerous goods shall comply with the requirements of this regulation, as appropriate, except when carrying dangerous goods in limited quantities‡ unless such requirements have already been met by compliance with the requirements elsewhere in this chapter. The types of ships and modes of carriage of dangerous goods are referred to in paragraph 2.2 and in table 19.1. Cargo ships of less than 500 gross tonnage shall comply with this regulation, but Administrations may reduce the requirements and such reduced requirements shall be recorded in the document of compliance referred to in paragraph 4.

2.2   The following ship types and cargo spaces shall govern the application of tables 19.1 and 19.2:

>   *.1   ships and cargo spaces not specifically designed for the carriage of freight containers, but intended for the carriage of dangerous goods in packaged form, including goods in freight containers and portable tanks;*

>   *.2   purpose-built container ships and cargo spaces intended for the carriage of dangerous goods in freight containers and portable tanks;*

>   *.3   ro-ro ships and ro-ro spaces intended for the carriage of dangerous goods;*

>   *.4   ships and cargo spaces intended for the carriage of solid dangerous goods in bulk; and*

>   *.5   ships and cargo spaces intended for carriage of dangerous goods other than liquids and gases in bulk in shipborne barges.*

---

* Refer to the Interim guidelines for open-top containerships (MSC/Circ.608/Rev.1).
† Refer to part 7 of the International Maritime Dangerous Goods Code.
‡ Refer to chapter 3.4 of the International Maritime Dangerous Goods Code.

3   Special requirements

Unless otherwise specified, the following requirements shall govern the application of tables 19.1, 19.2 and 19.3 to both "on-deck" and "under-deck" stowage of dangerous goods where the numbers of the following paragraphs are indicated in the first column of the tables.

3.1   Water supplies

3.1.1 Arrangements shall be made to ensure immediate availability of a supply of water from the fire main at the required pressure either by permanent pressurization or by suitably placed remote arrangements for the fire pumps.

3.1.2 The quantity of water delivered shall be capable of supplying four nozzles of a size and at pressures as specified in regulation 10.2, capable of being trained on any part of the cargo space when empty. This amount of water may be applied by equivalent means to the satisfaction of the Administration.

3.1.3 Means shall be provided for effectively cooling the designated under-deck cargo space by at least 5 l/min per square metre of the horizontal area of cargo spaces, either by a fixed arrangement of spraying nozzles or by flooding the cargo space with water. Hoses may be used for this purpose in small cargo spaces and in small areas of larger cargo spaces at the discretion of the Administration. However, the drainage and pumping arrangements shall be such as to prevent the build-up of free surfaces. The drainage system shall be sized to remove no less than 125% of the combined capacity of both the water spraying system pumps and the required number of fire hose nozzles. The drainage system valves shall be operable from outside the protected space at a position in the vicinity of the extinguishing system controls. Bilge wells shall be of sufficient holding capacity and shall be arranged at the side shell of the ship at a distance from each other of not more than 40 m in each watertight compartment. If this is not possible, the adverse effect upon stability of the added weight and free surface of water shall be taken into account to the extent deemed necessary by the Administration in its approval of the stability information.*

3.1.4 Provision to flood a designated under-deck cargo space with suitable specified media may be substituted for the requirements in paragraph 3.1.3.

3.1.5 The total required capacity of the water supply shall satisfy paragraphs 3.1.2 and 3.1.3, if applicable, simultaneously calculated for the largest designated cargo space. The capacity requirements of paragraph 3.1.2 shall be met by the total capacity of the main fire pump(s), not including the capacity of the emergency fire pump, if fitted. If a drencher system is used to satisfy paragraph 3.1.3, the drencher pump shall also be taken into account in this total capacity calculation.

3.2   Sources of ignition

Electrical equipment and wiring shall not be fitted in enclosed cargo spaces or vehicle spaces unless it is essential for operational purposes in the opinion of the Administration. However, if electrical equipment is fitted in such spaces, it shall be of a certified safe type* for use in the

---

* Refer to the Recommendation on fixed fire-extinguishing systems for special cargo spaces adopted by the Organization by resolution A.123(V).
* Refer to the recommendations of the International Electrotechnical Commission, in particular, publication IEC 60092 on *Electrical installations in ships*.

dangerous environments to which it may be exposed unless it is possible to completely isolate the electrical system (e.g. by removal of links in the system, other than fuses). Cable penetrations of the decks and bulkheads shall be sealed against the passage of gas or vapour. Through runs of cables and cables within the cargo spaces shall be protected against damage from impact. Any other equipment which may constitute a source of ignition of flammable vapour shall not be permitted.

3.3   Detection system

Ro-ro spaces shall be fitted with a fixed fire detection and fire alarm system complying with the requirements of the Fire Safety Systems Code. All other types of cargo spaces shall be fitted with either a fixed fire detection and fire alarm system or a sample extraction smoke detection system complying with the requirements of the Fire Safety Systems Code. If a sample extraction smoke detection system is fitted, particular attention shall be given to paragraph 2.1.3 in chapter 10 of the Fire Safety Systems Code in order to prevent the leakage of toxic fumes into occupied areas.

3.4   Ventilation

3.4.1 Adequate power ventilation shall be provided in enclosed cargo spaces. The arrangement shall be such as to provide for at least six air changes per hour in the cargo space, based on an empty cargo space, and for removal of vapours from the upper or lower parts of the cargo space, as appropriate.

3.4.2 The fans shall be such as to avoid the possibility of ignition of flammable gas/air mixtures. Suitable wire mesh guards shall be fitted over inlet and outlet ventilation openings.

3.4.3 Natural ventilation shall be provided in enclosed cargo spaces intended for the carriage of solid dangerous goods in bulk, where there is no provision for mechanical ventilation.

3.5   Bilge pumping

3.5.1 Where it is intended to carry flammable or toxic liquids in enclosed cargo spaces, the bilge pumping system shall be designed to protect against inadvertent pumping of such liquids through machinery space piping or pumps. Where large quantities of such liquids are carried, consideration shall be given to the provision of additional means of draining those cargo spaces.

3.5.2 If the bilge drainage system is additional to the system served by pumps in the machinery space, the capacity of the system shall be not less than 10 m^3/h per cargo space served. If the additional system is common, the capacity need not exceed 25 m^3/h. The additional bilge system need not be arranged with redundancy.

3.5.3 Whenever flammable or toxic liquids are carried, the bilge line into the machinery space shall be isolated either by fitting a blank flange or by a closed lockable valve.

3.5.4 Enclosed spaces outside machinery spaces containing bilge pumps serving cargo spaces intended for carriage of flammable or toxic liquids shall be fitted with separate mechanical ventilation giving at least six air changes per hour. If the space has access from another enclosed space, the door shall be self-closing.

REGULATION
19

3.5.5 If bilge drainage of cargo spaces is arranged by gravity drainage, the drainage shall be either led directly overboard or to a closed drain tank located outside the machinery spaces. The tank shall be provided with a vent pipe to a safe location on the open deck. Drainage from a cargo space into bilge wells in a lower space is only permitted if that space satisfies the same requirements as the cargo space above.

3.6   Personnel protection

3.6.1 Four sets of full protective clothing, resistant to chemical attack, shall be provided in addition to the fire-fighter's outfits required by regulation 10.10. The protective clothing shall cover all skin, so that no part of the body is unprotected.

3.6.2 At least two self-contained breathing apparatuses additional to those required by regulation 10 shall be provided. Two spare charges suitable for use with the breathing apparatus shall be provided for each required apparatus. Passenger ships carrying not more than 36 passengers and cargo ships that are equipped with suitably located means for fully recharging the air cylinders free from contamination need carry only one spare charge for each required apparatus.

3.7   Portable fire extinguishers

Portable fire extinguishers with a total capacity of at least 12 kg of dry powder or equivalent shall be provided for the cargo spaces. These extinguishers shall be in addition to any portable fire extinguishers required elsewhere in this chapter.

3.8   Insulation of machinery space boundaries

Bulkheads forming boundaries between cargo spaces and machinery spaces of category A shall be insulated to "A–60" class standard, unless the dangerous goods are stowed at least 3 m horizontally away from such bulkheads. Other boundaries between such spaces shall be insulated to "A–60" class standard.

3.9   Water-spray system

Each open ro-ro space having a deck above it and each space deemed to be a closed ro-ro space not capable of being sealed, shall be fitted with an approved fixed pressure water-spraying system for manual operation which shall protect all parts of any deck and vehicle platform in the space, except that the Administration may permit the use of any other fixed fire-extinguishing system that has been shown by full-scale test to be no less effective. However, the drainage and pumping arrangements shall be such as to prevent the build-up of free surfaces. The drainage system shall be sized to remove no less than 125% of the combined capacity of both the water-spraying system pumps and the required number of fire hose nozzles. The drainage system valves shall be operable from outside the protected space at a position in the vicinity of the extinguishing system controls. Bilge wells shall be of sufficient holding capacity and shall be arranged at the side shell of the ship at a distance from each other of not more than 40 m in each watertight compartment. If this is not possible, the adverse effect upon stability of the added weight and free surface of water shall be taken into account to the extent deemed necessary by the Administration in its approval of the stability information.*

---

* Refer to the Recommendation on fixed fire-extinguishing systems for special cargo spaces adopted by the Organization by resolution A.123(V).

3.10   Separation of ro-ro spaces

3.10.1 In ships having ro-ro spaces, a separation shall be provided between a closed ro-ro space and an adjacent open ro-ro space. The separation shall be such as to minimise the passage of dangerous vapours and liquids between such spaces. Alternatively, such separation need not be provided if the ro-ro space is considered to be a closed cargo space over its entire length and fully complies with the relevant special requirements of this regulation.

3.10.2 In ships having ro-ro spaces, a separation shall be provided between a closed ro-ro space and the adjacent weather deck. The separation shall be such as to minimise the passage of dangerous vapours and liquids between such spaces. Alternatively, a separation need not be provided if the arrangements of the closed ro-ro spaces are in accordance with those required for the dangerous goods carried on adjacent weather decks.

Table 19.1 – Application of the requirements to different modes of carriage of dangerous goods in ships and cargo spaces

Where X appears in table 19.1, it means this requirement is applicable to all classes of dangerous goods as given in the appropriate line of table 19.3, except as indicated by the notes.

Regulation 19.2.2 / Regulation 19	Weather decks (.1 to .5 inclusive)	.1 Not specifically designed	.2 Container cargo spaces	.3 Closed ro-ro spaces[5]	.3 Open ro-ro spaces	.4 Solid dangerous goods in bulk	.5 Shipborne barges
.3.1.1	X	X	X	X	X		X
.3.1.2	X	X	X	X	X		–
.3.1.3	–	X	X	X	X		X
.3.1.4	–	X	X	X	X		X
.3.2	–	X	X	X	X	For application of requirements of regulation 19 to different classes of dangerous goods, see table 19.2	X[4]
.3.3	–	X	X	X	–		X[4]
.3.4.1	–	X	X[1]	X	–		X[4]
.3.4.2	–	X	X[1]	X	–		X[4]
.3.5	–	X	X	X	–		–
.3.6.1	X	X	X	X	X		–
.3.6.2	X	X	X	X	X		–
.3.7	X	X	–	–	X		–
.3.8	X	X	X[2]	X	X		–
.3.9	–	–	–	X[3]	X		–
.3.10.1	–	–	–	X	–		–
.3.10.2	–	–	–	X	–		–

Notes:

1 For classes 4 and 5.1 not applicable to closed freight containers.

   For classes 2, 3, 6.1 and 8 when carried in closed freight containers, the ventilation rate may be reduced to not less than two air changes.

   For the purpose of this requirement a portable tank is a closed freight container.

2 Applicable to decks only.

3 Applies only to closed ro-ro spaces, not capable of being sealed.

4 In the special case where the barges are capable of containing flammable vapours or alternatively if they are capable of discharging flammable vapours to a safe space outside the barge carrier compartment by means of ventilation ducts connected to the barges, these requirements may be reduced or waived to the satisfaction of the Administration.

5 Special category spaces shall be treated as closed ro-ro spaces when dangerous goods are carried.

Table 19.2 – Application of the requirements to different classes of dangerous goods for ships and cargo spaces carrying solid dangerous goods in bulk

Class \ Regulation 19	4.1	4.2	4.3[6]	5.1	6.1	8	9
.3.1.1	X	X	–	X	–	–	X
.3.1.2	X	X	–	X	–	–	X
.3.2	X	X^7	X	X^8	–	–	X^8
.3.4.1	–	X^7	X	–	–	–	–
.3.4.2	X^9	X^7	X	$X^{7,.9}$	–	–	$X^{7,9}$
.3.4.3	X	X	X	X	X	X	X
.3.6	X	X	X	X	X	X	X
.3.8	X	X	X	X^7	–	–	X^{10}

Notes:

6 The hazards of substances in this class which may be carried in bulk are such that special consideration must be given by the Administration to the construction and equipment of the ship involved in addition to meeting the requirements enumerated in this table.

7 Only applicable to Seedcake containing solvent extractions, to Ammonium nitrate and to Ammonium nitrate fertilisers.

8 Only applicable to Ammonium nitrate and to Ammonium nitrate fertilisers. However, a degree of protection in accordance with standards contained in the International Electrotechnical Commission publication 60079, Electrical Apparatus for Explosive Gas Atmospheres, is sufficient.

9 Only suitable wire mesh guards are required.

10 The requirements of the Code of Safe Practice for Solid Bulk Cargoes are sufficient.

4   Document of compliance*

The Administration shall provide the ship with an appropriate document as evidence of compliance of construction and equipment with the requirements of this regulation. Certification for dangerous goods, except solid dangerous goods in bulk, is not required for those cargoes specified as class 6.2 and 7, as defined in regulation VII/2, and dangerous goods in limited quantities.

* Refer to the Document of compliance with the special requirements for ships carrying dangerous goods under the provisions of regulation II-2/54 of SOLAS 74, as amended (MSC/Circ.642).

Table 19.3 – Application of the requirements to different classes of dangerous goods except solid dangerous goods in bulk.

Class / Regulation 19	1.1 to 1.6	1.4S	2.1	2.2	2.3	3.1, 3.2 liquids ≤23°C15	3.3 liquids >23°C15 ≤61°C	4.1	4.2	4.3	5.1	5.2	6.1 liquids	6.1 liquids ≤23°C15	6.1 liquids >23°C15 ≤61°C	6.1 solids	8 liquids	8 liquids ≤23°C15	8 liquids >23°C15 ≤61°C	8 solids	9
.3.1.1	X	X	X	X	X	X	X	X	X	X	X	X	X	X	X	X	X	X	X	X	X
.3.1.2	X	X	X	X	X	X	X	X	X	X	X	X	X	X	X	X	X	X	X	X	–
.3.1.3	X	–	–	–	–	–	–	–	–	–	–	–	–	–	–	–	–	–	–	–	–
.3.1.4	X	–	–	–	–	–	–	–	–	–	–	–	–	–	–	–	–	–	–	–	–
.3.2	X	–	X	–	–	X	–	–	–	–	–	–	–	X	–	–	–	X	–	–	–
.3.3	X	X	X	X	X	X	X	X	X	X	X	–	X	X	X	X	X	X	X	X	–
.3.4.1	–	–	X	–	X	X	–	X¹¹	X¹¹	X	X¹¹	–	–	X	X	X¹¹	–	X	X	–	X¹¹
.3.4.2	–	–	X	–	–	X	–	–	–	–	–	–	–	X	X	–	–	X	X	–	–
.3.5	–	–	–	–	–	X	–	–	–	–	–	–	X	X	X	–	–	X	–	–	–
.3.6	–	–	X	X	X	X	X	X	X	X	X	X	X	X	X	X	X	X	X	X	X¹⁴
.3.7	–	–	–	–	–	X	X	X	X	X	X	–	–	X	X	–	–	X	X	–	–
.3.8	X¹²	–	X	X	X	X	X	X	X	X	X¹³	–	–	X	X	–	–	X	X	–	–
.3.9	X	X	X	X	X	X	X	X	X	X	X	X	X	X	X	X	X	X	X	X	X
.3.10.1	X	X	X	X	X	X	X	X	X	X	X	X	X	X	X	X	X	X	X	X	X
.3.10.2	X	X	X	X	X	X	X	X	X	X	X	X	X	X	X	X	X	X	X	X	X

Notes:

11 When "mechanically-ventilated spaces" are required by the International Maritime Dangerous Goods Code, as amended.

12 Stow 3 m horizontally away from the machinery space boundaries in all cases.

13 Refer to the International Maritime Dangerous Goods Code, as amended.

14 As appropriate to the goods to be carried.

15 Refers to flashpoint.

REGULATION

20 Protection of vehicle, special category and ro-ro spaces

1   Purpose

The purpose of this regulation is to provide additional safety measures in order to address the fire safety objectives of this chapter for ships fitted with vehicle, special category and ro-ro spaces. For this purpose, the following functional requirements shall be met:

> *.1   fire protection systems shall be provided to adequately protect the ship from the fire hazards associated with vehicle, special category and ro-ro spaces;*

> *.2   ignition sources shall be separated from vehicle, special category and ro-ro spaces; and*

> *.3   vehicle, special category and ro-ro spaces shall be adequately ventilated.*

2   General requirements

2.1   Application

In addition to complying with the requirements of regulations in parts B, C, D and E, as appropriate, vehicle, special category and ro-ro spaces shall comply with the requirements of this regulation.

2.2   Basic principles for passenger ships

> *2.2.1 The basic principle underlying the provisions of this regulation is that the main vertical zoning required by regulation 9.2 may not be practicable in vehicle spaces of passenger ships and, therefore, equivalent protection must be obtained in such spaces on the basis of a horizontal zone concept and by the provision of an efficient fixed fire-extinguishing system. Based on this concept, a horizontal zone for the purpose of this regulation may include special category spaces on more than one deck provided that the total overall clear height for vehicles does not exceed 10 m.*

> *2.2.2 The basic principle underlying the provisions of paragraph 2.2.1 is also applicable to ro-ro spaces.*

> *2.2.3 The requirements of ventilation systems, openings in "A" class divisions and penetrations in "A" class divisions for maintaining the integrity of vertical zones in this chapter shall be applied equally to decks and bulkheads forming the boundaries separating horizontal zones from each other and from the remainder of the ship.*

Guidance 20

G1   Vehicle, special category and Ro-Ro spaces

G1.1 Ventilation fans serving special category, Ro-Ro or vehicle spaces, cargo spaces and machinery used for operating bow or stern doors, should be situated in spaces separated from the special category Ro-Ro or vehicle spaces by 'A' Class divisions as specified in regulation 9. Fans with motors of less than 2kW used for mixing the air within a special category space in order to prevent stratification may be situated within the space subject to; the fan motors complying with the Merchant Shipping (Passenger Ship Construction; Ships of Classes I, II and II(A)) Regulations 1998, Regulation 60(3); and the fan blades being of a non-sparking type.

G1.2 Air pipes to tanks or voids should not terminate within a special category, Ro-Ro or vehicle space because they impair the 'A' Class integrity of the deck which separates such spaces. The air pipes should be taken to open decks or looped over within the special category space and taken out through the ships side.

3   *Precaution against ignition of flammable vapours in closed vehicle spaces, closed ro-ro spaces and special category spaces*

3.1   *Ventilation systems*

3.1.1 *Capacity of ventilation systems*

There shall be provided an effective power ventilation system sufficient to give at least the following air changes:

.1   *Passenger ships:*

Special category spaces	*10 air changes per hour*
Closed ro-ro and vehicle spaces other than special category spaces for ships carrying more than 36 passengers	*10 air changes per hour*
Closed ro-ro and vehicle spaces other than special category spaces or ships carrying not more than 36 passengers	*6 air changes per hour*

.2   *Cargo ships:*   *6 air changes per hour*

The Administration may require an increased number of air changes when vehicles are being loaded and unloaded.

3.1.2 *Performance of ventilation systems*

3.1.2.1 In passenger ships, the power ventilation system required in paragraph 3.1.1 shall be separate from other ventilation systems and shall be in operation at all times when vehicles are in such spaces. Ventilation ducts serving such cargo spaces capable of being effectively sealed shall be separated for each such space. The system shall be capable of being controlled from a position outside such spaces.

3.1.2.2 In cargo ships, ventilation fans shall normally be run continuously whenever vehicles are on board. Where this is impracticable, they shall be operated for a limited period daily as weather permits and in any case for a reasonable period prior to discharge, after which period the ro-ro or vehicle space shall be proved gas-free. One or more portable combustible gas detecting instruments shall be carried for this purpose. The system shall be entirely separate from other ventilating systems. Ventilation ducts serving ro-ro or vehicle spaces shall be capable of being effectively sealed for each cargo space. The system shall be capable of being controlled from a position outside such spaces.

3.1.2.3 The ventilation system shall be such as to prevent air stratification and the formation of air pockets.

3.1.3 Indication of ventilation systems

Means shall be provided on the navigation bridge to indicate any loss of the required ventilating capacity.

3.1.4 Closing appliances and ducts

3.1.4.1 Arrangements shall be provided to permit a rapid shutdown and effective closure of the ventilation system from outside of the space in case of fire, taking into account the weather and sea conditions.

3.1.4.2 Ventilation ducts, including dampers, within a common horizontal zone shall be made of steel. In passenger ships, ventilation ducts that pass through other horizontal zones or machinery spaces shall be "A–60" class steel ducts constructed in accordance with regulations 9.7.2.1.1.1 and 9.7.2.1.1.2.

3.1.5 Permanent openings

Permanent openings in the side plating, the ends or deckhead of the space shall be so situated that a fire in the cargo space does not endanger stowage areas and embarkation stations for survival craft and accommodation spaces, service spaces and control stations in superstructures and deckhouses above the cargo spaces.

3.2   Electrical equipment and wiring

3.2.1 Except as provided in paragraph 3.2.2, electrical equipment and wiring shall be of a type suitable for use in an explosive petrol and air mixture.*

3.2.2 In case of other than special category spaces below the bulkhead deck, notwithstanding the provisions in paragraph 3.2.1, above a height of 450 mm from the deck and from each platform for vehicles, if fitted, except platforms with openings of sufficient size

---

* Refer to the recommendations of the International Electrotechnical Commission, in particular publication 60079.

permitting penetration of petrol gases downwards, electrical equipment of a type so enclosed and protected as to prevent the escape of sparks shall be permitted as an alternative on condition that the ventilation system is so designed and operated as to provide continuous ventilation of the cargo spaces at the rate of at least ten air changes per hour whenever vehicles are on board.

3.3   Electrical equipment and wiring in exhaust ventilation ducts

Electrical equipment and wiring, if installed in an exhaust ventilation duct, shall be of a type approved for use in explosive petrol and air mixtures and the outlet from any exhaust duct shall be sited in a safe position, having regard to other possible sources of ignition.

3.4   Other ignition sources

Other equipment which may constitute a source of ignition of flammable vapours shall not be permitted.

3.5   Scuppers and discharges

Scuppers shall not be led to machinery or other spaces where sources of ignition may be present.

Guidance 20

G2   Power ventilation system

G2.1 Reference is made to MSC/Cir.729 – Design Guidelines and Operational Recommendations for Ventilation Systems in Ro-Ro Cargo Spaces. The requirement to indicate any loss of ventilating capacity is considered complied with by an alarm on the bridge, initiated by the fall-out of a fan motor starter relay. Arrangements should be provided to permit rapid shutdown of the ventilation system. These operations should be possible without entering the special category space. Ventilation ducts of a special category space:

.1 which is not part of the same horizontal zone should be constructed of steel and should be fire insulated to A–60 standard or fitted with an automatic fire damper in the separating division.

.2 which is part of the same horizontal zone should be constructed of non-combustible material.

G2.2 Ventilation ducts should not pass through machinery spaces unless fire insulated to A–60 standard.

G2.3 Scupper arrangements, for the sizing of scuppers and drainage pumps the capacity of both the water spraying system pumps and the water discharge from the required number of fire hose nozzles should be taken into account. Additional requirements for special category spaces below the bulkhead deck, pumping and drainage arrangements should be such as to prevent the accumulation of water on such decks. In respect of scuppers and drainage pumps, the following should be complied with:

G2.4 Exhaust fans should be of non-sparking type in accordance with IACS Requirement F 29, as revised.

G2.5 Installation of electrical equipment in special category spaces

The degree of protection of electrical equipment required will be realised:

.1   above a height of 450mm above the deck;

.1.1 by an enclosure of at least IP 55 as defined in IEC Publication 529 – Classification of Degree of Protection Provided by Enclosures; or

.1.2 by apparatus for use in zone 2 areas as defined in IEC Publication 60079 – Electrical Ap for Explosive Gas Atmospheres (Temperature Class T3).

.2   at or below a height of 450mm above the deck;

.2.1 the electrical equipment should be of certified safe type and wiring, if fitted, and should be suitable for use in zone 1 areas as defined in IEC Publication 60079 – Electrical Apparatus for Explosive Gas Atmospheres – (Gas Group II(A) and Temperature Class T3).

G2.6 In addition to motor vehicles with petrol in their tanks, motor vehicles propelled by liquefied petroleum gas (LPG) may also be carried provided the cylinders of LPG are properly secured. Likewise gas cylinders in boats, caravans and in other vehicles, where the gas is used solely in connection with its operation or business, may also be carried.

G2.7 The alarm signal given at the bridge or fire control station by the manual fire alarm system should be distinct from any other signal which does not indicate fire. Any call point for the alarm system situated in well ventilated vehicle deck spaces above the bulkhead deck, or in similar spaces having a specific flammable vapour hazard, should be mounted more than 450mm above the deck and should be suitably enclosed, unless of a certified safe type.

G2.8 As a minimum, they should be audible where the fire patrol makes their rounds such as key box locations and the routes specified on the fire patrol checklist. If necessary, extra antennas should be fitted to obtain effective communication.

4   Detection and alarm

4.1   Fixed fire detection and fire alarm systems

Except as provided in paragraph 4.3.1, there shall be provided a fixed fire detection and fire alarm system complying with the requirements of the Fire Safety Systems Code. The fixed fire detection system shall be capable of rapidly detecting the onset of fire. The type of detectors and their spacing and location shall be to the satisfaction of the Administration, taking into account the effects of ventilation and other relevant factors. After being installed, the system shall be tested under normal ventilation conditions and shall give an overall response time to the satisfaction of the Administration.

4.2   Sample extraction smoke detection systems

Except open ro-ro spaces, open vehicle spaces and special category spaces, a sample extraction smoke detection system complying with the requirements of the Fire Safety Systems Code may be used as an alternative for the fixed fire detection and fire alarm system required in paragraph 4.1.

4.3   Special category spaces

4.3.1 An efficient fire patrol system shall be maintained in special category spaces. However, if an efficient fire patrol system is maintained by a continuous fire watch at all times during the voyage, a fixed fire detection and fire alarm system is not required.

4.3.2 Manually operated call points shall be spaced so that no part of the space is more than 20 m from a manually operated call point, and one shall be placed close to each exit from such spaces.

Guidance 20

G3   Fire detection in Ro-Ro spaces

G3.1 Smoke detectors exclusively or a combination of smoke and flame detectors should be used in these spaces. The detector sections in these spaces may be provided with an arrangement, e.g. a timer, for disconnecting detector sections during loading and unloading. The central unit should indicate whether the detector sections are disconnected or not. The time of disconnection should be adapted to the time of loading/unloading. Manual release mechanisms should not be capable of being disconnected by the arrangement referred to above. A sample smoke detection system meeting the requirements of the Regulations should be accepted as an equivalent detection system.

G3.2 The fire detection system, excluding manual call points, may be switched off with a timer during loading/unloading of vehicles to avoid "false" alarms.

5   Structural protection

Notwithstanding the provisions of regulation 9.2.2, in passenger ships carrying more than 36 passengers, the boundary bulkheads and decks of special category spaces and ro-ro spaces shall be insulated to "A–60" class standard. However, where a category (5), (9) or (10) space, as defined in regulation 9.2.2.3, is on one side of the division, the standard may be reduced to "A–0". Where fuel oil tanks are below a special category space or a ro-ro space, the integrity of the deck between such spaces, may be reduced to "A–0" standard.

6   Fire extinction

6.1   Fixed fire-extinguishing systems*

6.1.1 Vehicle spaces and ro-ro spaces which are not special category spaces and are capable of being sealed from a location outside of the cargo spaces shall be fitted with a fixed gas fire-extinguishing system which shall comply with the provisions of the Fire Safety Systems Code, except that:

---

* Refer to the Guidelines when approving alternative fixed water-based fire-fighting systems for use in special category spaces (MSC/Circ.914).

.1   if a carbon dioxide fire-extinguishing system is fitted, the quantity of gas available shall be at least sufficient to give a minimum volume of free gas equal to 45% of the gross volume of the largest such cargo space which is capable of being sealed, and the arrangements shall be such as to ensure that at least two thirds of the gas required for the relevant space shall be introduced within 10 min;

.2   any other fixed inert gas fire-extinguishing system or fixed high expansion foam fire-extinguishing system may be fitted provided the Administration is satisfied that an equivalent protection is achieved; and

.3   as an alternative, a system meeting the requirements of paragraph 6.1.2 may be fitted.

6.1.2 Ro-ro and vehicle spaces not capable of being sealed and special category spaces shall be fitted with an approved fixed pressure water-spraying system† for manual operation which shall protect all parts of any deck and vehicle platform in such spaces. Such water spray systems shall have:

.1   a pressure gauge on the valve manifold;

.2   clear marking on each manifold valve indicating the spaces served;

.3   instructions for maintenance and operation located in the valve room; and

.4   a sufficient number of drainage valves.

6.1.3 The Administration may permit the use of any other fixed fire-extinguishing system* that has been shown, by a full-scale test in conditions simulating a flowing petrol fire in a vehicle space or a ro-ro space to be not less effective in controlling fires likely to occur in such a space.

6.1.4 When fixed pressure water-spraying fire-extinguishing systems are provided, in view of the serious loss of stability which could arise due to large quantities of water accumulating on the deck or decks during the operation of the water-spraying system, the following arrangements shall be provided:

.1   in passenger ships:

.1.1   in the spaces above the bulkhead deck, scuppers shall be fitted so as to ensure that such water is rapidly discharged directly overboard;

---

† Refer to the Recommendation on fixed fire-extinguishing systems for special cargo spaces adopted by the Organization by resolution A.123(V).

* Refer to the Guidelines when approving alternative fixed water-based fire-fighting systems for use in special category spaces (MSC/Circ.914).

.1.2.1 in ro-ro passenger ships, discharge valves for scuppers, fitted with positive means of closing operable from a position above the bulkhead deck in accordance with the requirements of the International Convention on Load Lines in force, shall be kept open while the ships are at sea;

.1.2.2 any operation of valves referred to in paragraph 6.1.4.1.2.1 shall be recorded in the log-book;

    .1.3   *in the spaces below the bulkhead deck, the Administration may require pumping and drainage facilities to be provided additional to the requirements of regulation II–1/21. In such case, the drainage system shall be sized to remove no less than 125% of the combined capacity of both the water-spraying system pumps and the required number of fire hose nozzles. The drainage system valves shall be operable from outside the protected space at a position in the vicinity of the extinguishing system controls. Bilge wells shall be of sufficient holding capacity and shall be arranged at the side shell of the ship at a distance from each other of not more than 40 m in each watertight compartment;*

    .2   *in cargo ships, the drainage and pumping arrangements shall be such as to prevent the build-up of free surfaces. In such case, the drainage system shall be sized to remove no less than 125% of the combined capacity of both the water-spraying system pumps and the required number of fire hose nozzles. The drainage system valves shall be operable from outside the protected space at a position in the vicinity of the extinguishing system controls. Bilge wells shall be of sufficient holding capacity and shall be arranged at the side shell of the ship at a distance from each other of not more than 40 m in each watertight compartment. If this is not possible the adverse effect upon stability of the added weight and free surface of water shall be taken into account to the extent deemed necessary by the Administration in its approval of the stability information.* Such information shall be included in the stability information supplied to the master as required by regulation II–1/22.*

    6.2   Portable fire extinguishers

6.2.1 Portable fire extinguishers shall be provided at each deck level in each hold or compartment where vehicles are carried, spaced not more than 20 m apart on both sides of the space. At least one portable fire-extinguisher shall be located at each access to such a cargo space.

6.2.2 In addition to the provision of paragraph 6.2.1, the following fire-extinguishing appliances shall be provided in vehicle, ro-ro and

---

* Refer to the Recommendation on fixed fire-extinguishing systems for special cargo spaces adopted by the Organization by resolution A.123(V).

special category spaces intended for the carriage of motor vehicles with fuel in their tanks for their own propulsion:

.1   *at least three water-fog applicators; and*

.2   *one portable foam applicator unit complying with the provisions of the Fire Safety Systems Code, provided that at least two such units are available in the ship for use in such spaces.*

Guidance 20

G4   Protection of special category spaces

G4.1 The control room or position where the valves are located should fulfil the requirements for control stations for the adjacent bulkheads and decks of the protected space.

G4.2 The fire extinguishers in special category spaces should be suitable for A and B Class fires. The extinguishers should have a capacity of 12 kg dry powder or equivalent.

G4.3 The bilge wells should be provided with high level alarms which give alarm in the control room for the water spraying system. The bilge well alarms should also be connected to the engine room alarm system.

Appendix

List of references in SOLAS text and explanatory guidance notes

Publications of the International Maritime Organization (available from the International Maritime Organization, Publications section, 4 Albert Embankment, London SAE1 7SR)

Assembly resolutions

A123(V) 25 October 1967 Recommendation on fixed fire extinguishing systems for special category spaces.

A565(14) 20 November 1985 Recommended procedures to prevent the illegal or accidental use of low flashpoint cargo oil as fuel.

A567(14) 20 November 1985 Regulation for inert gas systems on chemical tankers.

A654(16) 19 October 1989 Graphical symbols for fire control plans.

A752(18) 4 November 1993 Guidelines for the evaluation testing and application of low location lighting on passenger ships.

A756(18) 4 November 1993 Guidelines on the information to be provided with fire control plans and booklets required by SOLAS regulations II-2/20 and 41-2.

A760(18) 4 November 1993 Symbols related to life saving appliances and arrangements.

A830(19) 23 November 1995 Code on alarms and indicators 1995.

MSC Resolutions

1(XLV) Adoption of amendments to the International Convention for the Safety of Life at Sea 1974, adopted 20 November 1981, entered into force 1September 1984.

6(48) Adoption of amendments to the International Convention for the Safety of Life at Sea 1974, adopted 17 June 1983, entered into force 1 July 1986.

13(57) Adoption of amendments to the International Convention for the Safety of Life at Sea 1974, adopted 11 April 1989, entered into force 1 February 1992.

22(59) Adoption of amendments to the International Convention for the Safety of Life at Sea 1974, adopted 23 May 1991, entered into force 1 January 1994.

24(60) Adoption of amendments to chapter II-2 of the International Convention for the Safety of Life at Sea 1974, adopted 10 April 1992, entered into force 1 October 1994.

27(61) Adoption of amendments to the International Convention for the Safety of Life at Sea 1974, adopted 11 December 1992, entered into force 1 October 1994.

31(63) Adoption of amendments to the International Convention for the Safety of Life at Sea 1974, adopted 23 May 1994, entered into force: Annex 1 1 January 1996, Annex 2 1 July 1998.

57(67) Adoption of amendments to the International Convention for the Safety of Life at Sea 1974, adopted 5 December 1996, entered into force 1 July 1998.

61(67) Adoption of the international code for application of fire test procedures, adopted 5 December 1996, entered into force 1 July 1998.

98(73) Adoption of the international code for fire safety systems, adopted 5 December 2000, entered into force 1 July 2002.

MSC Circulars

MSC/Circ. 353 4 July 1983 Revised guidelines for inert gas systems.

MSC/Circ. 387 4 January 1985 Revised guidelines for inert gas systems.

MSC/Circ. 450/Rev.1 10 May 1988 Revised factors to be taken into consideration when designing cargo tank venting and gas freeing arrangements.

MSC/Circ. 451 24 September 1986 Guidance concerning the location of fire control plans for the assistance of shoreside fire fighting personnel.

MSC/Circ. 553 19 June 1991 Information on flashpoint and fire fighting media for chemicals to which neither the IBC code nor the BCH code apply.

MSC/Circ. 606 12 February 1993 Port state concurrence with SOLAS exemptions.

MSC/Circ. 608.Rev.1 5 July 1994 Interim guidelines for open-top container ships.

MSC/Circ. 642 6 June 1994 Carriage of dangerous goods – Document of compliance with the special requirements for ships carrying dangerous goods under the provisions of regulation II-254 of SOLAS 1974, as amended.

MSC/Circ. 671 22 December 1994 Lists of solid bulk cargoes which are non combustible or constitute a low fire risk or for which a fixed gas fire extinguishing system is ineffective.

MSC/Circ. 677 30 December 1994 Revised standards for the design testing and locating of devices to prevent the passage of flame into cargo tanks in tankers.

MSC/Circ. 699 17 July 1995 Revised guidelines for passenger safety instructions.

MSC/Circ. 729 4 July 1996 Design guidelines and operational recommendations for ventilation systems in ro ro cargo spaces.

MSC/Circ. 735 24 June 1996 Recommendation on the design and operation of passenger ships to respond to elderly and disabled persons needs.

MSC/Circ. 777 12 December 1996 Indication of the assembly station in passenger ships.

MSC/Circ. 799 9 June 1997 Guidelines for performance and testing criteria and surveys of expansion foam concentrates for fixed fire extinguishing systems of chemical tankers.

MSC/Circ. 849 8 June 1998 Guidelines for the performance location use and care of emergency escape breathing devices (EEBDs).

MSC/Circ. 850 8 June 1998 Guidelines for the maintenance and inspection of fire protection systems and appliances.

MSC/Circ. 909 4 June 1999 Interim guidelines for a simplified evacuation analysis of ro ro passenger ships.

MSC/Circ. 913 4 June 1999 Guidelines for the approval of fixed water based local application fire fighting systems for use in Category A machinery spaces.

MSC/Circ. 914 4 June 1999 Guidelines for the approval of alternative fixed water based fire fighting systems for special category spaces.

MSC/Circ. 917 4 June 1999 Guidelines for fire safety construction in accommodation areas.

MSC/Circ. 1002 26 June 2001 Guidelines on alternative design and arrangements for fire safety.

MSC/Circ. 1004 14 June 2001 Unified interpretations of the international code for application of fire test procedures (FTP Code) and fire test procedures referred to in the code.

MSC/Circ. 1009 8 June 2001 Amendments to the revised standards for the design testing and locating of devices to prevent the passage of flame into cargo tanks in tankers (MSC/Circ.677).

MSC/Circ. 1033 6 June 2002 Interim guidelines for evacuation analyses for new and existing passenger ships.

MSC/Circ. 1050 28 May 2002 Shipboard plans for fire protection appliances life saving appliances and means of escape.

Resolutions published as Codes

References to International Bulk Chemical, or IBC, Code are to the:

International Code for the Construction and Equipment of Ships Carrying Dangerous Chemicals in Bulk (1998 Edition).

References to Bulk Chemical, or BCH, Code are to the:

Code for the Construction and Equipment of Ships Carrying Dangerous Chemicals in Bulk (1993 Edition) and amendments adopted by resolution MSC 51(66) on 4 June 1996.

References to International Gas Carrier, or IGC, Code are to the:

International Code for the Construction and Equipment of Ships Carrying Liquefied Gases in Bulk (1993 Edition) and amendments adopted by resolutions MSC 32(63) on 23 May 1994 and MSC 59(67) on 5 December 1996.

References to Gas Carrier, or GC, Code are to the:

Code for the Construction and Equipment of Ships Carrying Liquefied Gases in Bulk (1983 Edition) and amendments adopted by resolution MSC 32(63) on 23 May 1994.

References to BC Code are references to the:

Code of Safe Practice for Solid Bulk Cargoes (2001 Edition).

International Maritime Dangerous Goods Code (IMDG Code)(2000 Edition).

Publications of the British Standards Institution

British Standards

BS 5306: Part 4: 2001 Specification for carbon dioxide systems.

BS 5396: 1976 Specification for seamless steel CO_2 containers for fixed fire fighting installations on ships.

BS 5430: Part 2: 1990 Specification for welded steel containers of water capacity 0.5L up to 150L.

BS 5445 –in part equates to BS EN 54 comprising:

    BS EN 54: Part 1: 1996 Introduction.

    BS EN 54: Part 2: 1998 Control and indicating equipment.

    BS EN 54: Part 4: 1998 Power supply equipment.

    BS 5445: Part 5: 1977 Heat sensitive detectors – point detectors containing a static element.

    BS 5445: Part 7: 1984 Specification for point type smoke detectors using scattered light, transmitted light or ionization.

    BS 5445: Part 8: 1984 Specification for high temperature heat detectors.

    BS 5445: Part 9: 1984 Methods of test for sensitivity to fire.

BS 5839: Part 4: 1988 Specification for control and indicating equipment.

BS EN 3 comprising:

BS EN 3: Part 1: 1996 Description, duration of operation, class A and B fire test.

BS EN 3: Part 2: 1996 Tightness, dielectric test, tamping test, special provisions.

BS EN 3: Part 3: 1996 Construction, resistance to pressure, mechanical tests.

BS EN 3: Part 4: 1996 Charges, minimum required fire.

BS EN 3: Part 5: 1996 Specification and supplementary tests.

BS EN 3: Part 6: 1996 Provisions for the attestation of conformity of portable fire extinguishers in accordance with EN3 part1 to part 5.

BS EN 354: 1993 Personal protective equipment against falls from a height. Lanyards.

BS EN 355: 1993 Personal protective equipment against falls from a height. Energy absorbers.

BS EN 358: 2000 Personal protective equipment against falls from a height. Belts for work positioning and restraint and work positioning lanyards.

BS EN 361: 1993 Personal protective equipment against falls from a height. Full body harnesses.

BS EN 365: 1993 Personal protective equipment against falls from a height. General requirements for instructions for use and for marking.

Publications of the International Standards Organization

ISO Standards

ISO 1716: 2002 Reaction to fire tests for building products – determination of the heat of combustion.

ISO 15371: 2000 Ships and marine technology – Fire extinguishing systems for protection of galley deep fat cooking equipment – Fire tests.

Publications of the International Electrotechnical Commission

IEC Standards

IEC 60034: Part 5: (2000-12) Rotating electrical machines – Part 5: Degrees of protection provided by the integral design of rotating electrical machines (IP Code) – Classification.

IEC 60068: Part 2: Section 1 (1990-05) Environmental testing – Part 2: Tests A: Cold

IEC 60079: Parts 0 – 20 Electrical apparatus for explosive gas atmospheres.

IEC 60092: Part 506: (1996-05) Electrical installations in ships – part 506: Special features – ships carrying specific dangerous goods and materials hazardous only in bulk.

Publications of the Department for Transport

(Merchant Shipping Notices (MSN), and Marine Guidance Notices (MGN) available from Mail Marketing (Scotland), Unit 6, Bloomsgrove Industrial Estate, Norton Street, Nottingham NG7 3JG)
Statutory Instruments and Instructions for the Guidance of Surveyors available from The Stationery Office

Merchant Shipping Notices

MSN 1665(M) The Merchant Shipping (Fire Protection) Regulations 1998: Fire fighting equipment.

MSN 1666(M) The Merchant Shipping (Fire Protection) Regulations 1998: Fixed fire detection alarm and extinguishing systems.

Marine Guidance Notices

MGN 31(M) Recommendation on the design and operation of passenger ships to respond to elderly and disabled persons needs.

Statutory Instruments

The Merchant Shipping (Emergency Information for Passengers) Regulations 1990. (SI 1990/660).

The Merchant Shipping (Crew Accommodation)Regulations 1997 (SI 1997/1508)

The Merchant Shipping (Passenger Ship Construction): Ships of Classes I, II and II(A) Regulations 1998. (SI 1998/2514).

Instructions for the Guidance of Surveyors

Survey of Crew Accommodation in Merchant Ships – Instructions for the Guidance of Surveyors (ISBN 0 11 552116 X)

Miscellaneous publications

European Council Directive 96/98/EC of 20 December 1996 on Marine Equipment. Amended by Commission Directives 98/85/EC of 11 November 1998 and 2001/53/EC of 10 July 2001. Published in the Official Journal of the European Communities.

Unified requirement F.29 revision 5, 1994. From International Association of Classification Societies.

Airport Services Manual, Part 1– Rescue and Fire Fighting (3rd Edition 1990). Reprinted August 2000 incorporating amendment 1. From International Civil Aviation Organization.

NFPA 12: Standard on Carbon Dioxide Extinguishing Systems, 2000 Edition. Published by National Fire Protection Association, Massachusetts, USA.